Australian Literature Today

In the Same Series

Australian and Indian Literature: Studies in Mutual Response
Ed. David Kerr and R.K. Dhawan

New Zealand Literature Today
Ed. R.K. Dhawan and William Tonetto

Australian Literature Today

Edited by

R.K. Dhawan
David Kerr

Indian Society for Commonwealth Studies

Published by
Indian Society for Commonwealth Studies
New Delhi 110 015.

ISBN 81-85218-70-6

Phototypesetting by
dataculture
New Delhi 110 024

Printed at
Mehra Offset Press
New Delhi 110 002

CONTENTS

POETRY

CREATIVE WRITING

Short Stories

Poetry

CONTRIBUTORS

Robert Adamson, Melbourne

Simon Curtis, Manchester

R.K. Dhawan, Delhi

Cynthia vanden Driesen, Perth

Tim Dunlop, Isaacs, ACT

Diane Fahey, Melbourne

M.D. Fletcher, St. Lucia

F.A. Inamdar, Surat

Victor Kelleher, Sydney

David Kerr, Melbourne

Tony Lintermans, Melbourne

Enrique Martinez, Australia

David Myers, Rockhampton

Basavaraj S. Naikar, Gulbarga

Judith Rodriguez, Melbourne

Thomas Shapcott, Melbourne

Alex Skovron, Australia

Peter Steele, Melbourne

Glen Thomas, Brisbane

Gerry Turcotte, Wollongong

Chris Wallace-Crabbe, Melbourne

Michael Wilding, Sydney

Australian Literature Today

R.K. DHAWAN

The avowed object of this project is to familiarize the English-speaking world with the contemporary Australian writing, and its significance in the world literature. Most of the articles and creative pieces included here were collected during my recent visit to Australia. These are highly representative of what Australian literature is today. Dr. David Kerr, my friend from Melbourne and the co-editor of this volume, was a great help in acquainting me with the literary scene in Australia.

II

Of course one wonders how Australian literature is different from the traditional English literature. Is it not a part of the great English tradition? The criterion to judge what constitutes Australian may be quite misleading. Should it be that Australian writer must be Australia-born? But we have successful writers whose works have indubitable claim to consideration were born elsewhere. Like Michael Wilding, Victor Kelleher and Yasmine Gooneratne. Is an Australian writer then one who ought to be a resident of Australia? Should his works be inspired by local scenes? Not really, for some great literature has been produced by Australian writers living overseas. Peter Porter, for example. Mere locality counts for little in literature. It is therefore not desirable to impose physical limitations on literature, for doing so is to miss its essential spiritual nature. Australian literature need not necessarily be concerned with a chosen theme, or the birthplace of the writer, or even the locality in which the author happens to have been living at the time of writing. Australian literature, like all great literature, is dynamic; it is the response of creative writers to the condition of life in Australia. A truly great writer would be one who successfully comes to grips with authentic feeling with the Australian environment, its character and its cultural syndromes. Literature, we all agree, is the whole expression of a literate community's life and activity, and this expression finds its outlet through language.

III

The women writers of Australia have produced sufficient work to merit world-wide attention. It is indeed stimulating and rewarding to find women's views and values at the centre of the literary stage shaping the contemporary issues as also the form of expression. The earlier women writers were adept in writing letters, for exchange of epistles was of utmost significance to the early migrants.

The tradition of realism offers women writers the possibility of exploiting female experience. In the recent times, therefore, women writers have shown their concern with some vital problems, like the cruel exploitation of black women by white men. Some women writers have revealed the inner recesses of their hearts and given expression to the area dear to their heart i.e. marriage and the position of women in society. Catherine Helen Spence is of the view that in the interest of women's self-realization, the institution of marriage should be discarded. The leader of the feminist movement is still Germaine Greer who in *The Female Eunuch* gave remarkable analysis of women's marriage. Greer regards the small nuclear family as a disaster and would like children to be reared by willing adults rather than by biological parents.

In several ways, Greer was reinforcing the feminist point of view projected by her contemporary Kate Millett, an American, who was a powerful force in the 1970s. In her book *Sexual Politics*, Millett describes the relation between the sexes as essentially political and for the establishment of patriarchal society, the status accorded to women has been a demeaning one. Greer, now 53-year old and settled in Britain, has been waging a life-long war against man's domination. In November 1991, she published a new book, *The Change*, a sensational study of the menopause. She says that a woman has no need to be apologetic after her menopause; it is a biological process and no blur on woman's femaleness. Greer's starting point for her radical theorizing has always been herself. Indeed she has survived on the strength of her indomitable personality and at the same time she is the spokesperson for her generation.

Two anthologies, brought out by Penguin, on women's writing make delightful reading. These are *The Penguin Anthology of Women's Writing* edited by Dale Spender and *Her Selection: Writing by Nineteenth-Century Australian Women*. In these two volumes of women's writing, Penguin seeks to put Australian women into the literary history of their country. Dale Spender highlights the thesis that Australian women writers have quite a different perspective from their male counterparts, and hence theirs is decidedly a different body of literature with some distinctive traditions.

Women's writing and feminism have given rise to another phenomenon in Australia—publishing by women's press. In Sydney and Melbourne especially, a number of women's publishing groups have sprung up, inspired perhaps by women in publishing groups in U.K. (In India too, feminist movement has given rise to women's press e.g. Kali for Women.) Aims of the Australian group include promoting the status of women in all areas of book publishing and providing a forum of discussion and exchange of ideas on issues related to women. The official launch of the Melbourne group was made, under the leadership of Marg Bowman, on 10 September 1988 with a session on "Forms and Themes in Recent Women's Writing." Women's organizations, such as these, will have a far-reaching impact on the shape and content of Australian publishing and women's writing.

IV

The arrival of Patrick White upon Australian literary scene was a great shot in the arms of Australian enthusiasts. Here was a writer who commanded respect internationally; his writings presented a challenge to critics. Award of the Nobel Prize in 1973 was a feather in his cap. Because White's works have been able to cast their spell on readers all over the world for more than thirty years, he has gained recognition, in India and elsewhere. as Australia's literary guru, an enchanter and sage whose words carry extra weight. White's death in September 1990 marked the end of a great era. During his life-time, White was an enigma; he was loved, he was hated. His writings often posed problems and common readers found it hard to relate White to his milieu. Perhaps no critic or book could project the writer in an objective and impassioned manner. This long-felt need has now been fulfilled by the stupendous biographical work on Patrick White, undertaken by David Marr. Entitled *Patrick White—A Life*, the book has been a phenomenal success. The astounding sale of the book speaks volumes about the popularity of Patrick White. The book is not only an account of White's own experience but the insights, misconceptions and characters encountered and the stories heard on which he drew to write his novels. The biographer collected as many as 2500 of White's letters from various countries which form the basis of this biography. Marr spent six years researching and writing. Towards the end he asked White why he had allowed *anyone* to write his life after saying so often and so vehemently that biographers should wait until he was dead. White replied that he was sick of the books academics had written about him and hoped a biographer might show him a 'real' person. Marr brought the final manuscript to White in July 1990 and White read through the entire text. White confessed that he "found the book so painful that he often found himself reading through tears."

V

The Australian literary scene is dominated by fiction. The National Book Council prize last year was split between two novels: *Longleg* by Glenda Adams and *Cloudstreet* by Tim Winton. Sydney writer Glenda Adams is a former winner of the Miles Franklin award. *Longleg*, the survival story of a boy abandoned by his mother who goes on searching for all his life, was the winner of the 1990 fiction section of *The Age* Book of the Year.

The West Australian Tim Winton has been recognized as one of Australia's most talented young writers. His novel *Cloudstreet*, the tale of two battling families sharing an old house, is an enthralling piece of fiction. Winton, it may be recalled, made his debut with *An Open Seminar*, an impressive novel, which has now been reissued by McPhee Gribble. This is an interesting, deftly-written novel about growing up, choosing those insights from childhood and early adolescence that are worth keeping.

The Great World is a powerful novel by David Malouf, Australia's prominent literary figure. A friendship develops between two prisoners of war, despite their early antipathy and their contrasting lives as civilians.

Mythology and reality are intricately intermixed in *The Kadiatcha-Sung* from Queensland Aboriginal writer Sam Watson. Black and white Australians stand juxtaposed in a deadly hunt positioned in a timeless past and uncertain future. In *The Speaking Land: Myth and Story in Aboriginal Australia*, Ronald Berndt and Catherine Berndt give us the rich stuff: one hundred and ninety five traditional myths and stories translated from the vernacular languages of about fifty or sixty storytellers from parts of Central Australia. The Berndts collected this material between forty and twenty years ago as the husband and wife anthropological team which has been a driving force in Aboriginal studies since the war.

In Nicholas Hasluck's latest novel *The Country without Music*, the story is told from different points of view, using a series of first-person narratives. While the novel is sub-titled "a novel," it is more a meditative fantasy than a text of character and action. The novel tells us about the decline and fall of an autocratic administrator and how this was accomplished.

Compared with *Illywhacker* and *Oscar and Lucinda*, Peter Carey's new novel *The Tax Inspector* is certainly short. The novel is both demanding and easy to read. Every word seems to belong there inevitably, but this seeming ease took 12 drafts written in Sydney, New York and a cabin by a lake in Canada. It is the story of the Catchprice family who own an outer suburban Sydney car dealership. The novel clearly intends to say something about the present-day Australia perhaps as seen from the vantage point of New York, where Carey now lives. It attempts to draw distinctions between the monstrous Catchprices—remnants of the old Australia—and those perplexed Greeks, Armenians and Italians who are drawn into their web of nastiness. The novel's action is contained within a week after the Catchprices get a visit from a tax inspector. The thematic focus is on Maria Tokis, the pregnant tax inspector, and her attempts to frustrate the taxation department's audit of the hapless Catchprice family's business enterprise. Peter Carey has already announced the theme of his next novel; it will be a story of an imaginary America. It will be America transformed, an America dreamed.

VI

There is a rich diversity of critical studies on Australian writing. During my visit I thoroughly read Bruce Bennett's *Spirit in Exile: Peter Porter and His Poetry.* This is one of the best critical studies on a living writer. Though Bennett's focus is on the poetry, he amply provides Porter's readers with the biographical data so that they can relate life and literature, and appreciate the poet's work. Bennett brings out strongly the importance to Porter of the loss of his mother at the age of nine, and Porter's overwhelming sense of the awfulness of his school days. Another publication of Bruce Bennett *An Australian Compass* has been well received in the literary circles. This is a useful study, easy to understand and full of keen observations. Bennett is Director of the Centre for Australian Studies, University of Western Australia, Perth. He is a strong advocate of the Australian Studies. *An Australian Compass* aptly fits in this critical framework. The reader feels greatly enthused by Bennett's great appreciation and reverence for Western Australia. The book is elegantly produced, and makes a rich contribution to the growing canvas of Australian literary studies.

VII

There are some prestigious literary journals which truly reflect the tone and temper of the contemporary Australian literature. *Westerly*, a quarterly review, is published at the Centre for Australian Studies, University of Western Australia, Perth. Each year, one special issue is devoted to some aspect of Australian cultural life. The journal is edited by Bruce Bennett, Peter Cowan, and Dennis Haskel. *Meanjin* is published quarterly at the University of Melbourne; *Scripsi* is published by Oxford University Press, Melbourne, and is brought out thrice a year; *Overland* is a quarterly literary magazine, ably edited by Barrett Reid and John McLaren; *Australian Drama Studies* is brought out by the Department of English, University of Queensland. There are some journals devoted exclusively to Commonwealth literature. These include *New Literatures Review* brought out by the University of Wollongong, and *CRNLE Reviews Journal* published by the Centre for New Literatures, Flinders University, Adelaide. Most of these journals and periodicals are liberally supported by the Literature Board of the Australia Council, Australian government's arts advisory organization. Great strides are thus being made in presenting Australia as a nation with a vital and unique literature and culture.

VIII

Australian studies overseas have been characterized chiefly by the study of Australian literature. There has been a growing interest in the study of Australia as a whole and Australian literature, in particular. In Europe, the European Association of Studies on Australia, last year, held their first gathering to discuss "The Making of a Pluralist Australia 1950-1990." The Robert Menzies Centre for Australian Studies, which is a part of Institute of Commonwealth Studies, London, has played a significant role in promoting Australian history and literature. The recently-formed Australian Studies Association of North America hosted a conference to discuss the developments and future prospects of Australian Studies in North America, Europe and Australia. Similarly, The American-Australian Foundation has planned to concentrate on promoting Australian and Pacific Studies at academic institutions throughout the United States and on improving interaction between Australian and American academic institutions.

In addition, a number of publications have been brought out by Australianials elsewhere. The Australian and New Zealand Study Group at the University of Hawaii began publishing a new journal entitled *Southern Crossroads* in September 1991, and the Cultural Affairs Office of the Australian Embassy in the United States produced the first issue of its journal *Miscellanea: Culture Australia* in August 1991.

In India, Australian studies have picked up considerably in the recent years. But in this country there is a great paucity of books on Australian literature. While British and American publishers have captured the Indian book market, Australian publisher has yet to reach here. The government of Australia, Centres of Australian Studies in Australia, Literature Board of Australia Council and academic organizations like Indian Society for Commonwealth Studies, can help in making books and journals on Australian literature available to Indian scholars. It is heartening to note that the Indian High commission has already taken some positive steps in this direction.

Recently the Australian government has announced the establishment of Australia-India Council. The objectives of the Council are to promote relations with India at trade, sports and cultural level. It will follow the working pattern of councils being run by the government like Australia-Japan Foundation, Australia-Indonesia Institute and Australia-New Zealand Foundation. It is hoped that Australia-India Council will help significantly in promoting Australian studies in India and Indian studies in Australia.

The Indian Society for Commonwealth Studies has played an important role in the promotion of Australian literature in India. The Society proposes to set up Centre for Indo-Australian Studies, following the pattern of Robert Menzies Centre for Australian Studies. It will promote publications on Australian studies and organize academic programmes in this area.

The Society publishes *The Commonwealth Review*, a bi-annual journal devoted to the new literatures in English. One issue of the journal, every year, is devoted to Australian literature. It also publishes bibliographies and books on Australian literature. Apart from publications, the Society organizes an annual conference in January where scholars from India and abroad participate. During the last three years, several scholars including Ms. Judith Rodriguez, Dr. David Kerr, Mrs. Rosemary Kerr, Dr. Terry Collits, Ms. Sylvia Lawson have participated in the annual meets. We hope more and more scholars will attend these and bridge the gap between Australia and India.

Perspectives of Contemporary Australian Literature on Culture-Clash between Australian and the Asia/Pacific Region

DAVID MYERS

For the last three decades Australia has been increasingly caught up in an irresistible transformation of its traditional political and economic stance in the Asia/Pacific region. The transformation is the subject of daily media analysis.[1] It is instructive to address ourselves to the question of how this transformation has been represented in contemporary Australian literature.

It is the purpose of this article to examine images of culture shock and culture clash in representative, postwar works of Australian fiction and drama. It is further the purpose of this article to analyze the moral and spiritual stance of Australian authors as they develop new images of typical Australians struggling to come to grips with alien cultures for which experience their education has given them virtually no preparation. Ultimately this article will focus on six works of contemporary Australian fiction which are set in the Asia/Pacific region and on the attempts by their authors—Koch, d'Alpuget, Drewe, Astley, Nowra and Stow—to bridge the gap between East and West in these novels through the mystic sacrifice of a scapegoat.

Contemporary Australian literature provides important insights into an Australian society that has changed rapidly and is still changing from a jingoistic outpost of British Empire whose inhabitants a mere fifty years ago believed in the superiority of the white race and in the "white man's burden" to bring true civilization to Asia and the Pacific. Contemporary Australian literature also gives evidence of a new Australian society that is painfully re-thinking its historical prejudices and learning new attitudes to the Asia/Pacific region.

Australia's new attitudes to the Asia/Pacific region are of course not the result of a sudden flash of moral vision. They are dictated by such factors as the end of European colonialism in East Asia, South East Asia and the Western Pacific and the rapid emergence of many Asian countries in this region as flourishing economic entities with considerable power and influence.

It has become an irritating platitude today to announce that Australia is part of Asia. It is irritating because few people have bothered to think the concept and its implications through. Politicians see this platitude as a way of striking a statesmanlike pose in which they point the finger of destiny towards the 21st century. Alternatively, opposition politicians make calculated and cynical appeals to traditional Australian xenophobia and to reactionary nostalgia for the so-called White Australia policy.

Economists see the Asian markets as a possible salvation for the ailing Australian economy. Conversely, it is argued, if we Australians ignore Asia either in insular smugness or in a fit of anachronistic loyalty to the British Empire of the past, it is direly predicted that Australia will fast become an economic colony of a new East Asian empire. Either way, Asia is apparently our fate for the foreseeable future.

If we accept that literature does not exist in some kind of esoteric or exalted vacuum and that much literature is most fruitfully studied as a socio-historical phenomenon not only because of the influences on the production and the reception of a literary work but also because social history provides a productive frame of reference for the detailed analysis of a literary text, then it will hardly surprise us to find instructive parallels between the more recent history of Australia's socio-political relations with the Asia/Pacific region and some of the important themes of contemporary Australian literature.

Historically, the Australian fear of Asia and prejudice against Asians—particularly against the Chinese and the Japanese—is an accepted fact that dates back to the race riots against the Chinese on the 19th century goldfields. Around the time of Australian Federation in 1901, there is well documented evidence of the motivations behind the infamous White Australia Policy and of the Australian fear of the "Yellow Peril" both among leading politicians and also in the press (see the racist cartoons in *The Bulletin* of this era). Historical events in the 20th century in the Asia/Pacific region have done little to allay Australian anxiety. Japanese military imperialism in W.W. II and more recently Japan's rise to world economic power, Communist revolutions during the 1950s and the 1960s in Korea, Malaysia and Vietnam, and the Indonesian takeover of Timor and West New Guinea (Irian Jaya) in the 1970s have done nothing to diminish the traditional Australian fear of Asia.

Nevertheless, in the last two decades Australia has begun to open up to the Asia/Pacific region in many different ways. The Whitlam Government recognized the people's Republic of China in 1972. The economic importance of our trade with Japan has skyrocketed. We have developed a liberalized immigration policy and Asian immigrants in 1988 formed approximately one third of the total immigrant intake for that year. Educationally the Asian Studies Council in 1989 began the task of implementing the FitzGerald Report which requires the Australian educational system to produce a reasonable number of "Asia-literate" graduates with a working knowledge of an Asian language, not just in the Humanities but also in the faculties of Commerce and Science/Technology within the next five years. The tourism boom from Japan to Australia and from Australia to Fiji, Noumea, Bali, Singapore and Hong Kong is of social as well as economic significance. In 1988 Australia hosted for the first time the Pacific Islands's Festival, presumably as a symbolic gesture that it now sees itself increasingly as a nation in the South West Pacific and not merely as an isolated ex-colony of British imperialism. The Australian government's pursuit of cultural and educational cooperations as the IDP (International Development Program), AIDAB and AUSTRADE and this has in turn resulted in the presence on Australian university campuses of thousands of young, full-fee paying Asian students seeking Australian academic qualifications. All of these factors have contributed to a slowly changing consciousness of Asia and the South Pacific among educated Australians.

On the other hand, the debate about the rapidly increased levels of Asian immigration to Australia reveals that there is still considerable fear and hostility among Australians towards East Asia. Nor is this fear and hostility restricted to the uneducated lower classes. Historian Geoffrey Blainey expresses severe misgivings about trends in Asian immigration to Australia when he says:

> Australia in the next decade will be under heavy pressure to accept more and more immigrants from nearer Asia, and especially from Hong Kong. The possibility of uncontrolled immi-

> gration cannot be dismissed.
>
> The Hawke Government in the last month has done something to increase that pressure by its pithy statements—made by senior ministers—that Australia should become more and more Asian.
>
> The time has now come for Mr Hawke to explain exactly what his government has in mind. Australia can gain much from sensible, selective migration from parts of Asia. But massive or inappropriate Asian migration—in defiance of public opinion—could prove a disaster.[2]

Whatever attitude we Australians take to this challenge from Blainey, it is clear that Australian society is now engaged in an upheaval which will take it away from its predominantly English ancestry and its European heritage towards closer ties with Asia. It is unlikely that this upheaval will be entirely peaceful because we are dealing with widely disparate cultures that have little or no understanding of each other. It is likely that there will be culture shock, fears of economic imperialism, religious bigotry and resentment of both changed immigration patterns and miscegenation. But the pressure to produce multinational economic communities and the relative geographic proximity of Australia and the Asia/Pacific region will inevitably triumph over parochial traditions and insularity.

The changing Australian consciousness of Asia is reflected in the themes and the authorial perspectives prevalent in contemporary Australian literature. On the one hand there are the novels of ex-soldiers and first hand witnesses of W.W. II which are unabashedly patriotic in tone and, understandably, anti-Japanese. Russell Braddon, for example, reopened the festering wounds of the Japanese maltreatment of Australian POWs in Burma/Thailand in W.W. II with his novel *The Naked Island* (1952). Nevil Shute evoked the plight of a group of Australian women and children who were POWs in Malaysia in his novel *A Town Like Alice* (1950).

On the other hand there are more recent Australian plays which launch a moral attack on the feelings of smugness and revenge masquerading as justice with which Americans and Australians greeted the ending of W.W. II with Japan. Public exultancy in the dropping of the hideous A-bombs on Hiroshima and Nagasaki and sanctimonious self-justification in General MacArthur's public execution of Japan's General Yamashita in the Philippines in 1946 are the satiric and tragic targets of American-Australian playwright Roger Pulvers.

Other Australian plays such as Alexander Buzo's *Norm and Ahmed* and John Romeril's *The Floating World* are harsh satires on the average Australian hypocrisy about race relations. Buzo's Norm is a garrulous Aussie who boasts about his fearless individualism, his independence and his racial open-mindedness. But when you blow away the hot air of his cliche-ridden rhetoric he is a cringing crawler to Establishment authority, a man who has sold his Australian birthright as a democratic individualist to become a cowardly conformist and alcoholic at the Leagues's Club, and a poisonous hater of all non-whites. Ahmed the polite, articulate Colombo-Plan student from Pakistan is duped by Norm's specious rhetoric and he pays the price when he is bullied and bashed by Norm. Average Australians, however, would certainly take exception to the slanting of the characterization in this play, if the figures are meant to be representative.

John Romeril's *The Floating World* (1975) also looks at the ways in which racial prejudice survives in Australia today. In *The Floating World* Les Harding, a yobbo Aussie digger with a beer gut, a foul mouth and rampant xenophobia goes on a P & O cruise to cherry-blossom Japan. But the cruise revives Les's traumatic memories of W.W. II when he was a Japanese POW on the infamous Burmese railway. He becomes insane, tries to run amok with a knife when the ship berths in Yokohama and has to be placed in a strait-jacket. It is understandable that many Australians can never forgive the Japanese for their abuse of Australian and Allied soldiers as slave labour in Burma. But would it be equally understandable if the Japanese could never forgive the Allies for the A-bombs dropped on women and children in Hiroshima and Nagasaki?

Because Australian patriotism is often based on boasts of military prowess in two world wars and on a tradition of white supremacy and rituals of macho-mateship, there are still problems today with educating a new generation of Australians towards cosmopolitan co-operation with Japan and to a lesser extent with China and South East Asia. Many well-educated Asians make the charge, with some justification, that Australians still tend to adopt a condescending attitude of moral superiority towards Asia on the basis of Australia's political stability, successfully functioning multiparty democracy and high living standards. The charge is based largely on Asian analysis of Australian media headlines about Asia. But Asian readers could, for example, misinterpret the thrust of Ian Moffitt's *The Retreat of*

Radiance which is about an Australian journalist who returns to China after an absence of many years to seek moral vengeance for a Nationalist massacre he witnessed there as an anguished and outraged observer. Nevertheless, Moffitt gives a philosophical dimension to his story which illustrates the fascination of Australian intellectuals with Asian religious and spiritual culture.

Contemporary Australian fiction is showing an increasing awareness of anti-Asian sentiment among average Australians. In his gargantuan saga *Illywhacker*[3] Peter Carey evokes the horror of the anti-Chinese riots at the Lambing Flat goldfields in 19th century Australia. He also invents a mysterious Chinese survivor of these riots, Goon Tse Ying, who escaped death by learning how to make himself invisible. Making yourself invisible is not a cheap magician's trick; it is the art of disappearing into the terror of imagining the pure hatred of a race riot (216) and is a protection against human malice. Goon becomes a successful businessman who towers "over every man I ever met in the size of his spirit, his indignation, his energy (and) his laugh." (*Illywhacker*, 210). Goon adopts young Herbert Badgery when he runs away from his unhappy home to become a frightened orphan boy whose "head was full of stories about John Chinaman: opium, slavery, how they ate the hands of Christian babies." (209) Goon overcomes young Herbert's fear and prejudice and in the brief dialogue which I shall now quote we hear the author Peter Carey speaking through Goon on the ironies of Australian racism. Goon asks young Herbert:

> "Why am I kind to you?"
>
> "Because you were an orphan, sir."
>
> "No," Goon said quietly. His voice became soft, amber, vaporous as the brandy on his foreign breath. "It is to show I am not a barbarian like them."
>
> In my confusion I thought he was referring to the Chinese. (212)

Peter Carey continues his ironic, surreal representation of Australian-Asian race relations when towards the end of his novel he introduces a baby called Hissao who is Herbert Badgery's Australian grandson but who nevertheless is born "snub-nosed and almond-eyed" because his Australian mother Emma was thinking hard about the Japanese bombing of Darwin which was taking place at the time of the birth. Carey also introduces a Mr. Lo who is an illegal immigrant from Penang fleeing Malaysian "conscription to fight the communists in the jungle." (509) Carey satirizes the Australian government's immigration policy with these words:

> The Australian government, having regard for the colour of Mr. Lo's skin and the shape of his eyes, did not wish him to stay. They had given him the same iniquitous dictation test that they had given Egon Kirsch, although they had done it in Dutch not Gaelic, and they did not wish him to stay. (502)

Mr. Lo seems prepared to spend the rest of his sad life locked up in a birdcage in Charles Badgery's petshop in order to escape detection from Australian immigration officials.

Australian consciousness of South East Asia has even penetrated into our children's literature. Allan Baillie has written an exciting boys's adventure story called *Little Brother* in which two Cambodian boys suffer through the insane Khmer Rouge murder of their family and of millions of educated Cambodians. The two brothers flee separately over distances of 600 kilometers to refugee camps on the Thailand border. This story is an eye-opener for Australian children whose country has never been ravaged by ideological fanaticism or by war. The story may also contribute young Australians's understanding of why we have Asian refugee immigration.

Allan Baillie has also contributed a Cambodian short story called *Snap* to the short story anthology *Home and Away*, edited by Rosemary Creswell (1987). Here Baillie ironically contrasts Australian photojournalist Brien with the Cambodian refugees at Nong Samet. Brien's brusque aggressiveness with his prying camera contrasts with the quirky philosophizing and talkative friendliness of one-legged Phan Mang. Brien wallows in secret self-pity at his recent divorce in Australia and has adolescent dreams of becoming a famous war-photographer. Phan used to be an "itchy bug cycle rider" before the war; now he is a widower with one leg. But the war which took away his family and his right leg has also presented him in this war-torn refugee camp with a beautiful new wife, Saro, who used to be a "Royal Classic Dancer" and was of course very much above Phan's humble station in life. Brien fails the test of courage and flees the Khmer Rouge attack on Nong Samet, but Phan stays on as "a soldier, a king" where he is needed. He refuses to flee to the transit prison of

Khao I Dang where the refugees beg for immigration to America, France or "even Australia." (*Home and Away*, 195) Like many contemporary Australian authors Allan Baillie reveals a narrative stance of self-deprecating irony and guilt contrast to the wars, the revolutions and the poverty that have plagued much of East Asia in the last fifty years.

Another of Australia's great fiction writers, Hal Porter, has set his first novel *A Handful of Pennies* (1958) and a collection of his inimitable short stories *Mr Butterfry and Other Tales of New Japan* (1970) in postwar Japan and has used this setting to study cliches of national identity for both Australians and Japanese. In *A Handful of Pennies* Hal Porter hovers ironically over the unbridgeable gap between Japanese and Australian culture. Porter is openly sarcastic about the "Occupation-Democracy" of the Allies as a grotesquely inapposite attempt to introduce Western-style politics, education, female emancipation and social laissez-faire into Japan. Japanese society, as depicted in this novel, reacts by making token attempts to please the victorious West while at the same time withdrawing under cover of their impenetrable language to sacred traditions and a feudally rigid social structure.

Porter remains sardonically distant from this culture-clash and takes sides only to the extent that he laughs openly at the gaucheness and bigotry of his fellow Australians. Porter's narrative technique is to devise antipathetic pairs of characters who represent the conflicting extremes in this clash. For example, Major Dugald deduces from Japanese war atrocities that the Japanese are all barbarians and must be treated with brutal contempt. But Major Everard-Hopkins, on the other hand, falls in love with the chaste restraint, the ceremonial politeness and the modest delicacy of Japanese food culture, clothing and arts and crafts and deduces that aesthetically it is the Australians who are the barbarians. As Porter himself puts it, Everard-Hopkins falls heavily for "astringency, for serenity, reserve, formality, for Autumn in a dozen brush-lines and insuperable grief in seventeen syllables!" (129)

Porter also stresses the dichotomy separating Japan and Australia by tracing the life and death of three interracial, sexual affairs. Imiko has a romantic but ill-starred romance with Captain Truscott who showers Imiko with expensive presents and erotic adoration, but when he abruptly returns to Australia alone, Imiko discovers that she can no longer return to the astringent simplicity, hard work and monotony of a traditional marriage in rural Japan. Her father's prophecy "Feed tiger—trouble later on" (111) has come true. She has pandered to her vanity and her self-indulgence with the full corrupting cooperation of the "Occupation-Democracy" and these qualities of character now contribute to her fall to the status of an urban prostitute. It may of course be a false, neo-romantic dilemma that Porter can see no middle ground between the hardship of Japanese peasant life and urban prostitution.

The other two sexual affairs in *A Handful of Pennies* are even less savoury. The Padre lusts after Oriental boy-girls and is deported in disgrace when he is caught in flagranti. Aggressive man-hunter Paula Groot contracts syphilis from her Japanese lover Kazuo and is also deported from Japan in disgrace. In both cases Hal Porter draws a strong distinction between Western moralizing and the hypocrisy of its punitive puritanism on the one hand and Japanese philosophical acceptance of the way of all flesh on the other hand.

Porter makes the point that these interracial sexual affairs work only on the level of short-lived lust or as prostitution. There is no question, among Porter's characters anyway, of a union of souls or minds. This is why Porter has the Japanese lover Kazuo say of Paula that "the map of her desires . . . was the reprint of any woman on heat; the map of her mind he would never understand beyond its outline." (*A Handful of Pennies*, 80) In the same passage Porter captures the envy that Kazuo feels for the "luxury, privacy, comfort and organization" of the Australian occupation forces but also the aesthetic contempt and horror that Kazuo feels for the tastelessness, wastefulness and vulgarity of their furnishings and personal lifestyle.

Above it all and remote from the turmoil of his characters in this Japanese-Australian culture-clash Hal Porter grins a sardonic and sometimes macabre grin. Not even at the end, not even in death does he relent from his apparent misanthropy and grant the reader the respite of pathos or sentiment. Instead he offers black humour. For example, Major Everard-Hopkins does not find the "well of ultimate peace" in his naive love of Japanese tradition; instead he dies of heart attack as an alienated observer of the orgiastic Japanese Festival of the Dead. (See 126-31) There are other examples of Porter's deliberate pessimism about Japanese-Australian interaction. Porter teases the reader's expectations when the hapless Australian virgin, Captain Wilkinson, comes tantalizingly close to being bedded by an attractive Japanese girl. Instead of a sentimental erotic union, however, Porter shows how the Japanese girl, who is, incidentally, married and a good mother, becomes a tart. Porter also sardonically chooses to have Captain Wilkinsone be bitten by a Japanese sacred horse and die of septaecaemia. It is fortunate that Hal Porter is not offering the characters in his novel as a model for future Japanese-Australian relations.

Whatever ironic admiration Hal Porter felt for traditional Japanese culture had been largely lost by the time he returned to Japan in 1967 and published *Mr Butterfry and Other Tales of New Japan* in 1970. In the story *They're Funny People* he is irritated by his Japanese guide's inability to unbend a little in spontaneous fellowship, by his apparent lack of intense emotions and individual substance. The guide Tadashi Yokamura wears a stereotyped, inscrutable Oriental mask with a tape-recorder instead of a voice that delivers remote-controlled trivial chatter about tourist attractions and antiquated etiquette. Only Tadashi's suicide note reveals the truth about his hidden self: he has been suffering silently from real or imagined humiliations inflicted on him by his office colleagues. His inner self thus also conforms to the stereotype that the West has of the Japanese: he is inwardly obsessed with saving face and with his pride of place in the business hierarchy. Hal Porter is repelled by the soulless aridity of Tadashi's lonely lifestyle.

To be fair, however, one must note that Porter is equally repelled by the lifestyle of his fellow Australian Mr. Butterfry in the short story of the same name. Porter renews a previous acquaintance with Mr. Butterfry dating back to the days of the occupation in Japan. Mr. Butterfry's youthful vision of winning a Japanese millionaire's utopia for himself by sharp dealing on the black market has now vanished. His Japanese wife has sold off almost all of his property in order to offer enormous bribes to further the careers of their two half-caste—and therefore virtually untouchable-daughters. Mr. Butterfry makes not the slightest attempt to hold back the rage and the bitterness he feels at having thus been made the dupe of Nature's reproductive cycle.

Let us make this cross-cultural comparison quite pointed. We have already noted that in the evening years of his Japanese life Tadashi Yokamura in *They're Funny People* politely hides his self-pity, writes a note of apology for his shortcomings and commits suicide in order to expunge his shame. In the evening years of his Australian life Mr. "Bluey" Butterfry wallows in open self-pity, rants and raves in drunken vulgarity and racist misanthropy and lives on to the bitter end holding everyone responsible for his life except himself. Hal Porter was a merciless observer of the defects in both the Japanese and the Australian lifestyles.[4]

These are only some of the plays, novels and stories which indicate a determination among Australia's literary artists to filter the often bitter lessons of racial, cultural and political conflict between Australia and the Asia/Pacific region through the cathartic purification of expression. This cathartic expression is continued in the six contemporary novels which I wish to examine in more detail in this article.

The six novels in question are Robert Drewe's *A Cry in the Jungle Bar* (1979), Christopher Koch's *The Year of Living Dangerously* (1978), Blanche d'Alpuget's *Turtle Beach* (1981), Randolph Stow's *Visitants* (1979), Thea Astley's *Beachmasters* (1985) and Louis Nowra's *Palu* (1987). That the first three of these novels together say something important about contemporary Asia to Australians has already been successfully contended by Helen Tiffin.[5] I am not aware of any detailed discussion yet linking *Visitants, Beachmasters* and *Palu* to the theme of culture-clash between Australia and the Asia/Pacific region.

A Cry in the Jungle Bar is the story of an Australian football hero, Dick Cullen, who has become an UNESCO expert on the role of water buffalo in Asian rural productivity. In the course of his midlife crisis and his alienation from his wife he suffers through unconsummated lust for Asian girls, fear of their ridicule and a conviction of his own physical emotional gaucheness. His inability to get to know Asia is compounded by his total linguistic and socio-cultural ignorance and by his foolish resolution to remain politically uninformed in the futile hope that this will make him a neutral bystander.

The Year of Living Dangerously shows how an ambitious Australian reporter, Guy Hamilton, on his first posting overseas, experiences the poverty, overcrowding, corruption and revolutionary violence of Indonesia towards the conclusion of President Sukarno's reign in 1965. In the course of the revolution and counter-revolution Guy learns from the tragic fate of Billy Kwan, a Chinese-Australian dwarf that Australians cannot remain apathetic and aloof from Asian suffering, while at the same time exploiting this suffering in order to make sensational media headlines and thus further their own careers.

Turtle Beach also shows an Australian journalist, Judith Wilkes, being confronted with Asian racial and political violence. Judith observes the plight of the Hoa-Vietnamese boat-people trying to seek provisional refuge in Malaysia in 1975 in the aftermath of the American agreement to undertake a military withdrawal from Vietnam in 1973. Judith also comes to grips erotically and philosophically with the volatile multiculturalism of Malaysia before she retreats to Australia as defeated and as baffled by Asia as Dick Cullen or Guy Hamilton.

Visitants is a haunting revelation of culture-clash between Australian government officials and isolated native villagers on the Trobriand Islands off the East Coast of Papua. It is a poetic tour de force as Randolph Stow allows us to see the clash from the differing viewpoints of multiple narrators both Australian and Papuan. The "visitants" are both the Australian intruders and also the supernatural beings who are worshipped by the natives as divine ancestors in a "cargo cult." The natives believe that these supernatural beings will return to their island in a spaceship from the stars bearing all the luxury cargo that will restore them to equality of power with the white intruders. In this expectation they spook themselves up into a frenzy in which they orgiastically break their sacred taboos and destroy their own culture and order. A certain price has to be paid before peace and stability can be restored to the community through mature leadership. Stow does not castigate the Australian territorial administrators in the way that Thea Astley satirically attacks the British and French colonists in *Beachmasters.* In fact Stow eschews dramatic effects and the superficial excitement of plot. Instead he infiltrates himself as invisible author within the limited perspectives of each of his narrators, revealing both the mysteries of human relationships and also the innermost souls of his character with understatement and restrained empathy.

Beachmasters tells the sad tale of a failed revolution on Trinitas, a tiny island in the South Pacific. Trinitas is a mythical and in itself insignificant member of an island-group about to be granted independence somewhere in the vicinity of Vanuatu. The Trinitas revolution is against British and French colonial rule but also against rule by the larger island in their group. Australia is implicated in this revolution historically through its brutal "blackbirding" of near-slave labour to the Queensland canefields in the 19th century and also through its plantation managers who are just as paternalistic and exploitative as the British and the French. The French are characterized politically by their devious machinations and the British by their snobbism and racial condescension. Thea Astley shows the abject failure of the colonial system to achieve any meaningful contact with Islander culture educationally, religiously, medically, in leadership style or in traditional family custom.

When the inevitable revolution occurs, it is done mainly in island style with a certain happy-go-lucky naivete. But there is a strong undertone of bitter resentment against European and Australian cultural imperialism, no matter how well meant this may have been. On the day of the uprising "hedmasta solwata" Woodful watches helplessly white drunken natives, his former pupils, vandalize the British colonial headquarters; one native compulsively grinds "a child's white plastic doll" (73) into the coral path with his bare feet and another former pupil yells:

> Don't explain nating. . . . Don't want to hear no explanations. Tri years you talk talk talk. Now it's my turn. You just go. (75)

Pere Leyroud reaches the conclusion after a lifetime as a missionary that he had no right to try to take away the Islander Gods and replace them with his own God; he further thinks that the Islander "yeremanu, the big men, were no different in their ritual ceremonies from the college of cardinals." (94) Doctor Trumble is even more the mouthpiece of Thea Astley's denunciation of "the criminality of colonialism" (160); Trumble admits after years on Trinitas that the Islanders prefer their "marasin," their form of herbal medicine and acupuncture and that he himself has only been an unwitting and important member of the "do-gooder brigands," used to disguise the economic exploitation that is the only reason for colonialism.

On the other hand the patriotic champion of traditional customs on Trinitas, half caste yeremanu Tommy Narota, finds himself at the end of his peaceful, comic revolution in prison, deserted and reviled by his own people. He has been used as a pawn first by American real estate sharks and then as a sacrificial scapegoat by French colonial machinations.

Palu has a great deal in common with *Beachmasters*. It also deals with the revolutionary yearning of a Melanesian people for independent nationhood, this time in Papua New Guinea. It also examines the tragic clash of a traditional, rural lifestyle with the new ways of Western urban democracy copied overhastily from the white man. The tribal rivalries of PNG, the economic incompetence of the people (or their indifference perhaps to national productivity) and their superstitious fears allow the lust for power of a few to triumph over democratic idealism.

Like *Visitants, Palu* and *Beachmasters* are also adventurous in terms of narrative perspective because Louis Nowra and Thea Astley have deliberately chosen to transfer their spiritual sympathies to a non-Australian main character. In *Beachmasters* Gavi Salway is the spiritual focus for a tragic study in divided loyalties. Gavi is a half-caste, teenage patriot of his tiny island. Unlike Dick Cullen, Guy Hamilton and Judith Wilkes, Gavi is therefore not an Australian onlooker aghast at foreign turmoil. He is personally torn apart by his naive involvement in abortive revolution. Similarly, the tragic heroine of *Palu* is also not an outsider Australian but a Melanesian woman. Like Gavi, Palu suffers as an idealistic, naive scapegoat who must be sacrificed in order to divert attention from political corruption and incompetence. Nowra daringly writes the novel from the first-person viewpoint of Palu herself as she awaits execution. Her vicious husband Emo who has become president of the republic of Papua New Guinea has accused her of being a witch so that he can get rid of her and her embarrassing predilection for truth. In a sense Palu is a latter day Antigone in reverse: she chooses the idealism of truth and the democratic state in preference to blind family loyalty and a corrupt dictatorship and she dies for her ideals.

All six novels, *A Cry in the Jungle Bar, The Year of Living Dangerously, Turtle Beach, Visitants, Beachmasters* and *Palu,* have a striking structural similarity. They all have at their heart the sacrifice of a scapegoat in order to appease the angry gods of revolutionary chaos and political or racial violence. In four of the novels this scapegoat is either bi-racial or bi-cultural. It is as though the necessity to re-establish social harmony after a tragic culture-clash between East and West demands human sacrifice.[6] A necessary step forward for a national culture is bought at the price of individual tragedy. This approximates to Hegel's theory of tragedy as the dialectic of world history moving forwards at the cost of the virtuous individual who is caught between two cultures.

In *The Year of Living Dangerously* it is the half-Chinese, half-Australian dwarf Billy Kwan who must die. Billy is murdered by President Sukarno's secret police because of his idealistic championing of the starving masses of Indonesia in 1965; Billy's sacrifice inspires a moral enlightenment in the representative Australian journalist Guy Hamilton.

In *Turtle Beach* it is the ex-Saigon bar girl Minou, who has become bicultural or half-Australian through her marriage to the Australian High Commissioner Sir Adrian Hobday, who must die. Minou commits satyagraha or spiritual self-sacrifice in order to save the lives of her fellow Hoa-Vietnamese boat people; her sacrifice may or may not have a delayed effect on Australian journalist Judith Wilkes. But it is certainly meant to have a moral effect on us the readers.

Visitants concludes with no fewer than five violent murders and suicides, but only one man dies the death of a sacrificial scapegoat in the name of racial harmony and that is Alistair Cawdor, the PO of Osiwa. The first man to die is the young native Teava. He is the accidental victim of the cargo-cult fanatics who raze his village to the ground in a self-destructive frenzy of orgiastic lust and greed for power. The second man to die is the evil, false Messiah of the cargo-cultists, Metusela. Metusela is fittingly dispatched from this life by the pure-hearted maiden Saliba with the sword of the King of France. In death Metusela looks like a transfixed Dracula. His murder could be interpreted as the allegorical triumph of good over evil.

It is also just possible to interpret the suicide of Alistair Cawdor in a positive way. Even in the depths of his dark night of the soul Cawdor is convinced that his spiritual home is in these Trobriand islands. In a blackly humorous way Cawdor accomplished with his death what he could not accomplish with his life, namely a spiritual union between white and black. As his dried blood covers his skin, it makes his skin look black and this is clearly intended as a macabre symbol.

In death Cawdor has tried to escape from the "visitants" of malaria and despair that have invaded his body. Just before his death he is given a fragment of a beatific vision in which he sees himself transformed into atoms and stars. His devoted houseboy Kailusa follows him into death. We grieve at their deaths but we are not filled with insuperable despair. It is as though Cawdor has achieved what little it was destined for him to achieve in one lifetime. Cawdor has also helped the young PO Tim Dalwood to grow into maturity and leadership in his place. In the Biblical sense the mantle of the prophet has been passed on.

In an ironic parallel development the aged tyrant Dipapa is murdered and his death permits the young Benoni to grow into maturity and leadership in his place. Although *Visitants* concludes with five deaths, it is neither gory nor melodramatic nor even unrelievedly depressing. On the contrary. It leaves us with a distant, implied hope of future social stability and harmony which are paradoxically achieved by murder and suicide and after the cathartic ritual passage of whole community through hysteria, fanaticism and evil.[7]

The sacrificial scapegoat in *Beachmasters*, Gavi Salway, does not die physically; but in an agony of remorse he is obliged to admit to himself that his naive gun-running for the revolution has caused the murder of his adored friend, the aged sage Lorimer. Gavi dies as a callow youth and is reborn at the end of the novel (and at the beginning of his exile) as reflective and potentially wise man who will live with his guilt and make something positive out of it.

Dick Cullen in *A Cry in the Jungle Bar* and Palu both await their imminent execution at the end of their novels. Admittedly Dick is anything but bicultural; his imminent death at the hands of Muslim rebels finds him as uncomprehending of the meaning of life and death as the ubiquitous, sacrificial water buffalo. In this novel it is we the readers who alone are meant to learn through his apparently meaningless death. We are meant to learn that Dick's narrow expertise in science and technology is grotesquely insufficient equipment for life; he needed a cultural, psychological, political and spiritual dimension that was totally lacking in his education in Australia.

How very different is the end for Palu; she goes to her execution in an ecstasy of spiritual triumph over her physical fate as an individual. She knows that superstitious rumours about her as a witch will be combined with her personal stories about the fireflies and the bird of paradise feathers and that she will become an immortal myth that will triumph over the bat demon of evil that her husband Emo has become in his corruption.

Sacrifice of the scapegoat hero or heroine is then a central myth in all six novels. This tragic myth suggests a new heroism and new dimension for the understanding of Australian national identity in Australian literature. Myths of Australian identity have traditionally been explored by measuring our classic heroes against the unforgiving outback bush. But as these six recent Australian novels make clear, new myths of national identity may now be formed out of the tragic culture-clash between Australia and the Asia/Pacific.

In this context it is intstructive to consider Trevor Shearston's novel *White Lies*, in which Sebo, an ageing witch doctor of the

Papuan New Guinean highlands and his son Yaru are brutally slaughtered in a clash of tragic pride between white missionaries and the superficially Christianized Gewa people. This bloody scapegoat sacrifice is in vain and the novel ends pessimistically with the Gewa people fleeing from the destroyed mission church to the sago swamps in superstitious dread of the witch doctor's ghost and also in fear of the white man's law and retribution. Shearston exposes the lust for power that lurks as evil "white lies" beneath the mantle of missionary Richard Weekely's Christian self-righteousness. The stubborn male pride and impatience of both Richard and Sebo have destroyed the tentative compromise that had been established between white "visitant" and black villagers.

In the novel's depressing sub-theme three white men who have sexually shared a black girl buy their way out of guilt with a cash payment to her and the illegitimate child. Women in this novel, both white and black, are portrayed as spiritually superior to men because they are humble rather than proud, comforters rather than confrontationists, healers rather than killers and silent bearers of the suffering which arrogant men have inflicted upon them. Trevor Shearston's *White Lies* is more soberly authentic than Louis Nowra's *Palu* but lacks the extra dimension of the Nowra heroine's dithyrambic triumph over death. It is left to Randolph Stow's *Visitants* to combine authenticity with tragic vision and to deliver this theme as understatement.

This culture-clash between Australia and its immediate geographic neighbours is exemplified by our different lifestyles in such activities as tribal bonding, systems of political government, religious traditions and superstition, food culture and sexual behaviour patterns. There are further tensions implicit in the issue of whether Australia and the western world are exploiting the mass poverty of some parts of Asia and the Pacific in a form of economic imperialism. Our societies are also very much at variance in having widely different attitudes towards the freedom of the mass media from government censorship.

These problems of culture-clash are compounded by Australian ignorance of Asian languages and by the demeaning use of Pidgin in the Pacific Islands (called Seaspeak by Thea Astley). Asia and the South Pacific have a popular aura for Australians of an exotic but dangerous antidote to our tradition of stuffy British respectability. Australia has a popular reputation in the Asia/Pacific of high living standards for all, immense living space, a democracy that works and a prejudice against Asians and islanders. These two vastly different images are projected many times onto the pages to *The Year of Living Dangerously, A Cry in the Jungle Bar, Turtle Beach, Beachmasters* and *Palu*.

The protagonists of the first three of these novels are all Australian careerists who are talented in their field and who perceive their posting to Asia as a career challenge and as a privileged working holiday from the monotony and the predictability of the Australia they know too well. Nevertheless all three novels end with the careerists yearning to escape from their shocking experiences in Asia. They fall victim to home-sickness because of their experience of culture shock, their fear of violence and corruption, their horror of mass poverty, their feelings of disorientation (that is, losing their patriotic bonding with Australian rituals) and their problems with food, climate and sex. Structurally each novel begins with the protagonist at a high point in his/her career, filled with optimism, curiosity, elan, excitement and professional pride. Inexorably all three protagonists are drawn into the maelstrom of Asian politics, experience intense sexual excitement and frustration, discover their own vulnerability and their ludicrous inability to put things right in Asia as they would have liked to according to their naive Australian standards of justice, democracy and a fair go for all.

Judith Wilkes, Guy Hamilton and Dick Cullen all experience an intense need to escape back to the safety and the refuge of Australia: two succeed in making this escape, the third is presumably shot by revolutionary terrorists. The Australian protagonists retreat from Asia, horrified and defeated. It is, however, fair comment to add that two at least of the protagonists are also defeated either by their own personal problems or by the depressing weight of approaching middle age.

What is the precise nature of the culture shock which they have experienced? A complex answer is needed to this question but the origins of the answer may well lie in the sharp discrepancy between vague Australian expectations of exoticism and excitement in Asia and the sometimes depressing and horrifying reality which they encounter.

In *Turtle Beach* d'Alpuget makes clear that there are still many Australians who are attracted to South East Asia only by their anachronistic nostalgia for the "romance of the British Raj—the rubber boom, the sporting sultans, the servile Chinese." (58) But the Selangor Cricket Club in Penang, as d'Alpuget presents it now, is a drinking hole for the upper classless of the many races who have formed an uneasy financial and constitutional truce with one another. There are vegetarian Hindi Tamils, pig-eating Chinese businessmen, debonair Muslim tunkus and sultans, and boastful Sikhs. This multiracial society would constitute an exotic romance on its own if it were not for d'Alpuget's clear-headed representation of the financial and racial tensions. The background to the novel is provided by the 1969 racial riots in which mobs of young Malaysians murdered Chinese and then Indians shouting "We've got the pigs! Now for the cows!" (51) This hatred is extended in the present tense of the novel to the Malaysian fishermen's slaughter of the Hoa-Chinese boat-people fleeing from Vietnam. At the same time the Sultan Tunkus strip forests so that the Japanese woodchip industry can pay for their luxuries and arrogance. The ex-colonial British retain their capital investments, while the Indonesian generals threaten stability from the south and the Chinese communist threaten from the north. And in the heart of the country there is a rebirth of Muslim fundamentalism which is enforced by Muslim vigilante groups. (128, 258) This is less a picture of exoticism and more a picture of intolerance, greed and a grim battle for power and prestige.

Similarly in *A Cry in the Jungle Bar* Drewe implies through his frustrated stumblebum of a protagonist, the representative Australian Dick Cullen, that irrationally we Australians are still seeking some exotic mystery in the Asia/Pacific region, a mystery that has nothing to do with contemporary Asia and much to do with the embroidered legends of the East Indies spice trade and the literary legends created by Rudyard Kipling, Joseph Conrad, Robert Louis Stevenson and Somerset Maugham. A much more appropriate symbol for contemporary Asia, contends Drewe, is bubalus bubalis, the ubiquitous water buffalo. The water buffalo stands symbolically for everything that we aggressive, dissatisfied, questing Westerners never attain because we place all of our faith in activism, materialism, rationalism, science and the changes demanded by reform and ever greater efficiency. But the water buffalo is an unquestioning traditionalist, a creature with a dreamy physiognomy who passively accepts the hard grind of daily work and whose routine has not changed in thousands of years. Through his routine the water buffalo attains the serenity of fatalism and the dubious honour of being the chosen victim sacrificed to the blood-thirsty goddesses.

Protagonist Dick Cullen's ludicrous quest for an exotic Eastern princess in the mythical jungle bars of south eastern Asia leads almost inevitably to his mundane and depressing encounter with a Third World barrio prostitute while her child sleeps in the next room. He is then stabbed by a pimp and bled like a sacrificial buffalo until his coup de grace is administered at dawn by Muslim revolutionaries. *A Cry in the Jungle Bar* is a deeply pessimistic novel and in it the Australian quest to understand or even just to experience Asia ends in frustration, failure, disease and violent death.

It is usefully representative that Drewe chooses for his protagonist a man who embodies the old Australian myths of success as football hero. As a schoolboy he once achieved "the Mt. Everest of a Himalayan Career," as his pederastic old schoolmaster eulogized at the time. This phrase rings ever more ironically as poor Dick Cullen stumbles from marital failure to sexual flop. Even in his successful UNESCO career in Asia—during which he flies around the real Mt. Everest in a small aeroplane—he has become so repulsed by Asia that he longs only to withdraw to the neutral world of some air-conditioned intercontinental Hotel and wash Asia down the plughole.

Cullen tries instinctively to export some of his Australian pop culture to the Philippines; that is, he packs down in a solipsistic scrum with the palm tree in the front garden every morning, much to the amused condescension of his Filipino chauffeur. But when he is accosted by archetypically Australian football fans in the Jungle Bar, he discovers that he has lost his rugger-bugger sociability, his bonds of Australian mateship. He is no longer Australian and yet he feels rebuffed by Asia; symptomatically for Australian culture today he stands at the crossroads and the crossroads are in a No Man's Land where his sense of belonging has been lost.[8]

In the private sphere the protagonists of Drewe, Koch and d'Alpuget experience sexual misadventures and feel alienated by the confusing religions and superstitions of Asia. In the public sphere they are given a taste of the socio-political authoritarianism, the nepotism and the corruption of some Asian governments, and are exposed to the contestant threat of Marxist or Muslim revolution. Let us begin this analysis with the socio-political sphere.

Dick Cullen in *A Cry in the Jungle Bar*, Guy Hamilton in *The Year of Living Dangerously*, and Judith Wilkes in *Turtle Beach* all experience paternalistic dictatorship and the very real threat of Muslim or Marxist revolutions in the Philippines, Indonesia and Malaysia respectively. Underlying their self-protective attitudes of either feigned apathy towards politics or repulsion for both dictatorships and armed revolution is the smug feeling that Australia has socio-political stability and a working participatory democracy in which corruption is allegedly minimal (except in Queensland). But the threat of revolutionary unrest portrayed in these novels is not always Marxist in origin. As often as not the unrest has its origins in racial hatred. In *A Cry in the Jungle Bar*, admittedly we hear of Agitprop and impotent Marxist cadres in Bangladesh and Sri Lanka, but the only real challenge to the dictatorship of the Philippines is organized not by Marxists but by Muslim fundamentalists in the south. In *The Year of Living Dangerously* the counter-revolution portrayed consists of the rightwing military slaughter of Marxists in 1965 but this movement was also partly motivated by a racial hatred of overseas Chinese. In *Turtle Beach* the often impoverished Malaysian Muslims hate both the resident Indians and the Hoa-Chinese boat people arriving as refugees from Vietnam. Australians reading about racial tensions in these three novels inevitably reflect on the relative homogeneity of Australian society and wonder to what extent our social stability will be threatened by our ethically correct policy of multiculturalism and Asian immigration. In this socio-political sense these three novels are reinforcing the image of Asian society that is broadcast by our mass media. And it is not accidental that two of the three protagonists in these novels are journalists.

All three novels are concerned with the obvious contrast between the freedom of the mass media in Australia from government censorship (though not necessarily from a private owner's censorship) and governmental control of the press in Indonesia, Malaysia and the Philippines. These fictional accounts of journalists and the role of the media in Asia have their tragic real life equivalent in the murder of the three Australian journalists who were covering the Indonesian invasion of Timor in 1975. In *The Year of Living Dangerously* Guy Hamilton has to find ways to circumvent Indonesian censorship in order to get his reports out to Australia and in *Turtle Beach* Judith Wilkes is refused official admission as a journalist to the refugee prison camps because the Malaysian government considers that these camps are not to be included in ''all the news that's fit to print.'' Ted Orosa, the Philippine journalist in *A Cry in the Jungle Bar* poses as a crusader against corruption and nepotism but when he unwittingly offends President Marcos in one of his column items, he disappears without trace.

The surface blandness of Australian society is arguably based on a convention that the horrifying, the ugly, the extreme and most reminders of sickness, poverty and death are tidily swept up and hidden behind respectable institutional walls. *A Cry in the Jungle Bar*, *The Year of Living Dangerously* and *Turtle Beach* all reveal aspects of Asian societies in which this compulsive and fearful tidying up has not been done. Monsters, cripples, mutilated beggars, lower class prostitutes, piles of stinking refuse, an inability to overcome mass poverty and insanitary living conditions are all depicted in these three novels as the inevitable reverse side of the exotic chaos and colour so beloved of Australian tourists in Asia. The protagonists of these three novels also enjoy their escape from the boring blandness of Australian society but they pay the penalty, to varying degrees, of their experiment with Asian turbulence. Dick Cullen is assassinated, Guy Hamilton loses the sight of one eye and Judith Wilkes suffers various personal, religious and political traumas.

A similar structure of escape from the blandness of Australia and defeat in the turmoil of Asia is to be observed in Ian Moffitt's *The Retreat of Radiance*. Quinn, the eighteen year old protagonist in this novel pays a high penalty for his vainglorious adventurism as a junior reporter in the Chinese civil war of 1948. Quinn loses his innocence to the murderous General Keh when he witnesses war atrocities committed by Keh on the sacred, Taoist mountain of Hua-shan in Shensi and at a Buddhist monastery called the Retreat of Radiance on a peak above the town of Kweilin. Moffitt's novel is an exotic and grotesque war-thriller but ultimately it provides only a shallow and melodramatic account of the corruption of a naive Australian conscience in East Asia and an implausible quest for revenge. Quinn feels the same need to test his worth in Asia as Judith Wilkes, Guy Hamilton and Dick Cullen. The mythical testing of Australian youth which until recently was traditionally located by Australian art in the vast outback or at Gallipoli has now been replaced by the hero's confrontation with Asia, in which the hero is required to show nobility of soul in spite of personal failure and amid the pervasive presence in Asian society of corruption, gargantuan greed, racial hatred, ideological fanaticism and evil. What seems to have remained constant is the predilection of Australian fiction to celebrate an average kind of bloke who vaguely believes in a fair-go for all and who becomes a noble-hearted hero as he blunders at first innocently and then stoically deeper and deeper into failure.

Barnes and Birrel create another such Aussie hero in the figure of John Cooper in *Water from the Moon*. Cooper hopelessly underestimates the level of Indonesian corruption when he honestly tries to establish viable settlement sites in Sumatra for Javanese transmigrate. His bewildered integrity and not quite credible naivety are of course no match for the intrigues of the Indonesians and the Dutch in their conniving to fleece the world bank with the grotesque farce of transmigrasi. Despite its poetic title, presumably borrowed from a wistful line in *The Year of Living Dangerously*, *Water from the Moon* remains in the sphere of competent journalism. It is more successful with its well informed, politico-financial expose than with its one-dimensional characters.

The other major area of culture-shock for the Australian protagonists of these novels is that of religion and superstitious rituals. This is not to imply for a moment that Christianity is not as much based on irrationality, dogma, superstition and ritual as are Buddhism, Hinduism and Islam. But the Australian practice of religion is shrouded in respectable understatement and is in any case eroded by widespread materialism, hedonism, belief in scientific rationalism, and apathetic agnosticism. The Asian people, as they are portrayed in these three novels, are unabashed in their religious practices and unembarrassed by any need to pretend that they are one hundred percent rational and scientific as human beings. The religious rituals portrayed in *A Cry in the Jungle Bar* range from the noisy processions of demonstrative Philippine Catholicism, through the sacrifice of young water buffalos to the angry goddesses of the Hindus (particularly to Kali the Terrifying), the faith-healing of priest-doctors in the Philippine highlands, the domestic "science of lizards" (131) which provides omens for the future, and the stoning to death of two compositors in the university press of Bangladesh because they published a book entitled "Literacy in Thirty Hours" (the book was seen as an insult to the Prophet). In *Turtle Beach* Judith Wilkes is horrified by the religious rituals of the festival of Thaipusam in which Hindu dancers in a state of trance pierce their flesh with fish hooks and skewers to which they attach topes dragging the Kavadi, the sacred monstrance. In *The Year of Living Dangerously* Guy Hamilton is oceans removed in temperament from the obsession of Kwan, the Chinese-Australian dwarf, with Brahma, Vishnu and Shiva. It is not until Guy has suffered anguish, terror and guilt at end of the novel that Guy has even begun to learn the meaning of Kwan's statement: "Unless we love God and reverence life, we are bound for extinction." (134)

As long as the Australian protagonists of these novels continue in a state of wealth and health and feel protected by the materialistic advances of Western science, they can afford to be amused and/or appalled by the superstitious rituals performed in Asia for a kaleidoscope of gods and goddesses. But how quickly they too turn to superstition and ritual if they are threatened in their well-being. How sadly we watch Dick Cullen's wife Margaret pilgrimage to a faith-healer in the Philippine highlands and feel the trauma ourselves as she has a nervous breakdown in his surgery. And is Dick's daily battle in his solipsistic scrum with the palm tree any more rational than Asian rituals which are likewise intended to ward off old-age, sickness and death?

The most personal and the most traumatic of the culture-shocks experienced by the three protagonists of these novels is definitely in the area of sex. Dick Cullen feels repelled by his frigid wife and is "ravaged by awe and lust" (*A Cry in the Jungle Bar*, 116) for the flirtatious but seemingly unattainable Miss Fernandez. The glacial Chinese girlfriend of chic Muslim ZM seems equally unattainable. In fact Dick is portrayed as a middle aged man who has lost his earlier self-confidence and now blunders around eaten away by shame that his physical bulk must seem clumsy to Asians and yet secretly thinking to himself that Asian girls should be attracted to him because he is always the most powerful male physically in the room.

Guy Hamilton after some hesitation follows an American journalist to a decidedly unromantic midnight tryst at the cemetery where throngs of cheap prostitutes are to be had for a pittance. But he is repelled as much aesthetically as he is fearful of VD. Other journalists in *The Year of Living Dangerously* choose voyeurism, Billy Kwan opts for ethical self-control while King Wally is drawn to homosexual relations with the boygirl banshees of Djakarta. The prospect of exotic sex in Asia often loses its allure for the novels's characters, however, when they are confronted with the daily living conditions of the Asian cities. Even Judith Wilkes's affair in *Turtle Beach* with the quietistic and fastidious Hindu Dr Kanan is aborted when she is offended by his ecstatic dancing around the mutilated Kavadi-bearers and by his fastidious refusal to "pollute" himself by interfering in the suffering of others.

Dr Kanan on the other hand is offended by Judith's outspoken socio-political passion to change and to reform. Kanan sees world history as repetitive cycles of death and rebirth on the spiritual wheel of all being. Judith sees world history as the struggle for progress, enlightenment and democratic civilization for all. When Judith tries to prevent Minou from committing sacrificial suicide, she is severely chided by Kanan who says:

> All you Westerners rush, rush. Satyagraha—you say "self-sacrifice"—is a very noble act. You would have interfered and prevented her doing the noble thing she had decided upon. Western people know nothing about sacrifice. Even to fast for a week or to be chaste is impossible for you. (271)

This is hardly an original insight into alleged differences between oriental fatalism and occidental activism, but it is effectively used as a device to illuminate the dichotomy in characterization in *Turtle Beach.* Nevertheless, the chasm between the alleged religious beliefs of a society and the actual behaviour patterns of individuals remains unbridged by either eastern or western society.

Hal Porter is far more ironic than Blanche d'Alpuget in his assessment of what he sees as the parodistic relationship between individual behaviour patterns and traditional myths of national identity. For example, the Japanese woman Suzuki depicted in a miscegenous relationship in *A Double Because It's Snowing* is unconsciously parodistic of our cliched expectations. Sexually she appears on the surface to be the compliant, Asian playmate of the narrator who also appears on the surface of things to be a normal member of the triumphant army of occupation. But both male and female are victims of misleading cliches. The Western male is not a conquering hero who reduces the Japanese girl to shameful concubinage and thus to ostracism from her xenophobic society. On the contrary. He is a shy virgin, a Mummy's boy who is amazed to discover for the first time that he feels like other men, "like dinkum effing Aussies, like blokes." Male and female are re-enacting the historic encounter of the first American consul general Townsend Harris with his Japanese mistress O-Kichi, but with an ironic difference. The Australian male's life becomes a tragic failure because he lacks the courage at a vital stage of his youth to choose his Japanese girlfriend in preference to his dominating mother. This is no traditional seduction according to cliched myths of national identity.

Artistically the Japanese female Suzuki may seem on the surface to be an embodiment of cliched calendar pictures of cherry-blossom Japan. But she is really a quasi-prostitute. Hal Porter uses his customary stylistic technique of hyperbole undercut by self-mockery in order to capture the pathos and irony of the couple's parodistic re-enactment of betrayed love.

An odd footnote to the Australian alienation from Asia portrayed in these novels is the fact that the Australian characters are after all experiencing aspects of Asia that have been largely westernized. As Galash says in *A Cry in the Jungle Bar* about the Philippines: this is a culture that has experienced "three hundred years in a convent and forty in Hollywood." (33) Drewe allows his characters to note that Philippine businessmen offer "crypto-American cocktail parties," force themselves to eat the "expensive masculine food of white businessmen" in public places and that erotically Philippine society exists in a "time warp of bobby-soxers and double-malteds." (167) This Americanized time-warp in South East Asia is evident in *Turtle Beach* when Judith Wilkes reacts to esoteric Tunku Bibi and scented Dr. Kanan by thinking:

> This is a 1920s Hollywood version of the East. . . . Mystical princesses, and men who tart themselves up like whores. (135)

But this Americanization is either a thin veneer of affectation from the ruling classes or merely superficial sentimentality. It has little to say about the daily realities for the masses of Asia.

There is a very revealing passage in *Turtle Beach* in which d'Alpuget's protagonist Judith compares men's traditional condescension to women with Australians's traditional condescension to Asians. These are two vital areas of social change in Australia today:

> When women everywhere were downtrodden at least they were in the main treated gently, like pets, because they were so vulnerable. Now we have claimed equality but we've not won respect, merely hostility. She recalled suddenly what it was that she had disliked about the Singaporeans. They had been no more brusque than Australian airport staff; they had, however, not been submissive. One expected Asian flunkey to be submissive, like women. (76-77)

It is interesting here that we are dealing not with the racial hatred of an uneducated woman but with the realization by a liberal, cosmopolitan feminist that she has been unconsciously conditioned by the imperialist European ideology of white supremacy. She feels obliged to rethink herself racially as she has already rethought herself sexually and socially. It is food for thought that Judith's lines about the Singaporean airport staff remind us of the satiric condescension to Indonesian airport staff at the end of the film *The Year of Living Dangerously*. In this film the dashing Australian hero makes his illegal escape to romantic bliss while Indonesian bureaucrats in Customs fumble and bumble with his taperecorder looking for seditious material. It will be in similar locales but in much less self-heroicizing circumstances that Australians wiil be rethinking and expressing their attitudes towards the countries of Asia in the years ahead. It is not unreasonable to argue that the six novels, *A Cry in the Jungle Bar*, *The Year of Living Dangerously*, *Turtle Beach*, *Visitants*, *Beachmasters* and *Palu* have provided a literary impetus to this rethinking of the religious, social and economic culture-shock that we Australians experience in the Asia/Pacific region today.

The far-sightedness and open-mindedness of Australia's literary authors needs now to be matched by our governmental policy-makers, our economic leaders and our media reporters if traditional Australian fear and hostility towards Asia are to be defeated. Gerard Henderson, director of the NSW Institute of Public Affairs claimed in a recent article that "our Bicentennial Year has been marked by a rebirth of intolerance and insularity," particularly with regard to the public debate on our immigration policy, the resentment felt for Asian-Australians who are economically successful in Australia, and the concern about Hong Kong and Japanese investment in Australian property. Henderson goes on to say:

> The essential task facing all of us is to make Australia a more productive and competitive nation so that we can take advantage of all available opportunities—particularly in the booming Asia-Pacific region.
>
> It is the height of Bicentennial folly to expect that there will be any economic salvation for Australia in resorting to insularity and hankering for the days when, by means of our immigration and protection policies, we tried to pretend that Asia didn't exist.[9]

Contemporary Australian literature has led the way to Australian intellectual awareness of the Asia/Pacific region. Who will now lead the way to a complete re-education of non-literary Australians?

NOTES

1. The Australian media are obsessed with Australia's economic relationship with North East and South East Asia, not with our cultural relationships. The main function of Australia's changing cultural attitude to Asia, according to our media, is to improve our business prospects with the region. For example, Westpac's chief manager in Singapore is reported as saying that many Australian businesses had failed in South East Asia because they "didn't want to understand the culture. Especially in Malaysia and Indonesia, you need patience, but some just found it all too hard." (*The Weekend Australian,* March 24-25, 1990, p. 27) For a literary evocation of Australia's dubious business relations with Indonesia, see Barnes and Birrell, *Water from the Moon* (Penguin, 1989). The agreed media stereotypes at the moment on Australia and Asia are that Australia is "a First World country on the way to becoming a Third World one" and that Australia is already seen by Asians "as a playground for Asia and as a resources backyard." (*The Weekend Australian,* March 24-25, 1990, p. 27) The Australian novels analyzed in these articles offer a non-stereotyped view of human and cultural relationships between Australians and Asians but are on the whole no less pessimistic about culture-clash and culture-shock.
2. Geoffrey Blainey, "A Dangerous Myth," in *Prose Writing for Australians,* ed. Alan Mahar and John Powers (Nelson Wadsworth, 1985), pp. 25-26.
3. Peter Carey, *Illywhacker* (University of Queensland Press, 1985). Other novels and short story anthologies analyzed are: Roy Barnes and James Birrell, *Water from the Moon* (Penguin, 1989). Rosemary Creswell, ed., *Home and Away, Travel Stories* (Penguin, 1987). Hal Porter, *A Handful of Pennies* (University of Queensland Press, copyright 1958, ed. by Mary Lord, 1980). Hal Porter, "A Double Because It's Snowing" in *Selected Stories* (Angus and Robertson, 1971). Ian Moffitt, *The Retreat of Radi-*

ance (Collins, 1982). Robert Drewe, *A Cry in the Jungle Bar* (Picador, 1988, first published by Collins, 1979). Christopher Koch, *The Year of Living Dangerously* (Grafton Books, 1986, first published by Michael Joseph, 1978). Randolph Stow, *Visitants* (Secker and Warburg, 1979). Blanche d'Alpuget, *Turtle Beach* (Penguin, 1981). Thea Astley, *Beachmasters* (Penguin, 1985). Trevor Shearston, *White Lies* (UQP, 1986). Louis Nowra, *Palu* (Picador, 1987).

4. In his analysis of *A Handful of Pennies* and *Mr Butterfry and Other Tales from New Japan,* Toshiko Kishida argues that Hal Porter's representation of "modernized Japan" was harsh and distorted, partly because of Porter's narrow focus on "the seedier side of (urban) society" and partly because Porter allegedly did not attempt on either of his twelve month visits to Japan to involve himself in "the true richness . . . of cross-cultural encounters" (Toshiko Kishida, "Hal Porter's Japan," unpublished paper at the sixth national conference of the Japanese Studies Association of Australia, July 1989). Kishida further argues that Porter's attempts to maintain a posture of detached observation of Japanese culture fail because of his conservative-romantic prejudices in favour of preserving purist-nationalist traditions in both Japan and Australia. There is admittedly a problem with the reinforcement of negative stereotypes about the Orient in Porter's Japanese stories just as there is also a potential problem for many readers with the intensity of Porter's rancour and misanthropy, but nevertheless Porter must be conceded an indisputable talent for the lively evocation of "the grotesque, the absurd, the ugly, the macabre" (Leonie Kramer) in both Japan and Australia.

5. Helen Tiffin, "Asia and the Contemporary Australian Novel," in *Australian Literary Studies,* Vol. 11, No. 4, 1984, pp. 468-79. Tiffin focuses in this article on the ways in which Asian philosophies (Hinduism, Buddhism and Taoism) are being used by some contemporary Australian novelists to challenge "the way we perceive our psychic relationship with the universe." (p. 479) I am more concerned in this brief article with cataloguing ways in which the admittedly ironicized, average Australian protagonist of these novelists resist the implicit challenge of Asian lifestyles in the sexual, social and political sphere as well as in the question of religious faith. It is unlikely that Australian readers of

these novels will be convinced that they should embrace either satyagraha (self-sacrifice) or the quietistic fatalism inherent in much Asian philosophy. For that matter it seems unlikely that many Asians pay more than lip-service to these doctrines either.

6. Rene Girard emphasizes this restoration of social harmony as the function of the sacrifice of the scapegoat. Girard sees the scapegoat "as a being who submits to violence without provoking a reprisal; a supernatural being who sows violence to reap peace," (p. 86) as a "surrogate victim" "whose death purges the community of its ills—as the subsequent restoration of public tranquillity clearly testifies." (p. 95) *Violence and the Sacred* (The John Hopkins University Press, Baltimore, 1977).

7. Hassall is not prepared to be quite so positive in his interpretation of the conclusion of *Visitants*. Hassall focuses less on the political outcome for the community and more on the bleakness of Stow's depiction of Cawdor's personal tragedy. In this perspective Hassall is correct in emphasizing Cawdor's fear that "the universe is as empty as the cave of the dead at Budibudi." (Anthony J. Hassall, *Strange Country. A Study of Randolph Stow* [University of Queensland Press, 2nd edition, 1990,] p. 145) Hassall therefore accords less importance to Cawdor's beatific vision of his self-transformation into atoms and stresses rather the "despair and terror . . . of a spirit divided against itself." (p. 145) Stow himself commented that Cawdor has had "an illumination" and "that it doesn't matter if his physical body dies, the elements will reform and all will be well." (as quoted in Anthony J. Hassall, "Interview with Randolph Stow," *ALS*, 10, 1982, pp. 311-25).

8. Tiffin unsympathetically sees Cullen as "a sort of Australian 'Norm,' [who] drags his dysenteric bulk through [to him] incomprehensible Asian worlds." Tiffin also claims that Cullen and his "pseudo-Western 'buddies' blunder through Asia like blind men in a room full of strange but delicate objects." (*ALS*, 1984, p. 471) There is some truth in this view on the personal or erotic level, but none whatsoever when applied to the clash of western science and superstitious Asian tradition in the matter of water buffalo culture. There are even moments in *A Cry in the Jungle Bar* when Cullen reveals sharply satriric insights into the discrepancies between Asian philosophy and Asian reality. For example, see Cullen's drunken remarks on the relationship be-

tween the Teaching of Buddha and the promotion of the precision tool-making industry (pp. 133-34) or Cullen's ironic condescension to the empty rhetoric of the Bangla Academy meeting of "intellectuals to Resist Famine." (p. 99) Cullen is more than a blunderer. Indeed it is possible to interpret him as a tragic figure rather than as a buffoon.

9. Gerard Henderson, *The Australian*, Monday, January 2, 1989, p. 7.

What Kind of Truth? Fiction from the 1890s

DAVID KERR

It is a curious feature of the discussion of Australian fiction that it is judged against standards of truth—and also, paradoxically, as "beautiful lies." Brian Kiernan, who coined the latter phrase, was drawing attention to both necessary and deliberate distortion of history by the makers of fiction—if nothing else he could always point to the Australian tradition of tall tales and leg-pulls, fantastic exaggeration designed to suggest the weird nature of the Australian landscape and the way it impacted on the psyche of those who lived and worked in the outback.

Truth, it must be admitted from the outset, is a slippery customer—so much so that one might almost be tempted to say there is no standard for judgement and let the liars, whether beautiful or otherwise, take the floor. However, to abandon a central sense of justice, worth and rectitude, to give up notions of essential truth, no matter how difficult they may be, seems cowardly.

Truth, except of factual detail of time and place, is not a fixity—rather it is a direction, a governing principle in ordering discourse. To judge a work of art one must first seek to define its way of seeing the world and representing experience. How is it approaching the raw material of experience to shape it and give it meaning? For example, when Russel Ward wrote *The Australian Legend*, he was seeking to define the Australian ethos as it had developed from the peculiar conditions of the settlement and development subsequent to the European invasion of the Australian continent in 1789. He offers an account of the effect of frontier life on the development of democratic civilization, pointing out the role of that kind of life in the development of an egalitarian society. Further, he points to the difficulty experienced by those whose cultural standards were derived from Europe in assimilating and giving artistic expression to what they experienced. Artists who wrote from a European perspective were writing truth as they saw it, but it could not be an enduring truth. As settlers and their children adjusted to the land they would begin to meet it on its own terms—that is, on modified European terms, so that a transplanted society could develop new forms and standards for appraising and judging itself.

The early colonial writers, seeing the world through European eyes, wrote novels in which Australia presented itself as a savage land to be tamed: a land without culture, without traditions, ripe for exploitation. Over time the newness and strangeness made an impact, and the special features of the land and the society developing on it began to demand attention. However, there was a gulf between the harsh reality and the romantic tradition available to Australian writers, who were more in tune with Sir Walter Scott or Charlotte Bronte than with the emergence of realism in George Eliot's *Adam Bede*.

Consequently, telling things as they were within the context of romance writing presented a problem. Solutions were various. Rolfe Boldrewood and Marcus Clarke adapted the romantic tradition to their subject matter; Joseph Furphy rejected the traditions of romance and actively subverted them, and Henry Lawson, though less elaborately, took a similar path. Barbara Baynton undercut romantic expectations with a cold precision not even found in Lawson.

Of the writers of romantic adventure Marcus Clarke, with his fictional account of convict life in *His Natural Life*, is pre-eminent. His detailed research of the horrors of a period which had come to an end only a generation before he wrote his novel stamps with authenticity his story of love, nobility and self-sacrifice, set against a background of venality, brutality and savagery.

This history of James Williams, convict, recovered for us by Marcus Clarke, offers a graphic illustration:

> This fellow was sentenced in 1822, at the age of 19, to seven years' transportation for pocket-picking. He arrived in 1823, was assigned, and in 1824 sentenced to an additional seven years. Placed in a chain-gang he was insolent, and received 25 lashes. The week after his punishment he refused to work, and received (sic) 25 more. Before three months had elapsed he had suffered 50 lashes. In two months' time he effected his escape, was recaptured, sentenced to 100 lashes, and loaded with the heaviest irons permitted by the convict regulations. . . . [After

> further crimes] he was condemned to "life in irons." He was sent to Port Arthur, and, held securely in that terrible prison-house, died in 1849 at the age of 45. [He] passed 20 years in irons, and received during his life more than 1000 lashes. Imagination refuses to picture the mental conditions of this admirable example of the convict system.[1]

In romantic fiction this kind of material becomes transformed into a version of the archetypal battle between good and evil. Rufus Dawes, the suffering convict, retains a form of dignity despite the harshness of his punishment which nothing could alleviate. Even the consolations of religion were offered in the form of threats of damnation rather than through the forgiveness of a suffering saviour. It was the kind of environment that forced young children to suicide. Despite the failures of the representatives of the Church in this book, it is a story built around the concepts of sin and redemption, and of the victory of truth. In those senses it is romantic and idealistic, despite the harsh realism of the descriptions of the prison system.

II

Joseph Furphy (Tom Collins) deals with the struggles between stockmen, bullock-drivers and station owners for control of the land and its resources. His tone is that of philosophic ironic reflection on events. John Barnes says of his work, "Such fiction may be truer than truth itself, since the latter, often anomalous and untypical, is always part-hidden from view."[2]

Furphy challenges the view that European culture had no natural place in Australian literature where that literature dealt with outback life. In doing so he parts company with earlier novels, such as *Geoffrey Hamlyn*, in which Australia was portrayed as alien and Europe as the norm. His chief work, *Such is Life*, is designed to give a sense of authenticity though being based on a journal, from which extracts are taken at various intervals to give a sense of the life the narrator was leading. The technique allows the writer reflect on events, on literature, philosophy and political justice, while gradually building a narrative which, while not following "the flowery pathway of the romancer,"[3] nevertheless in time unfolds a story of the people encountered on the track.

Furphy's purpose is the comic exploration of concepts of truth and justice in Australian society of the early 1880s, and to achieve his purpose he frequently interrupts his story to point a whimsical moral. The relationship between his philosophic disquisitions and his narrative is generally ironic: what sounds fine in theory never quite works out in practice. For example, his discussion of truth suggests that the whole world is, or should be, bent on justice:

> Yet I do cling . . . to Plato's beautiful thought, that no soul misses truth willingly. . . . Chastened by contemplation of levelling mortality, awed into truth, by the spectacle of whole world made kin by that icy touch of nature, the belated soul seeks refuge in a final justice . . . found on the conception of equal spiritual birthright. . . . Why is your idea of earthly justice so widely different. . . . Better silence than falsehood; better no religion at all—if such a lack is possible—than one which concedes equal right beyond the grave but denies them here. (87-88)

In one episode he illustrates both his bias in favour of justice and the absurd and tangled guises in which this can present itself. In brief a bullock-driver is caught trespassing on a squatter's grass. The narrator, Collins, intercedes for the bullock-driver, and the station-owner is prepared to be lenient, but a European visitor takes a more legalistic view and would whip the miscreant into submission. The station owner, however, controls the situation and metes out a mixture of leniency and justice coupled with a warning, rather than "crushing the poor devil" as he might legally have done. (239-42) The episode points to the English style of relationships between the common man and the "gentleman" and contrasts this with the "Jack's as good as his master" form of egalitarianism emerging in the Australian colonies.

However, with the idealization of the frontier hero there is a danger of slipping away from a higher kind of truth into a higher kind of falsehood. Russel Ward alludes to something of the kind when he writes:

> Practically every book on the Australian outback contrasts very favorably the "independence," the "freedom," and closeness to "Nature" of the bushman's life with the drabness and meanness of life in the cities. It is the principal theme of

> Furphy, Lawson and Paterson, epitomized in the latter's enormously popular "Clancy of the Overflow."[4]

First one should modify Ward's statement. While Paterson represents this kind of easy antithesis, Lawson (as I will show) does not. In fact, Lawson and Paterson conducted an extended argument in verse on this very subject, in which Lawson was merciless in his account of the miserable existence in the bush. Furphy's position is somewhat ambiguous. His interest is not so much in asserting the value of bush-life as opposed to city life; rather it is to write an ironic account of class pretensions, the irony being all the sharper because the narrator as a proponent of egalitarianism is not quite free of the temptation to consider himself an educated gentleman and therefore a cut above the rest.

Consequent on his ironic stance, the "higher kind of truth" Furphy offers might with equal justice be characterized as "beautiful lies," as this snippet from his account of the ideal horse-rider amply demonstrates:

> Perfect horsemanship is usually the special accomplishment of the man who is not otherwise worth his salt, by reason of being too lazy for manual labour, and too slenderly upholstered on the mental side for anything else. (279)

For Furphy should be understood as a social moralist who creates as his vehicle a legendary form using as his raw material the characters and incidents of the Australian bush. His higher truth carries with it a good deal of judicious selection and exaggeration, as he sees resemblances throughout his story between Australian bush folk-lore and the literary legends handed down by Shakespeare, the traditional tales of King Arthur, the mythology of Ancient Greece. In *Such is Life,* he ironically names one station "Runnymede," and underlines his choice of name by likening all stations to Medieval baronetcies, both in their social organization and in their traditions. However, he is at pains to point out that his materials are gleaned from experiênce, and that the kind of distortion he offers is built on careful observation and will lead the discerning reader closer to the truth than novels of the *Geoffrey Hamlyn* type which he explicitly castigates. (164)

As I have hinted, Furphy does not exempt his narrator from his ironic gaze. When Collins becomes interested in the charms of Mrs.

Beaudesart, a lady of superior birth who had fallen on hard times, he loses sight of his egalitarian stance, and allows himself to add slight lustre to his antecedents to impress her:

> And such was her hypnotic power, or my adaptability, that in the atmosphere of Runnymede I became a Conservative of the good old type, and actually enjoyed the communion of soul necessarily subsisting between a pedigreed lady and a pedigreed gentleman. (211)

However, unlike in Arthurian legend, the fair lady he is sent to save is the unprepossessing Ida, who serves as the unlikely focus for a concentration on the virtue of otherwise of the "low-born" seeking independence. Against Ida Mrs. Beaudesart has developed a class-based rancour. Of Ida's ill-starred father she is moved to say:

> But he aimed at independence—i n d e p e n d e n c e ! A fine word, Mary [she would not call her Ida], but a poor reality. This idea of independence is much too common amongst people. . . . I'm afraid you wilfully overlook . . . the divine command to do our duty in that state of life it has pleased God to call us. (213)

Collins does little enough for Ida, and instead of being prepared to carry off Mrs. Beaudesart, his main aim is to escape her—especially when he learns she believes he will certainly marry her! A different view of the claim of independence, together with an unstated realization that Mrs. Beaudesart has views and tendencies that Collins would reject outright except that he would not offend a lady, leads him to encourage Moriarty the storekeeper to spread false rumours about him so that Mrs. Beaudesart will be put off from pursuing her romantic intentions. Collins was never a knight in shining armour, but in the Australian context the Arthurian legend must be turned completely on its head as the man becomes quarry for the woman, and the hero conspires in undermining his own reputation to ensure his freedom.

III

Whereas the truth in Joseph Furphy must be approached through an ironic re-interpretation of legend, together with an analysis of the changing class relationships within Australian society (and that is to give the merest hint of the complexity of this writer), the route to a grasp of the essence of Henry Lawson's vision is less circuitous, though to the general reader possibly more compelling.

Henry Lawson (1867-1922) offers a more complete identification with the working man and the battler that we find in *Such is Life*. His own tragic life and impoverished circumstances no doubt conspired to curtail his literary output. Nevertheless, he was able to construct a world from his experiences of outback life and his memories of childhood (he was born in a slab hut in Grenfell on the NSW goldfields).

His vision of outback life was generally bleak. It was an alien landscape in which men and women struggled and died more or less in isolation from their fellows and at war with the harsh extremities of climate and unproductive soil. Stories range from the black humour and ironies of "The Bush Undertaker" to the weariness and defeated struggle expressed in "Water them Geraniums" and the partially subverted optimism of "Joe Wilson's Courtship."

Underlying all these stories is a vein of violence and madness, which good nature and a civilized spirit struggles, generally vainly, to overcome. The tone is conversational, laconic, with a substratum of bitter humour which even shows through in stories with a positive outcome. Here is a brief passage from "Joe Wilson's Courtship" which gives a sense of the complex tonal quality of what is a simple tale:

> I drifted back to the river slip-rails and leant over them, in the shadow of the peppermint tree, looking at the rows of river-willows in the moonlight. I didn't expect anything [from Mary] in spite of what Jack said.
>
> I didn't like the idea of hanging myself: I'd been with a party who found a man hanging in the Bush, and it was no place for a woman round where he was. And I'd helped drag two bodies out of the Cudgegong in flood, and they weren't sleeping beauties.[5]

Joe's bleak vision, based on grim experience, undercuts the comic illusion of a romantic lover's death and fairy-tale rescues that the scene suggests. However the vision of the story as a whole is hopeful: life is affirmed, though there is a sense of masked reluctance at the ending where, in giving permission for the marriage Mr. Black confines himself to, "Oh! I suppose that's all right, Joe." (39)

Death is never very far away in a Lawson story. In "The Bush Undertaker," the ghoulish becomes familiar in a story that parodies the Christmas symbolism of hope by telling the story of a sheepherder who, at Christmas is led to the dried out body of a dead man who he is able to identify as Brummy Usen, drunkard and wastrel. He celebrates the festive season by dragging the remains back to his hut to prepare his burial. During the night he is disturbed by a black goanna which he shoots from the ridge pole of the hut. Finally he digs a grave for Brummy and gives him some kind of burial service. His reverence in the face of the mystery of death is no doubt macabre and comic, but the story conceals a larger issue. At its opening he has dug up the bones of an Aborigine: at its end he inters the bones of a white man. The former represents successful adaptation to the land, the latter failure. Lawson's truth is not the truth of a reporter, rather it is the truth of a visionary who senses the pain and futility of the adaptive process in the lives of settlers whose cultural roots are far away in a land of white christmases and civilized rituals.

In particular Lawson shows sympathy for the sufferings of women. In "Brighten's Sister-in-Law" the angle of view is generally indirect. In a primitive environment where a woman is expected to solve all difficulties with her hands and her will, nothing much else being available, the strains can be overwhelming. After an exhausting struggle to save a child in convulsions the narrator sneaks a look at the woman who has persisted and prevailed:

> She was staring straight before her—I never saw a woman's face change so suddenly—I never saw a woman's eyes so haggard and hopeless. Then her great chest heaved twice, I heard her draw a long shuddering breath, like a knocked-out horse, and two great tears dropped from her wide open eyes down her cheeks like rain-drops on a face of stone. And in the firelight they seemed tinged with blood.[6]

The sadness of the Joe Wilson stories is based firmly on the contrasts between the civilized life the women such as Mary had left behind and the hardship and poverty to which they had been brought, the outcome of which is foreshadowed for Mary in the miserable lot of those who had gone before. Not only is there the "haggard Bushwoman," Mrs. Spicer from "Water them Geraniums," there are the passing references to the selector who had abandoned the property they acquired because his wife had died there. As in "The Drover's Wife," women were left to run the selections while their men went off driving to make some extra money. Where a husband proved provident the situation was difficult enough, but in cases where he was a drifter and/or a drunkard the situation was hopeless.

A description of the town of Gulgong "a wretched remnant of a town on an abandoned goldfield" where the men "when at home, most asleep or droning over the pipes or hanging about the pub" while "the women, mostly hags, blackened each other's and the girl's characters with their tongues"[7] gives a sense of the cultural poverty women not yet defeated by circumstance were forced to endure. It was a life like this that Joe feared for Mary; yet his weakness with drink kept him from returning to the relative comfort of the city. The long-gone gentility of Mrs. Spicer's past underlined the fact that being well brought up was no barrier against the kind of dissolution and decay that had overcome her. As Lawson emphasizes by writing Bushwoman with a capital "B," she is representative of a type of struggling poverty that was integral to a selector's life. Joe reflects on it like this:

> And I think the saddest and most pathetic sight on the face of God's earth is the children of very poor people made to appear well: the broken worn-out boots polished or greased, the blackened (inked) pieces of string for laces; the clean patched pinafore over the wretched threadbare frocks. Behind the little row of children . . . I always see the worn face of the mother.[8]

IV

Barbara Baynton (1862-1929) brings the sharpest focus on the central truth of the harshness of living in the outback—more commonly called the Bush when she was writing. In the introduction to *Barbara Baynton*, the editors Alan Lawson and Sally Krimmer write:

> The landscape Barbara Baynton chose to write about was particularly brutal, as were its inhabitants. . . . Baynton shows men lacking compassion in their attitude towards women. . . . The bush is constantly portrayed as a lonely, hostile place, antago-

> nistic to its inhabitants who depend on it for survival. . . . Here is found no noble sentiment but rather a savageness man has retained from his beginnings to enable him to cope with his brutal surroundings.[9]

In Baynton there is a lowering menace that one does not find in Lawson. She sees the land as malevolent, with beauty transformed to terror and man metamorphosed to animal cunning in his efforts to survive. In "Scrammy 'And" [the title refers to a deformed hand], man and dog are alike— "there was a suggestion of dog in his movements; and in the dog, as he rounded up the sheep, more than a suggestion of his master."[10] As for the landscape at sunset, romance is sent packing with this baleful description:

> The eyes of the sheep reflected the haze-opposed glory of the setting sun. Loyally they stood till a grey quilt swathed the setting sun. In their eyes glistened luminous tears materialized from an atmosphere of sighs. The wide plain gauzed into a sea on which the hut floated lonely. Through its open door the hut gleamed like the red steaming mouth of an engine. Beyond the hut a clump of myalls loomed spectral and wraith-like, and round them a gang of crows cawed noisily, irreverent of the great silence.[11]

The story grows out of the setting. The images of sadness, of man-made hell, of domesticity and finality, all fleeting present in the above paragraph, crystallize as the story develops. An old sheep-herder is left alone with his dog when the property owner has to take his wife to town to give birth. The first part of the story is humorous and domestic as the old man's life is sketched. He conducts a monologue with his dog, the latter offering imagined replies to his questions and comments on the sheep, the supper, a cabbage-tree hat, the fire, and so on. The old man is clearly sick and in pain. He postpones eating, considers taking some pain-killer, counts his horde of money, remembers "Scrammy 'And" whose request for money he had refused. At this point he hears a disturbance and panics when he remembers he has left the axe outside. The story then shifts to "Scrammy," who has returned and plans murder.

The story illustrates the contrasting effects of isolation on two men, both from the "old country," one having retained his humanity, the other twisted mentally and maimed physically from his time as a convict. It is a constructed story, which uses a contrived but believable set of circumstances to underline a truth about the sufferings inflicted on men and women in the Australian bush.

Even more contrived is the story "The Chosen Vessel," in which links are drawn between Catholic piety and the failure of men to perceive and respond to the real plight of women. In brief, a woman, left alone in a remote location while her husband goes shearing, is raped and murdered by a swagman. On the night she was killed, a horseman on his way to vote at an election sees her in the distance as she runs through the dark towards what she hopes will be safety, but mistakes her for a vision:

> All the superstitious awe of his race and religion swayed his brain. The moonlight on the gleaming clay was a "heavenly light" to him, and he knew the white figure not for flesh and blood, but for the Virgin and Child of his mother's prayers.[12]

He feels convinced by his vision that he is chosen by God: We are not told his response when he is told the truth of his supposed vision. In the final paragraph the man who has committed the crime and his accomplice, the dog, are both nominated as guilty of spilling of blood. However, the story has been constructed to suggest something deeper. The implication is heavy that in the sentimental piety of the religion of the young man and his mother lies an evasion of reality which is the root cause of the brutal death the young woman suffered. Further, the title points to the sacrificial blood which is poured in atonement—there is an intimate connection between the fate of the young woman and the guilt of her murderer. The blood of the murdered is necessarily the sacrificial offering for sin. The chosen vessel is not the self-deceived young man: it is the woman whose plight he misconceived.

Barbara Baynton's vision of Australian life in the 1890s is built of similar elements to Lawson's vision: it is clear they are looking at the same broad picture. There is, however, deceptive simplicity in Lawson which contrasts markedly with the deliberate drawing together of elements in Baynton to construct a picture that challenges one to look deeper, confronts one with a savagery in mankind as active destroyer that Lawson rarely approaches. Her truth is, for that reason, less general than Lawson's. Where he appears to be working nearer the mainstream of outback life, she is working at the margins. There, work is complementary, and from combining what each has to offer a fuller understanding of the nature of reality at that period of history may be gleaned.

There is, however, another truth—that of the black Australian, invaded, enslaved, almost wiped out by white settlement. But that is another story.

NOTES

1. Marcus Clarke, "Convictism," in *Marcus Clarke*, ed. Michael Wilding (St Lucia: University of Queensland Press, 1976), p. 514.
2. John Barnes, "Australian Fiction in the 1920s," in Geoffrey Dutton, ed., *The Literature of Australia* (Penguin, 1976), p. 179.
3. Joseph Furphy, *Such is Life*, in John Barnes, ed., *Joseph Furphy* (University of Queensland Press, 1981), p. 1.
4. Russel Ward, *The Australian Legend* (Melbourne: OUP, 1966), p. 252.
5. Henry Lawson, "Joe Wilson's Courtship" in *Joe Wilson* (Chippendale: Ellsyd Press, 1987), p. 36.
6. Henry Lawson, "Brighten's Sister-in-Law," *ibid.*, p. 51.
7. Henry Lawson, "Water them Geraniums," *ibid.*, p. 59.
8. *Ibid.*, p. 67.
9. Sally Krimmer and Alan Lawson, eds., "Introduction," *Barbara Baynton* (Portable Australian Authors, St. Lucia: University of Queensland Press, 1980), p. xviii.
10. *Ibid.*, "Scrammy 'And," p. 28.
11. *Loc. cit.*
12. "The Chosen Vessel," *ibid.*, p. 87.

Colonial Conflict in Tom Gibson's *A Soldier of India*

BASAVARAJ S. NAIKAR

There are quite a few Indian English novels which deal with the colonial encounter between the British and the Indians around 1947, like Chaman Nahal's *Azadi* and Raja Rao's *Kanthapura* and so on. But those dealing with the earlier encounters between the two around 1857 are very few considering the number of historical events that took place in the mid-nineteenth century. Gidwani's *The Sword of Tipu Sultan* is, perhaps, the only novel which covers that part of history. It is indeed very unfortunate that Indian English writers have failed to give artistic expression to the earliest encounters between the Indians and the British, though that is still an inexhaustible mine of historical wealth. But such a lacuna being filled in by an Australian writer like Tom Gibson is indeed a very happy achievement deserving congratulations by the Indians. His novel *A Soldier of India* provides an example of how a historical novel could be written without indulging in chauvinism or sentimentalism or even false glorification. It might be said without any hesitation that Indian English writers would benefit a lot from the study of this classic work from the Australian novelist.

The central theme of the novel is the ambivalent relationship between the Rani (Laxmi Bai) of Jhansi and the East India Company represented chiefly by Captain Martin Lalor. In the depiction of the paradoxical situations involving contradictory feelings of love and hatred; attraction and repulsion; sensuous indulgence and professional responsibility and so on, the author brings in a wealth of facts and meticulous details which do a lot for the fictional construction of history and enable the reader to visualize the entire scene clearly before his mind's eye. As declared by the publisher's blurb, it "graphically and movingly depicts the fears, hardships, bloodshed, loves and hatreds of those historic days when British mastery of the fabulous Indian subcontinent trembled and wavered on the brink of disaster."[1]

Martin Lalor who plays an active role in the struggle with the native chiefs of India, is, of course, accompanied by other British officers like Adrian Meadows, Sir Julian Wentworth, his daughter Alicia Wentworth, Skene, Gordon and Dunlop who are camping in a bungalow at Jhansi surrounded by the ferocious mutineers. Martin Lalor tries to save himself and his companions from the mutineers and finally escapes from the bungalow, after having killed a leader of the group of native fighters namely Karim. Before that, Adrian is killed by the mutineers, thus reducing Alicia to the level of a forlorn. Lalor escapes from there along with the forlorned Alicia and is offered protection and shelter by the Queen Laxmi Bai of Jhansi. Though Lalor's life is so far directed by a single-minded purpose, it is now characterized by a dilemma. The extra care and affection that he shows to Alicia induces amorous love in her for him, but unfortunately for her he refuses to rob her of her virginity, though, of course, he had his native beloveds in the past. Lalor is thus thrown into a dilemma, while he is duty-bound to protect her from the native mutineers, he fails to satisfy her amorous desires.

Now that he has temporarily escaped from the native mutineers and been enjoying the protection offered by Rani Laxmi Bai of Jhansi, he has a little time for breathing. But he is not totally free from worries. He is thrown into such an unexpected situation that he cannot easily escape from there. Although the Queen has offered shelter to him and Alicia Wentworth, she, being a very shrewd and practical lady, does not allow him to go away from there. She, of course, allows Alicia to go to Saugor in order to join her own countrymen camping there. The Queen wants to retain Lalor there for very diplomatic reasons in that she wants to have him as her "insurance policy" and as a witness to her loyalty to the British. She even allows Alicia Wentworth to go away from Jhansi only because she expects the latter to convince the British officers about her allegiance to the British. Lalor has fallen into such a dilemma that he can neither accompany Alicia to Saugor nor allow her to go away without him. He knows the firmness and pertinacity of the Queen of Jhansi's decision and tries in vain to change it. Forced by the unexpected predicament he allows Alicia to go away to Saugor while he stays back at Jhansi enjoying the hospitality offered by the Queen.

The situation into which Lalor is thrown is such that he cannot escape from there. He has, in fact, no choice at all. The Queen makes it mandatory on his part to stay there not only as an "insurance policy" but even fight for her by organizing and training her own army, against the king of Orchha. The entire situation is a highly dilemmatic one for Lalor. He has to displease Alicia by not accompanying her to Saugor, in order to please the Queen of Jhansi by his obedience to her. Similarly, he has to incur the wrath of the Queen, if he decides to leave her by accompanying Alicia. Either way, he has to displease somebody. It is precisely because of his mature understanding of the political situation prevalent in India at that time that he chooses the lesser danger and, therefore, decides to stay on at Jhansi. Compelled by the exigency of situation and lack of choice, he trains up the Queen's soldiers by disguising himself as Lal Bahadur in native dress. He, thus, helps the Queen of Jhansi to defeat the King of Orchha with his expert military knowledge and planning in his capacity as a Commander. As a reward for his loyalty and dutifulness, the Queen allows him into her bed.

> "Now you must open the lock that has been about me these years, Lalor," she said almost inaudibly. "Only you have that key."
>
> When he held out his arms, she slipped into his embrace. He kissed her passionately and she clung to him. He could feel her voluptuous but strong body writhing in his arms. When he began kissing her cheeks and neck, she gave a deep sigh and murmured in Hindi which he could not catch. They stayed held in each other's arms for a long time, their lips seeking each other's hungrily or buried in each other's neck. He caressed her long hair and firm back, intoxicated by her perfume and nearness. After a final lingering kiss, he packed her up and carried her, so sensually warm and yielding, to her bedroom.
>
> When they had given each fully to the other and passion was temporarily spent, they lay nakedly in each other's arms, wet with perspiration from their exertion but, as lovers do, neither cared. Outside, the rains came steadily down and thunder grumbled against the occasional glint of lightning. She lay pillowed on his right shoulder and he stroked her hair gently. Her skin was like glistening brown satin.
>
> Eventually she whispered: "Lalor, dearest one, you must stay

> here forever and be my prince. Everything is changing now. The whole of India is in turmoil."(146)

The political relation between the Queen and Lalor is thus supported by emotional (or sexual) relation. In fact, the Queen wants to exploit the sexual relation to fôrtify her political stature. She suggests to him that he should stay there permanently as the Commander in Jhansi publicly and as the lord of her heart privately. Being a woman she wants to surrender herself totally to him and expects a similar dedication from him. But Martin Lalor, being primarily a soldier and only secondarily a lover, does not want to mix up the two relations i.e., political and sexual. He, therefore, decides and manages to escape from Jhansi without intimation to the Queen.

Lalor joins his own people, after leading a life of disguise as Lal Bahadur at Jhansi. He reports himself back to duty. Coloner Mercier, Acting Political Agent for Central India and Brigadier Charles Hasted make enquiries about Alicia Wentworth. Lalor tells them how she was escorted to Saugor. Further they want to know details about the murder of British men and women at Jokhan Bagh. Lalor confesses his ignorance about that. But he tries to convince these authorities how the Rani of Jhansi was loyal to the British and how she had her own problems with the sepoy and so on. But the British authorities who are dead-set against the Rani offer ample evidence about her enmity towards them. Now, anyway, the circumstances call for Lalor's assumption of his duty as a British officer. He is, therefore, compelled to participate actively in the attempt to vanquish the Rani. From the role of a lover, Lalor has now to change to the contradictory role of an enemy. Obviously he has to fight against the kingdom of Jhansi. The British authorities try to exploit Lalor's intimate knowledge of Jhansi to their best advantage. Like a true servant of the Company, Lalor also does his best to organize the military force against the Rani. In the heart of his hearts, Lalor knows that the Rani may have to lose her life in the battle. Like a good lover he wants to prevent her from that. He, therefore, meets her privately at dusk and even appeals to her to surrender to the British. She not only refuses to surrender but even accuses him of betraying her love.

> "Manu, for the love of Mary, don't be a bloody fool; Save yourself and your people while you have this chance. This will be the last time that the British will extend the hand of peace to

you."

Silence. He glanced up at the wall about him and saw bearded faces, the whites of their eyes showing as they stared down at him.

"Lalor, in those days which now seem so long ago, when we were together," she said slowly, "I thought that you and I both would fight for my people. You did once, or do you try now to forget that? I also realize that I was stupid to have such dreams, just as I thought you could be my prince. I take some poor consolation that I am not the first woman to be deserted and betrayed by her man." (195)

Martin Lalor tries to convince and even appeal to the Rani to surrender her kingdom to the British. But she is firm in her determination and clearly and resolutely refuses to do so.

> The great Lord Krishna will give me what reason and wisdom I require. But include me in your prayers, Lalor. I am sure that I will need all the prayers I can. (195)

Disappointed by her intransigence and non-compromise, he returns to his camp. The dilemma having been resolved and the course of action having become clear, Lalor applies himself wholeheartedly to the cause of capturing the kingdom of Jhansi. He not only plans the *modus operandi* of attack, the division of soldiers, sequence of marching, but leads the main column with his dynamism. His intimate knowledge of the city of Jhansi and the palace of the Rani comes in handy for his systematic attack. Eventually the kingdom of Jhansi is captured and the Rani is reported to have been killed at the final stage. The Union Jack begins to fly on the top of the palace. The British Commanders including Lalor congratulate themselves on the highly difficult achievement and celebrate it with whisky. Captain Lalor feels sorry at heart for the death of the Rani who had shared his bed, in the past. Yet he heaves a sigh of relief on his achievement of success.

But things are not so simple as he perhaps thinks. Before he gets used to the newly-acquired happiness, it is disturbed once again, rather very disconcertingly when he receives a warrant to the effect he has to face a court-trial. Captain Lalor is, naturally, shocked out of his wits. But yet like a true soldier he decides to face it boldly. What surprises him most is the fact that the person who has been responsible for his trial is none other than Alicia Wentworth herself whom he had taken care of so meticulously after the murder of her father. The main complaint against him in the court is that he had betrayed the East India Company not only by helping the Rani against the King of Orchha, but by being her paramour as well. Martin Lalor's bonafides are thus highly suspected, in spite of his deep-seated loyalty to his Government. But his frankness and honesty help him a lot to clarify the doubts of the jury. He explains how he was compelled by the exigencies of life to be the prisoner of the Rani of Jhansi and, therefore, had to obey her out of sheer necessity. In other words, he says he had become a puppet of the situation. As for the sexual relation between the Rani and himself, he does not deny it at all, because it was in line with the behaviour of several other British officers who had native mistresses. Lalor explains how he wanted to send away Alicia Wentworth to the British regiment at Saugor, although he was not allowed by the circumstances to accompany her. His honesty and frankness help him clarify the doubts raised by the court. He explains as follows:

> But I earnestly ask you to realize the background, what pressures were on me to cause me take the decisions I did. I don't plead that these, on looking back, were necessarily the best or right decisions but in those days, they seemed to be the only choice to me. As two such decisions are the main burden of the prosecution's case against me, I will concentrate solely on answering these.
>
> The first principal accusation against me is that I ensured or allowed Alicia Wentworth to go to Saugor while I allegedly chose to remain at Jhansi with the Rani, either through political affiliation or sexual attraction or the hope of riches—I'm not sure what you are meant to think, possibly all these reasons. I'll simply re-iterate . . . that in my considered opinion at the time, Miss Wentworth's mental and physical condition would not permit her to remain a refugee, a semi-prisoner, in a native court in Jhansi. I had to balance this up against the dangers of her journeying to Saugor but I decided that this was the lesser of two evils. Looking back, I now know I was wrong.
>
> The other and main accusation against me is that I commanded the Rani's forces against an alleged ally, the Raja of

> Orchha. . . . So I will now repeat simply that in July, when the battle against Orchha was fought, the Rani was a decided loyal adherent of British interests and she stated so in writing to Saugor. . . . However, she was rebuffed and left isolated and soon became conscious that she was being blamed for the mutineers' massacre of the women and children at the Jokhan Bagh. So she drifted into the enemy camp for some form of survival. . . . To go back to Orchha's invasion in July, all I knew was that the Rani had taken over responsibility in the absence of the British for law and order in Jhansi territory and Orchha, a completely unknown quantity as far as I was concerned, had attacked her. Orchha, in my opinion then and now, was out to make capital out of British misfortune. And I'll say solemnly to you, as I have done to Colonel Mercier and Sir Robert Murray, many times, we lost the Rani to our cause through unfounded rumour, prejudice and neglect.
>
> To the charge against me, my conscience is clear. I repeat that I am in no way guilty. I have served my Regiment, the Army and Queen honourably and to the best of my ability for fifteen years. 1857 was no exception. (268-69)

Because of all these reasons Martin Lalor yielded to the Rani's plan of sending Rao Chaudri with Alicia as an escort. But he is shocked out of his wits by the final revelation by Alicia that she was raped by Rao Chaudri all through the journey until she reached Saugor. Alicia complains against him as follows:

> "The Rani had some kind of hold over him. He listened to her and ignored me. He became determined to pack me off to Saugor." Suddenly her voice rose hysterically and she leaned forward in the witness chair, rigid and wild-eyed. "He seemed to abandon me, to desert me! Yes, he deserted me, just when I needed him most! On the journey to Saugor! The road to Saugor! Saugor! Saugor and another imprisonment, another hell, all alone." (265)

Alicia Wentworth who was secretly in love with Martin Lalor could not, like any woman in general, tolerate his sexual attachment to the Rani. Martin Lalor has, therefore, the paradoxical misfortune of being misunderstood by all those whom he tried to help in his own way.

Because of his sexual relationship with the Rani, his political loyalty is suspected by the British East India Company. When he escapes from the clutches of the Rani of Jhansi, he is accused by the Rani of the betrayal of her love. And again because of his love for the Rani, he has to face the court-trial caused by Alicia Wentworth. The circumstances are so contradictory and harassing that they are enough to drive him simply mad. But he survives all this crisis only because of his extra-ordinary strength of soul and courage and powers of endurance. Finally when he is exonerated of all the charges, he leaves India for good to serve in the army in America. He ultimately dies there in a bomb-blast. Alicia Wentworth, unable to recover from the traumatic experience, goes back to England and dies a natural death at her own hearth.

The entire novel is written in a beautiful realistic style. There is no scope for either romanticization or idealization. The colonial conflict has been depicted from the outsider's (British) point of view. That explains why the native political affairs remain mysterious to the British eyes. Whatever details are learnt by the British about the Indians are only such as are gathered through espionage and reports. For example Rani Laxmi Bai's ambivalent relationship with the Indian rioters, her enmity towards the King of Orchha and her secret alliance with Tantia Topi etc. are all learnt by the British officers only through espionage and the information, hence, remains scanty as compared to the details of the British activities. Himself a Commander of a regiment, Tom Gibson has been extra-ordinarily able to delineate the British point of view. In capturing the details of the British soldiers's difficulty of depending upon the Indian cooks, and servants and yet fighting against the Indian kingdoms, their systematic use of military tactics and maintenance of their solidarity against the Indian patriotism etc. are all depicted by the novelist in abundantly picturesque and realistic detail. The internal hierarchical system of the British military, the details of military weapons and modes of attack have been captured minutely and meticulously. As a result of the dominance of the colonizer's point of view, the feelings and ideologies of the colonized party are naturally either neglected or kept to a minimum. But yet the novel succeeds in offering a very authentic picture of the pre-Independent Indian scene. One wishes the author had ended the novel at Martin Lalor's departure to England, thus making it very effective. The novelist's description of what happened to Lalor and Alicia Wentworth after their leaving India is not, strictly speaking, relevant to the central theme of the novel.

NOTE

1. Tom Gibson, *A Soldier of India* (London: Robert Hale, 1982).

Uniting the Hemispheres: David Malouf's Fiction

DAVID KERR

One of the perennial problems for all societies is self-definition, a coming to self-knowledge. For countries like India and Australia, with their different kinds of colonial experience, the locus of art and history seems, if one confines one's attention to the last 200 years, to be centred on the divided nature of experience, and on the establishment of an identity which, while it may draw from its colonial past, moves on to something better, something which in many ways represents a denial of India further, for it is plain that the nature of the problem in each country is not strictly comparable. I mention it merely to point out that for Australian writing there has been a sort of inevitability about the pursuit of self-knowledge through an exploration of antecedents, and an effort, as far as possible, to concurrently reclaim them, outstrip them and be rid of them. It is not surprising that there is a danger of a kind of cultural schizophrenia setting in.

In the writing of David Malouf we have a contemporary and sophisticated exploration of the Australian psyche, in which the effort to reconcile and transcend opposites in his own background and experience is the driving force behind the writing. In the early eighties when I did a series on educational radio I asked Malouf about his vision of Australia. He replied:

> Once we would have said to ourselves, "I am an Australian. I know how Australians think everywhere." That is simply no longer true. (Different cities) . . . have very different modes of being and behaviour. . . . After living ten years in Sydney that is still a place I can't fathom. Sydney seems to believe in a very existential way in style, in costume, in assumed roles. I find that alarming . . . disturbing. Queensland, which is a very old-fash-

> ioned place and belongs to a very old-fashioned Australia . . . is deeply devoted to the notion of character and fate.[1]

Malouf, in these words, suggests an intellectual possession of what it means to be Australian, but in the work which inspired the comments, *Harland's Half Acre,* he attempts to push into a deeply-felt response to the Australia he has discovered—an Australia that is only now beginning to emerge in our national literature. This novel represents Malouf's first direct confrontation with Australian experience, his first detailed, longitudinal look at Australia's socio-cultural development. For the first time Europe enters obliquely, an unexpected bombast in a chapter that stands apart from the rest, with consequences that are disproportionately traumatic for the bewildered onlookers. That is, memories of the holocaust precipitate in a marginal situation an horrific and bizarre murder that twists out of frame the lives of the narrator and his friend Harland, the artist-recluse.

It is, for Malouf, a work of unaccustomed detail. The earlier novels are spare by comparison. Possibly hinting at a perception that had gathered force, Malouf, in the interview I had with him, commented on our literature's failure to register the great variety of the Australian landscape. We are not merely a wide, brown land, he pointed out. To him Queensland is green, tropical, lavish. That may account for the tonal richness in this novel.

To this reader the shift has not been entirely successful. The earlier novels expanded in the mind through the power of suggestion. Malouf, through controlling his perspective on his material, worked to achieve his effect through careful selection of significant moments and deployment of metaphor. It was the method of a poet working in prose.

Johnno, Fly Away Peter, and *An Imaginary Life* may each, in their distinct ways, be seen as part of Malouf's effort to reconcile his Australian with his European heritage. He, as Martin Leer has implied, has seen Australia "from the edge." His map, as Leer says,

> is a map of the imagination, a topography of the mind, of the self which involves nationality. It is a map "burned into" the narrator's mind which affects not only the way he thinks about Australia, but the way he sees his own position in the universe, in space and time.[2]

The impulse to create such a map comes from Malouf's own background, with his father's family coming to Brisbane from Lebanon in the 1880s, and his mother (also Jewish) coming from middle-class Edwardian London in 1913.[3]

Of the two his mother seems to have possessed the stronger influence. She wished to model the life of the growing boy on what would have been acceptable in Edwardian London. In *12 Edmondstone Street,* he writes:

> Forbidden to use the local slang, or to speak "Australian," we grew up as in a foreign land, where everything local, everything outside the house that was closest and most ordinary, had about it the glow of the exotic. The effect on me was just the opposite of what my mother must have hoped. "Gimme," I would snarl when my sister and I were out of earshot—playing Australian and tough. (33)

Malouf admits that Australia then was "a foreign land," and that his possession of the idiom—possibly of the whole culture—was at this time horribly self-conscious.

He is being drawn—inevitably—two ways. His parentage, his family memories, have their source and substance in Europe, yet are locked away, almost inaccessible to the young Malouf. All around him is the slow ambience of Brisbane, ramshackle, temporary, casual, despite substantial Victorian public buildings. He is an outsider to both worlds, impelled through the power of his imagination to draw them together, to make them whole.

He attempts to accomplish his task by looking closely at particular things—at rooms, at landscapes, at moments in time—and seeing in these particularities universals that have permanent existence for all mankind.

As Leer points out, "The claustrophobic room and the infinite void are the extremes of Malouf's vision."[4] The mother's room in *Harland's Half Acre* provides the setting for the playing out of the strange power-relationships of the family. The original for that room is probably to be found in *12 Edmondstone Street*. In this autobiographical exploration of childhood, the places Malouf is able to explore from memory are given fictional form in other works.

The pressure—it is almost a passion—to get at the reality of objects, places, is explained this way:

> The house is a field of dense affinities, laid down, each one, with an almost physical power, in the life we share with all that in being "familiar" has become essential to us, inseparable from what we are. We draw back magically, magnetically, to our own sticky fingerprints. Even in their ghostly state, on objects long since dispersed. They haunt us. Set loose in a world of *things*, we are struck at first by their terrible otherness. It drives to a fury.*(9)*

The search to recover the past is difficult, memory plays tricks, time and space become fluid, the old house of memory refuses to disentangle itself from later variants. For Malouf this has advantages, for

> it is the whole house I want to go back to and explore, rediscovering, room by room, what it was I first learned there about how high, how wide the world is, how one space opens into another, and from the objects those rooms contained, and the habits and uses they were caught up in . . . what kind of reality I had been born into, that body of myths, beliefs, loyalties, anxieties, affections that shapes a life, and whose outline we enter and outgrow. (12)

But the process of entering into, of absorption, is more immediately present in the writing than the outgrowing is. It shows up in his accounts of people, in the returns he makes in poetry and fiction to the same objects.

In his poem *Early Discoveries* his grandfather is defined as "strange" through his cultivation of a mediterranean garden in his Brisbane backyard. In the later prose account, however, he is seen rather as "very mild and familiar," and his strange knowledge and experience is inferred from Malouf's more recently acquired historical knowledge:

> it was hard to believe he had known a place where whole villages could be wiped out in a single afternoon. The shop (in South Brisbane) was such a backwater. Our own afternoons, so warm and still, seemed far from even the echo of violence. And the language with which his cronies went over it all, the fearful history, the litany of names, the village jests and insults, was so softly guttural and cooing. (6)

His grandfather possessed unimaginable knowledge. At first this was little more than object of wonder, but before long Malouf began to question how this knowledge, where it was of trauma, might affect a person who was physically far removed from its source. The explosive outburst of destructive violence became a subject for Malouf in its own right. In the story "Sorrows and Secrets" (*Antipodes*, 43) the suicide at the end acts as a disorderly eruption in an otherwise well-ordered universe—or so it seems. Far more powerful, however, is the murder-suicide in *Harland's Half Acre*, where the memories of the holocaust break through the surface-kindliness and warmth of the Jewish musician, and wreak inexplicable havoc in an otherwise tranquil environment.

That, of course, was the result of war. It is through this, especially, that Malouf rediscovers Europe, its depth of history, its buried memories, and places it in relation to a land with no history to speak of, and no memories. Possibly it is that fact which has permitted the translation of Europe in Australia into something from which Europeans may learn about themselves.

It is through war that we are able—it is an unintended by-product—to gain a perspective on the Age in which we live, and the rupture that has occurred with the past. In Australia, in a sense, there has been a double rupture—the one geographic, the other historic. That may account for the anachronistic quality of Australian society, when compared with American and urban Europe. In *12 Edmonstone Street*, Malouf puts it this way:

> A degree of gravity, at this moment, is essential. The Wireless has it. We are in the age of certainties. . . . It gives a visible presence, a tangible form, to words that might otherwise, in this quiet backwater have nothing to attach themselves to.
>
> Freedom. Destiny. The easy life we have grown up in, white for the most part, British almost entirely, in spirit Protestant, has never been under threat. If there are those among us whose freedom has been lost, who have been dispossessed, we do not see them. . . .
>
> We do not know it yet but the war is already won.
>
> The other thing we do not know is that all the values it was meant to embody, even in us, are already lost. (37)

Whether some of those values were worth preserving is not here stated. Some of them, assuredly, were not. A puritanic, punishing morality is something Malouf does not regret. The grand, flourishing rhetoric of freedom, even when it was most trumpeted, never in the past prevented enslavement of classes or races. The age of certainties was, in most respects, an age in which the confident proclamation of enduring values had never been a barrier to behaving quite otherwise. Malouf's prose betrays this indirectly. Before the war the dispossessed existed, but had not entered our consciousness. We were comfortable. complacent and insensitive to wrongs that did not affect our own social class.

The war put an end to the circumstances in which complacency like that could long endure. Malouf's fiction, in large measure, may be interpreted as an exploration of that forced coming to consciousness of the Australian people.

Johnno breaks the ground, but it is through *Fly Away Peter* that Malouf's theme reaches it maturity. *Harland's Half Acre* brings the story up-to-date by concentrating on the post-1945 period.

Fly Away Peter explores a complex set of metaphors in an effort to explain the destructive madness that lies just below the surface of mankind. The birds in the story have a visionary grasp on the whole of creation that is both sympathetic and complete. Man, on the other hand, wishes to subdue by violence. Jim's father exemplifies what Malouf means.

> There was in Jim's father a kind of savagery that Jim kept at arm's length; not because he feared to be its victim in a physical sense—he had been often enough and it was nothing much, it was merely physical—but because he didn't want to be infected. It was of a kind that could blast the world. It allowed nothing to exist under its breath without being blackened, torn up by the roots, slashed at, and shown when ripped apart to have a centre as rotten as itself. . . . No, the baleful look his father turned on the world had no reason, it simply was. (6)

The power of the older generation to infect is not, in the end, something Jim can entirely evade. When war breaks out Jim does not enlist at once. It is only after the deaths at Gallipoli that he begins to question his decision. His father's wish that he should go was not the deciding factor—Jim remained healthily sceptical of his father's motives. Rather it lay in his own understanding of what was happening:

> If he didn't go, he had decided, he would never understand, when it was over, why his life and everything he had known were so changed, and nobody would be able to tell him. He would spend his whole life wondering what had happened to him and looking into the eyes of others to find out. (55)

He is caught up in events in which he has no ideological commitment, and which he scarcely understands. The masses have been swept away by mob feeling and rhetoric Jim Saddler, of more introspective temperament, goes to satisfy his sense of personal destiny.

Throughout the novel Jim, the native Australian, with little or no sense of his European heritage, is counterpointed with Ashley Crowder, the Establishment figure, who, with enlightened judgement of the intrinsic value of the area of land he owns, has employed Saddler to record its bird-life—to act as warden. He is a curious mixture of old-world values and social status and new-world egalitarianism. Malouf treats him lightly but with affection.

On his inherited property he is in tune with the Australian character of the place in a way that his father and grandfather never were:

> They had always had in mind a picture they had brought from "home," orderly fields divided by hedgerows, to which the present landscape, by planning and shaping, might one day be made to approximate. But for Ashley this was the first landscape he had known and he did not impose that other, greener one upon it; it was itself. . . . For all his cultivation, he liked what was unmade here and could, without harm, be left that way. (11)

His relationship with Saddler lightly parallels the emerging egalitarianism of Australian society. They did not comprehend each other, but accorded each other recognition and respect. War divides their fates. Crowder goes as an officer, Saddler as a private.

Throughout the passages of war action in the novel (after Chapter 9), Crowder slips from view. Only near the end, with Saddler wounded and dying, does he make a brief reappearance, to conduct Saddler's spirit into the timeless world where he joins the legions of the dead digging their way back home.

Immediately prior to this, as a kind of footnote to the larger action, he is allowed to speculate on the significance of the conflict.

> Ashley, whose mind was of the generalizing sort, had seen quite clearly from the beginning that what was in process here was the emergence of a new set of conditions. Nothing after this would ever be the same. War was being developed as a branch of industry. Later, what he had learned on the battlefield would travel back, and industry for now on, maybe all life, would be organized like war. The coming battle would not be the end. . . And having learned . . . what the terms were—and in expiation of the blood that was on his hands—to resist. (112)

It is the working-class Australian, Jim Saddler, who bears the brunt of what the front-line has to offer, who suffers and dies, and it is his death that Imogen Harcourt ponders on the last pages of the novel.

He is a representative figure, whose enlistment leads Jim into the strange-familiar territory of Europe—a Europe acting out in violence and in blood its complex and ancient destiny. Whereas Jim knew how Australian marshland would look from the air before he had ever seen it that way, Europe is a world "unlike anything he had ever known or imagined. It was as if he had taken a wrong turning in his sleep, arrived at the dark side of his head, and got stuck there." (58)

In a similar way to Henry James's fiction, Malouf chronicles the interaction of innocent colonials with their worldly-wise European ancestors, and in Jim Saddler explores the journey from innocence to experience. In the cauldron of war, he discovers a core of self that he had not previously exposed.

There are several stages in this process. The first is a preliminary stage in which friendships are made, eyes are opened to different ways of thinking, feeling and acting. In this stage Jim gets to know Clancy Parkett, and is introduced to the wonders of his life. (74)

But with incredible suddenness the world changes. "Often, as Jim later discovered, you entered the war through an ordinary looking gap in a hedge and on duckboards . . . that led to the war." (76)

Jim has to become properly accustomed to many things rapidly. At each step closer to the front-line there is a further breaking down of the normal order of life. Farmland gives way to muddy trenches with walls caved in, seepage, dead bodies, and an increasingly vile smell compounded of gas, mud, rotting, planks, and corpses. The troops being relieved look worse than ghosts.

The first climax in the war action is the death of Clancy, who is literally blown out of existence. "The body's wholeness, he saw, was an image a man carried in his head. It might persist after the fact." (83)

Jim believes he must be dead and yet aware of his body's continued existence. When he realizes this is all that remains of Clancy he screams a silent scream of nightmarish agony. Similarly, in the same incident, Eric loses his legs, and Jim is forced to look on the solitary nature of man's existence, its existential hopelessness.

What, given this hopelessness, are we to do? That, in essence, is what Saddler is forced to learn.

When he confronts the bully Wizzer in a shell hole during an attack which goes wrong, he comes close to giving up to blind panic than at any other time.

He has already encountered Wizzer in the training camp. This acts as a prelude for what is to come.

> Jim found himself defending whatever it was in him that Wizzer rejected, and discovered that he needed this sudden confrontation to see who he was and what he had to defend. Enemies, like friends, told you who you were. (63)

This is part of Jim's encounter with the dark side of his head, where he will find his inheritance from father, and all that is dispensable of European tradition. In the shellhole, this process reaches its climax:

> It was eerie, nightmarish, to be fighting for your life like this in a shellhole out of battle, and with an unknown assailant.(90)

Then Jim recognizes that it is Wizzer he is fighting.

> Overhead the sky was split. A livid crack appeared in the continuity of things, a line of jagged light through which a new landscape might have been visible. The crack repeated itself as sound. Jim's head was split this time and the further landscape in there was impenetrably dark. (90)

This is the low point of Jim's experience. He is perilously close to joining Wizzer in his abject retreat. Saddler's temptation represents a longing for a more primitive state where responsibility for oneself is abandoned to the unchecked power of instinct. But Jim returns to the nightmarish landscape where he must live. Although "scared silly" Jim sees it does not matter whether he is killed or not. (94) Until he reaches that point he has not assumed control over his own life.

He has, in fact, accepted his own death as the ambiguous slide from "corpses" to "other living figures" seems to imply.

His return to the fighting places him outside time. Being liberated from the fear of death he is equally liberated from a consecutive view of time. To put it another way, what might follow has no more claim on his attention than what was or what is. He now possesses the whole living picture from moment to moment as a four-dimensional whole:

> He saw it all, and himself a distant, slow-moving figure within it: the long view of all their lives, including his own—all those who were running, half-crouched, towards the guns, and the men who were firing them; those who had fallen and were noisily dying; the new and the old dead, his own life neither more nor less important than the rest, even in his own vision of the thing, but unique, because it was his head that contained it and in his view that all these balanced lives for a moment existed: the men going about their strange business of killing and being killed, but also the rats, the woodlice under the logs, a snail that might be climbing up a stalk, quite deaf to the sounds of battle, an odd bird or two, like the couple of wheat-eaters . . . in a field like this. (117)

At this point, the fact that he is an Australian in Europe has slipped entirely from view. Social, political and cultural perceptions no longer matter. What Malouf has done is to make use of the notion of distant connection with something unfamiliar—with, in effect, the buried part of one's mind—in order to explore the universal question of men's relationship with the universe. In the context Malouf establishes, Jim's perception becomes a metaphor, which he approaches from a variety of perspectives—with each angle of attack having ultimately the same objective.

Only thus is the most difficult achievement in the novel made possible—integration of Imogen Harcourt into the fabric of the work.

Jim Saddler first meets Imogen Harcourt when she is photographing a bird he, from a concealed position, is watching. It is worth quoting Malouf on this episode, as it is central to his whole purpose.

> KERR: That then is perhaps what life is about—this ability to hold complex interactions and relationships in your head.
> MALOUF: Yes, and to bring that to some point of different being. . . . There is a moment when they first meet, when they are both in fact looking at the same bird and don't realize they are doing it. She is attempting to take a photograph of it and he is looking through his binoculars and she does take a photograph of the bird. . . . When the young man looks at the pictures he realizes that somewhere in that blur behind the bird is him. He has been there all the time. He has not got into the picture but he was there and she is fascinated, in watching him watch the picture, by the fact that he is at that moment concentration on her photograph of the bird in much the same way that he concentrated on the bird when she took the picture; but for her at that moment he is the one who is there as vividly as the bird is in the picture, and that is her perception of *absolute presence*. That is why she even used that word, "absolute presence." . . . It is what it is all about.[5]

It is Imogen, who on learning of Jim's death, affirms that he has existed, that he exists. "It was," she reflects, "that intense focus of his whole being, it's me, Jim Saddler, that struck her with grief, but was also the thing—and not simply as an image either—that endured. That in itself . . . as it for its moment was. That is what life meant, a unique presence, and it was essential in every creature. . . . A life wasn't for anything. It simply was." (132)

And the novelist's task, so it seems, is to capture and affirm that individuality that stands above history and the flux of circumstance. Episodes of Jim Saddler watching the migratory dunlin, work two ways to this end. First, the absolute presence of the bird is affirmed through the intensity of observation Saddler turns upon it. Second, the dunlin possesses a map of the world that is prior to experience, just as Saddler knows what his local territory will look like in advance of seeing it from the air. In some ways the dunlin's vision of its world is larger, more complete. Jim, through losing touch with his deeper instinctive knowledge, is in the position occupied by most of the human race. He is only half-aware of what she is, of what he might be.

A clue to what Malouf has done with Saddler, with the dunlin, with the change and growth he goes through, may be gleaned from a comment in the interview on the question of time. I had suggested Malouf may have been inferring in this novel an *An Imaginary Life* that mankind may have had some form of prior existence.

> Well I think two things on that. One might be a different shape to time. We say prior only if we think of time as being linear, but maybe time is not linear, maybe it is cubic rather than linear. But it is true also that here are various ways in which we must be in tune with other creatures and other things in the world because we are made out of the same substances . . . there is a kind of tunnel open between us and them which we have forgotten about. I assume that what the fall means is that we have lost some kind of continuity between ourselves and the rest of creation. I think I am always wanting to try and find ways back to that continuity. That is certainly largely what *An Imaginary Life* is all about.[6]

The journey in Malouf is therefore from a position in which the desire to achieve a reconciliation of opposites is transcended and replaced by an overview of time, place and circumstance where all creation is held in balance in the imagination. It is like the vision that, arguably, God might have of the universe, a vision which contains all that Yeats's golden bird sings about—what is "past, or passing or to come." From that perspective the apparently irreconcilable worlds of one's ancestry and of one's present life become part of an extended living fabric in which new life is always coming into being as the old decays. It may appear to be a reductionist, a simplifying vision: it is not. For in it both the complex relationships, the beauty and the terror, the flux is not reduced to a simplicity, rather it is apprehended whole: both the conscious and the subconscious are brought into a relationship, the present reality is seen to be a working out of the dark side of the mind: the hemispheres are in communication, growing towards a union.

NOTES

1. Interview with David Malouf, October 1983.
2. Martin Leer, "At the Edge: Geography and the Imagination in the Work of David Malouf," *ALS*, p. 3.
3. For a detailed discussion, see Samar Attar, "A Lost Dimension: The Immigrant's Experience in the Work of David Malouf," *ALS*, vol. 13, no. 3, May 1988.
4. Martin Leer, p. 4.
5. Interview.
6. *Loc. cit.*

The Theme of Entrapment in Peter Carey's Fiction

M.D. FLETCHER

In an important analysis of "post-colonial" writing, Ashcroft, Griffith and Tiffin have argued for the centrality of metonyms to that enterprise. Post-colonial writing in "settler" countries—Australia, Canada, New Zealand, the United States—has differed from its counterparts elsewhere. In Australia in particular, the theme of entrapment or imprisonment—reflecting white Australia's origins as a penal colony—has been a major metonym.[1]

Throughout Carey's fiction, both literal and figurative entrapment are invoked; and while naturally one must be careful not to see figurative entrapment everywhere, Carey is usually quite overt in that respect. His fictions abound with actual prisons and cages, which perhaps serve as metonym for Australian society. But he also is fascinated by the construction of entrapping structures, as Graeme Turner reminds us,[2] and often that involves individual, figuratively entrapping structures.

Carey has indicated in an interview that *Illywhacker* marks his attempt to come to terms with Australia,[3] but many of the themes and motifs of *Illywhacker*, and of *Oscar and Lucinda*, are anticipated in *Bliss*, including that of imprisonment or entrapment, and in this essay I look at some of the ways in which that theme is deployed in those three novels.

As Laurie Hergenhan notes in his *Unnatural Lives: Studies in Australian Fiction about the Convicts*, Foucault has changed our thinking about imprisonment by demonstrating how its characteristics permeate other modern power relations.[4] The similarity between prison and an asylum is the most obvious point, but, in addition, the ability to observe unseen provided by the panopticonic design of Bentham's reformed prison heralds a transition to self-surveillance and what Foucault calls the "capillary" surveillance of social self-surveillance or surveillance by the whole society rather than by outsiders from above. Carey depicts a number of these themes in the three novels discussed here.

The major protagonist in *Bliss*, Harry Joy, is literally taken into custody by the police and later committed in an asylum. Harry also sees himself as literally trapped in Hell, and the terms "trapped" and "prisoner" are employed by Carey to describe other situations in the novel as well. Hasall, in particular, has suggested that Harry's wife (Bettina) and children (David and Lucy) are depicted as "trapped in the socially approved roles he (Harry) has imposed upon them," while David and Bettina and Bettina's lover Joel "are trapped in other people's stories and kill themselves."[5] In addition, Harry and his employee, Alex Duval, are similarly trapped in marriage, in advertising, and finally in the asylum itself.[6] Some of these points seem questionable, while others require elaboration.

Bettina's desire to become a "hot shot" in advertising has been thwarted by Harry's refusal to bring her into the business, and his expectations and perceptions of his children do not correspond to reality, but the imagery of entrapment is not prominent in those cases (although David seems entrapped in his own romantic fantasies).

Hasall's comparison of Alex and Harry is more telling, however. Carey is explicit in describing the game in which Alex's wife is able to trap him time after time, even having him released from the sanctuary of the asylum for that very purpose, and he is inventive in creating the nightmare which embodies Alex's experience of that entrapment. Similarly, while Harry does not initially feel trapped in his own marriage, he is certainly ensnared in the deal with Bettina that secures his release from the asylum.

Harry is trapped in the city and in advertising by his love of comfort, just as Alex is trapped in the dishonesties of advertising by his fear of losing his livelihood. It is appropriate, then, that after Alex is mistaken for Harry and committed in the asylum, Harry is in turn committed and in effect "becomes" Alex. Alex already has the name Harry Joy when the real Harry arrives, and once re-labelled the real Harry begins to act like Alex.

Hassall's third point, that those who are in someone else's story (Bettina, David, Joel) kill themselves, also warrants extension. In this context it may be illuminating to compare Harry's trip to the police station with his incarceration in the asylum. He is taken to the police station for driving an unroadworthy vehicle after a circus elephant sits on his little red Fiat. He finds himself close to serious trouble because his story is the retelling of an old joke and totally implausible. Although he is man-handled by the arresting officers, he manages to tell an original story, and although there is not even a pretence of relevance to the condition of his automobile, he is released.

In the asylum, on the other hand, Harry has no more stories to tell. Although he tries to follow Honey Barbara's advice and avoid the double bind of claiming persecution and thus opening himself to the diagnosis of paranoia, he is trapped in the warders's definition of reality, even "becoming" Alex once he is assigned that name.

Finally, the theme of people being entrapped within certain perceptions of reality also is carried by Harry's belief throughout most of the novel that he is imprisoned in Hell. In a conceit reminiscent of Don Quixote, Harry believes he is in Hell and that actors are playing the roles of this family and acquaintances to fool him. His imposition of that frame influences his interpretation of events to confirm his perceptions, and his actions on that assumption even create responses from others that re-enforce his suspicions.

In *Illywhacker* the forms of imprisonment once again are literal as well as figurative. The story begins with Herbert, the "Illywhacker," telling the story of his life and that of his family. In mid-life Herbert spends a long period in gaol. In Herbert's terms, being in gaol forces him to shrink, to assume a character that does not attract attention or retribution and even to become physically shorter, leaving him permanently changed. Compare, from *Bliss*, Harry Joy's stay in the asylum, where he begins to take on the actual personality of Alex Duval.

Before being gaoled, Herbert had enjoyed travelling about the countryside with Leah. After leaving gaol he is reunited with Leah, now freed from caring for her invalided husband, but he no longer has much to offer—he simply wants to be taken care of by his family. A high level of self-surveillance is employed to adjust to conditions in gaol, and the experience of gaol carries over into civilian life as a continuing state of reduced expectations.

In another sense, however, these characteristics were present in Herbert as a young man. *Illywhacker* is about lying, and the liar may be entrapped as well as liberated by lying. As Helen Daniel argues, from the very beginning of his relationship with his wife, Phoebe, and her family, he becomes trapped in his own lie about the snake he has with him—that is a pet, a lie designed to impress Phoebe—and causes her father's death in the process of attempting to substantiate his lie.[7]

Daniel also suggests that Herbert's marriage to Phoebe does not last because Phoebe flees "the cage she perceives as Herbert's life."[8] More specifically, Herbert, orphan that he is, is continually building homes to create a family, from which Phoebe flees as she attempts also to escape from the entrapment of having children, as she equates Herbert's idea of home and family with prison.[9] In this sense Herbert as a young man anticipates Herbert as an old man looking for a family in which to be cradled.

The story of Herbert is paralleled by the story of his son, Charles, and Charles's wife, Emma. In his youth, Charles is trapped at the Chaffey farm for months during a drought. Les Chaffey has taken apart his motor bike, and Charles cannot leave until it is reassembled. This episode results in Charles and Emma meeting, however. Once married, Charles and Emma happily manage an enormous pet emporium but the turning point in their story occurs when Emma begins to live in one of the pet cages after a misunderstanding with Charles.

Ultimately, the emporium is refinanced with Japanese money as a human display emporium for tourists. The theme of colonization as imprisonment, and of indigenes seen as exotics on display, is clear here. The denouement is anticipated not only by Emma's taking up residence in a cage but also by Herbert's desire to be taken care of like a pet. Even before the emporium is re-organized for the display of humans, Herbert has been observed at the window of his room between letters of the pet shop's neon sign, similar in effect to the bars of a cage or prison cell. In a final (or perhaps initial) twist, Herbert was already giving his spiel from the beginning of the book from inside the human pet emporium, despite giving the impression at the outset of being an independent raconteur.

The theme of imprisonment in *Oscar and Lucinda* is carried somewhat differently by the two title characters. Lucinda finds the entire world a prison, entrapped in the conventions and expectations of her society "even without (the) whalebone and elastic" that she refuses to wear.[10] She is even admonished to shorten her stride, failing to wear the conventional clothing that would inhibit it automatically—and compare Honey Barbara in *Bliss*, whose stride is contrasted to the hobbled walk of city women and who strikes David as disconcertingly "wild and untrammeled."[11]

Inadequately socialized as a woman (according to her mother's mea culpa), Lucinda must be kept in her place by the gaze of men in groups and by the Foucauldian "capillary" surveillance of everyone—the lawyer, Ahearn, the glass blower, Phelps, and even her maid, Mrs. Smith—admonishing her to stay within accepted boundaries.

Oscar, on the other hand, experiences a series of prisons of various types. Throughout the novel he is entrapped in his religious belief, making a series of extremely painful and important life decisions on the basis of throwing lots or flipping coins. Travelling to Australia from England by boat, he is trapped below deck by his fear of water, and has to be hoisted onto the boat initially in a cage.

Working in a room fully of clerks for d'Abbs, Oscar is subjected to the "panopticonic" oversight of Jeffris, under which everyone works silently even though there are no articulated rules. During the journey to the outback with the glass church, he is literally Jeffris's prisoner, and is confined to a wagon designated "the Ladies Compartment" to add to his ignominy. Finally, of course, he dies entrapped in the glass church as the river water rises through cracks in the glass and the door to the church jams.

Oscar and Lucinda together conspire to construct an entrapping misunderstanding as elaborate and cleverly constructed in its way as the glass church itself. As in a classic romance, they deepen the misunderstanding in a minuet of steps, the differences being that the classical romantic resolution fails to occur. Lucinda eventually prays for Oscar to release her from "the prison her foolishness had made for her,"[12] but divine intervention is not forthcoming.

Lucinda, afraid that Oscar will think she has him in mind for marriage, pretends to a continuing and exaggerated passion for Hasset well after he has left her life both physically and emotionally, including keeping letters on the mantelpiece, so she will not lose Oscar's company altogether. When she thinks he might be ready to reciprocate her interest in him, convention as well as the fear of appearing too bold hold her in check, and she waits for Oscar to speak first.

Oscar is crushed by her deception concerning Hasset, as he loves her already. He fears revealing his love for her, lest she be offended and withdraw or even refuse to see him. Indeed, assuming himself to be in competition with a clever, "manly" Hasset, Oscar sees his only hope as appearing to be saintly—as unselfishly good and, of course, not pressing his suit. His Christianity compounds this approach, leading him to hope that self-sacrifice may be the road to desires fulfilled.

Lucinda and Oscar conspire, then, to invert each others's meanings to maintain the edifice of misunderstanding. They enter into the wager of whether or not Oscar can deliver the glass church to Hasset in the outback by Palm Sunday, which ends in his journey into the heart of darkness with Jeffris and his death trapped in the glass church.

NOTES

1. Bill Ashcroft, Gareth Griffiths and Helen Tiffin, *The Empire Writes Back: Theory and Practice in Post-Colonial Literatures* (London: Routledge, 1989).
2. Graeme Turner, "American Dreaming: The Fictions of Peter Carey," *Australian Literary Studies*, 12 (4), October 1986, p. 435.
3. "Peter Carey's Interview with David Sexton," *Literary Review*, 84, June 1985.
4. Laurie Hergenhan, *Unnatural Lives* (Brisbane: University of Queensland, 1983).
5. A.J. Hassall, 'Telling Lies and Stories: Peter Carey's *Bliss*," *Modern Fiction Studies*, 35 (4), Winter 1989, pp. 645, 639.
6. *Ibid.*, p. 646.
7. Helen Daniel, *Liars: Australian New Novelists* (Ringwood: Penguin, 1988), p. 171.
8. *Ibid.*, p. 173.
9. Peter Carey, *Illywhacker* (Brisbane: University of Queensland Press, 1985, paper edition, 1986), p. 205.
10. Peter Carey, *Oscar and Lucinda* (Brisbane: University of Queensland Press, 1988, paper edition, 1988), p. 251.
11. Peter Carey, *Bliss* (Brisbane: University of Queensland Press, 1981, paper edition 1990), pp. 203, 211.
12. *Oscar and Lucinda*, p. 410.

From Empire Feudalism and Racism to Commonwealth Citizenship: The Views of Four Female Intruders in the Colonial Tropics

A Comparison of Ruth Prawer Jhabvala's *Out of India* with Karen Blixen's *Out of Africa*, Jeannie Gunn's *We of the Never Never* and Doris Lessing's *The Grass is Singing*

DAVID MYERS

It is in the spirit of Commonwealth internationalism that I venture today to compare Ruth Prawer Jhabvala's perspectives on Indian society with Baroness Karen Blixen's views of life in Kenya, with Aeneas Gunn's experiences in Australia's tropical Top End and with Doris Lessing's savage insights into the Rhodesian South Africa of her childhood. All four of these women were European intruders in the Commonwealth tropics in periods ranging from the turn of the century to the end of World War II. That is, they were acute observers of the power and the decay of the British Empire in its tropical colonial realities and they were personally involved in different aspects of interracial relationships between white Europeans and the indigenous inhabitants of Africa, India and Australia.

As one reads Ruth Prawer Jhabvala's *Out of India*, Karen Blixen's *Out of Africa*, Jeannie Gunn's *We of the Never Never* and Doris Lessing's *The Grass is Singing*, one is always conscious of reading the perspectives of free-spirited and forthright female artists who were beyond the influence of the Empire explorers, senior administrators and powerful financiers who expressed the economically and politically dictated orthodoxy of the male power-elite of this era. The characters in these women's fictions are therefore not predetermined by racial prejudice. Rather they are the results of a free exploration of "the other," toward which the authors feel impelled with similar mixtures of love, compassion, bemusement, admiration and irony.

In order to narrow the focus of this paper, I thought it best to concentrate on the following four aspects of cultural behaviour patterns as observed by Jhabvala, Blixen, Lessing and Jeannie Gunn: acceptance of the European intruder into a colonial or ex-colonial society; male-female relationships; bourgeois convention versus adventurous non-conformism; European rational materialism and activism versus Indian/African fatalism, passivity and stoic spirituality.

I am very conscious in this paper that I am not comparing the views of four sociologists who work with questionnaires, statistics and graphs and who work with would-be scientific definitions of class, race, religion and gender behaviour. On the contrary. I am comparing the intuitive views of four gifted female artists who offer personal insights into the scientifically unknowable personalities of their fictional characters. There are clearly advantages and disadvantages to the path of the artist and the literary critic as opposed to the path of the sociologist. The imagination, intuition, empathy and stylistic brilliance of the artist may be counter-weighted by possible limitations of personality and experience. The brilliance of the artist may be further counter-weighted by the possibly pedestrian or pedantic horizons of the literary scholar. In any case one should not expect the results to have anything to do with the impersonal, balanced but purely external overview of the sociologist.

What is particularly important to me in the topic of this paper is that it puts the study of literature into the context of an international commonwealth of nations in a way which has nothing to do with European conquest and mono-cultural arrogance and everything to do with a female, European intruder's curious and admiring exploration of a foreign culture as part of her quest for personal fulfilment. I believe that one of the greatest services that literature can perform is the exploration and comparative illumination of foreign cultures for a wide readership.

Let us commence our study by considering the terms of acceptance of the European artist-intruder into a colonial or ex-colonial society. In comparing these four women's perspectives on the tropical extremities of what was then the British Empire, it is perhaps inevitable that the first focus is on their relationship to the indigenous inhabitants of the then colonies.

Karen Blixen adopts feudal stance: she assumes that the Kikuyu people need her patronage and the benevolent protection of her wealth, her coffee plantation work, her big game rifle, her connections with upper class English government officials and safari-hunters, and her medical and educational care. She runs her house like an aristocratic castle and her farm like a grand, pre-industrial, feudal estate. The correct crystal glassware for chilled champagne (or for Chambertin 1906) together with the family silver is as a matter of course imported from Denmark.

This is all understandable insofar as Karen Blixen was after all Baroness Blixen in a remote part of post W.W. I Kenya which remained blissfully unaffected by the cataclysmic changes that shook European society to its foundations in these years. Nevertheless, when Baroness Blixen infers that her friends Denys Finch-Hatton and Berkeley Cole belong to a bygone age of dualism and chivalry, she might just as well have been writing of herself (from our contemporary point of view):

> No other nation than the English could have produced them, but they were examples of atavism, and theirs was an earlier England, a world which no longer existed. (184)

Baroness Blixen, who was never too tired to go fishing for a classical allusion or two, compared Berkeley Cole with d'Artagnan and Don Quixote and her beloved Denys Finch-Hatton with Sir Philip and Francis Drake. Perhaps she believed the reflected glory would also shine on herself or perhaps like all lonely people she couldn't resist a little wishful day-dreaming. She even extended this day-dreaming to the religious sphere, comparing herself having late evening conversation with Denys Finch-Hatton in her well-lit house in Kenya with Saint Clare and Saint Francis "entertaining one another upon theology" late in the evening Umbria. (141)

Baroness Blixen was in the habit of quoting bravado German to her beloved Denys ("Frei lebt wer sterben kann") and she also held a shaking lantern to his rifle while he shot two lions after dinner. But when Denys was away on safari (which was most of the time) Karen was more than capable of shooting her own lions. In fact she confesses that at one stage "I could not live till I had killed a specimen of each kind of African game." (207) But perhaps it is understandable that her Amazonian steeliness melted when confronted with Denys

Finch-Hatton alias Francis Drake. Denys himself was quite accustomed to shooting anything on four legs. Perhaps Denys shared with Ernest Hemingway the puzzling perversion of seeing a non-existent connection between killing and virility and dignity and romance. Such was the nature of the grand, feudal era of Kenya in the 1920s and 1930s.

Karen Blixen is quite open about her faith in the aristocracy and her contempt for the bourgeoisie. She keeps Scotch deerhounds because they help to produce the correct "feudal atmosphere" (67) and treasures a letter which is addressed to her as "Lioness Blixen." (68) As she and Berkeley Cole hand out British Empire medals after W.W. I to the Masai chiefs, she reflects:

> The ceremony could only have been carried through so well by two parties of noble blood and great family traditions; may democracy take no offence. (191)

Indeed she even divides up the history of Kenya into the Berkeley era and the post-Berkeley era. The Berkeley era was allegedly the time of "the Happy Hunting Grounds" but the post-Berkeley era was marked by a catastrophic drop in the "standard of gallantry" and the changing of the colony to a mere "business proposition." (193) One wonders whether the Kenyans saw their history in this light.

Baroness Blixen views her stay in Kenya not as a quest for happiness or an attempt to do anything so crassly bourgeois as to make money, but rather as an aristocratic fulfilment of her mission as an idea of God. She says that she does not expect justice or happiness from God but rather mystery, tragedy and "the infinite power of imagination." (30) She compares herself with the African natives, saying that she shared their "unadulterated liking of danger—the true answer of creation to the announcement of their lot—the echo from the earth when heaven had spoken." (30) Stylistically this is likely to stir us on first reading, but upon reflection it looks rather more like adolescent, neo-romantic bravado with little relationship to reality.

In fact one could argue that Baroness Blixen experiences a preconceived Kenya which she re-creates according to her class prejudices. She is most romantically self-indulgent when she adores the Masai who are "both aristocracy and proletariat" (178) and therefore fit to share in her theological concept of tragedy as the idea of God. She is most openly satirical about the bourgeois British doctor who refuses to treat natives because "he had before now, practised to the elite of Bournemouth." (223)

Within the posturing limitations of her feudalism, Karen Blixen creates a gracious vision of her interaction with Kenya, a vision which is based to a large extent on her admirable moral foundations, namely self-discipline and the determination never to complain about her lot but rather to filter experience through philosophy and so seek for beauty. Her failed marriage must have been a very bitter experience and her subsequent ten years in Kenya must often have subjected her to feelings of loneliness, listlessness and futility. But never once does she complain. Her noblesse oblige and her self-discipline ensure this. One simply does not speak of one's woes or one's ills. This would show a lack of breeding.

Karen Blixen and her ilk felt spiritual awe for the majesty of the landscape and the flora and fauna of the Kenya high country. There is a reverence and an exaltation for the privilege of living in Kenya and escaping from boring Europe. This extends to the lions that they kill, to the exhilaration of flying, to the exotic wild game reserve of the Masai and to the beauty of the seasons of the year.

This exaltation produces a style which is inevitably elevated, salted with quotations from classical literature and spiced with brilliant metaphors. The style also expresses the results, however, of scientific observation which forbids such vulgarities as sentimentality or uninformed effusiveness.

If Karen Blixen romanticizes and aestheticizes her baronial life on a Kenyan high country coffee plantation, Doris Lessing unmasks, only one generation later, the soulless greed and racism inherent in maize and tobacco farming in the sun-baked, Southern Rhodesian lowlands. Doris Lessing focuses her outrage equally on the rape of the earth and on the rape of the African natives who are reduced from human beings to animals kept as press-gang labour. (114)

When Doris Lessing creates Mary and Dick Turner in *The Grass is Singing*, there are no mists of mythology or notification through classical quotation. There is no privacy for the characters, no intimate sphere of perversion and shame which noblesse oblige leaves unexpressed. Instead there is a merciless laying bare of despair, sexual and racial perversion, incompetence, prejudice, ignorance and self-pity.

This is the other side of the British colonial experience. Poverty and farming failure produce a low self-esteem among many of the white farming immigrants. But it is their unacknowledged guilt in exploiting indentured black labour which according to Doris Lessing produces in them the extremes of hatred and loathing of the African natives of Rhodesia and South Africa—the despised kaffirs as they are called. (It would not be irrelevant to compare *The Grass is Singing* with some of the literary portrayals of poor whites and their hatred of blacks in the deep South of the USA in the last century.)

In this radically different context, the fellow Europeans of the white female "protagonist" are no longer noble-spirited, as they are portrayed by Karen Blixen. They are mean, money-grubbing, ungenerous, conniving and malicious. They do not love the African landscape, they exploit it in a rapacious manner for short-term gain and long-term degradation. There is no spiritual inspiration from the land and the seasons, but only curses against the heat, the drought, the plagues and the sullen unresponsiveness of the over-worked, underpaid native labour.

Lessing captures the hypocrisy of British racism in the Empire through the blustering harangues that white farmers deliver to the brow-beaten "kaffirs" about the dignity of labour. Mary Turner, for example, is a poor white in *The Grass is Singing* whose loathing and fear of the blacks is epitomized by the fact that "she hated more than anything, with a violent physical repulsion, the heavy smell that came from them, a hot sour animal smell." (115) She harangues the blacks who ask for permission to leave her employ and ends her speech with

> a short homily on the dignity of work, which is a doctrine bred into the bones of every white South African. They would never be any good, she said (speaking in kitchen kaffir which some of them did not understand, being fresh from their kraals) until they learned to work without supervision, for the love of it, to do as they were told, to do a job for its own sake, not thinking about the money they would be paid for it. It was this attitude towards work that had made the white man what he was: the white man worked because it was good to work, because working without reward was what proved a man's worth. (114)

Mary Turner's nervous breakdown and her husband Dick's collapse into insanity are an ironic and even tragic commentary on the hypocrisy of this silly speech. Even though Dick Turner is more lenient than Mary is with his indentured black labour, he is so only because he is desperate to cajole them into staying and continuing to work for him.

Dick's abiding and tragic virtue is that he deeply loves the earth of his farm. His reward is that his fellow white farmers regard him as an incompetent farmer. Dick refuses to grow tobacco because he considers it to be "a factory crop" which is unworthy of the land. He is sad that the British mining companies have stripped his land completely of trees, so he plants one hundred acres of eucalyptus in order to atone for this rape of the soil. He is derided as a fool by his fellow whites because eucalyptus are not a cash crop. But he is the only character in the novel who genuinely loves the land and the goodness which it can produce if it is cared for (see p. 123). Dick is deliberately contrasted with the typical white farmers of Rhodesia who grew fabulously wealthy from maize in W.W. I and from tobacco in W.W. II. Charley Slatter is typical of these British farmers:

> He had five hundred acres of the most beautiful rich dark soil, which in the old days had produced twenty-five and thirty bags of mealies to the acre. Year after year he had squeezed that soil, until by now he got five bags an acre if he was lucky. He never dreamed of fertilizing. He cut down his trees (such as remained when the mining companies had done) to sell as firewood. . . . His attitude to the land was fundamentally the same as that of the natives whom he despised; he wanted to work out one patch of country and move on to the next. (170)

Dick receives no reward for his love and nurturing of his land. Instead he watches while his wife's perverted fear and loathing of the blacks warps after years of failure, humiliating poverty, isolation and sickness into a "coy, coquettish" dependence on her black servant, Moses. Moses enjoys the power of becoming her paternalistic boss and murders her only after she betrays his authority to a young, white visitor.

Her fellow white European farmers learn nothing from her nervous breakdown and murder and her husband's fall into insanity. Their only concern is to protect the reputation of the white community with a cover-up and whitewash. It cannot be leaked out that middle-aged Mary Turner did the unthinkable: she loved her black servant. The ludicrous lie is invented that Moses murdered her in a robbery attempt. The purpose of the cover-up is to keep the black population in a state of unquestioning subservience. The blacks cannot be allowed to think that they are any better than animals, that they have erotic, political and economic power.

At least they have this power potential. The key to unlocking this potential power is of course education. But the only place where the blacks in the decades before the end of the W.W. II could get even a partial education in Rhodesia was the Christion mission. This is why Charley Slatter hates the mission-educated Moses. He knows that the missions give the blacks a dangerous taste of refinement and even dignity, a sense of Christ's doctrine of the equality of all souls before God. Missions and the "nigger-loving" government are the enemies because they are determined to modify the attempt by the farmers to reduce the blacks to the level of whip-driven oxen.

In her autobiographical account of her year in Australia's tropical Northern Territory Jeannie Gunn sketches characters who share Charley Slatter's contempt for all blacks. She herself, however, shows a benevolent "paternalism" towards the Aborigines and frequently a spontaneous admiration. The contempt for Aborigines in this work is expressed by some of the old Territory hands in the vast tropical, cattle stations of the Top End. Equally of course they express their resentment of women like Jeannie Gunn daring to defy the taboo against the presence of women in the Australian Outback. The old Territory cattlemen of this era at the turn of the century hate the wild, nomadic restlessness and rebelliousness amongst the black stockmen working on the white men's stations.

In contrast with this prejudice and greed is the tolerant openness to other cultures and the gentle love which Jeannie Gunn feels for the Aborinine women. One needs to contrast Jeannie with Doris Lessing's Mary Turner who calls the African blacks "filthy savages," (110) who swings a "sjambok (whip) jauntily on her wrist," (112) who loathes selling "kaffir truck to stinking kaffirs" (94) and who, because of her perverted repression of her own libido, feels a loathing (which is really an envy) for "the exposed fleshiness of them, their soft brown bodies and soft bashful faces that were also insolent and inquisitive, and their chattering voices that held a brazen fleshy undertone." (94) By contrast Jeannie goes swimming in the billabongs with the lubras and the children, shares their native tucker and learns their folklore. Jeannie also feels spiritual reverence and curiosity about Aborigine creation myths.

It could be argued that Jeannie Gunn was, in terms of inter-racial friendship, well ahead of her times in an Australia which was still openly racist against both Aborigines and Chinese at the time of

Federation in 1901. Nevertheless, Jeannie's narrative reveals some of the old-fashioned graciousness of Karen Blixen in Kenya in the 1920s. Jeannie is also to some extent and with much less money, an isolated grand dame in the man's world of the Northern Territory and she insists on creating a household which expresses civilization and refinement. She is saved from pretentiousness and the pitfalls of snobbism by her sense of humour and her lively curiosity about her new environment.

Although Jeannie shares with Doris Lessing's Mary Turner suffering from the isolation, the heat, the hardship and the shock at her new "Never-Never" environment, she is never at risk of lapsing like Mary into self-pity or despair because she is supported by her unswerving love and admiration for her husband. She cannot be saved, however, from the tragedy of losing her husband to a similar malarial fever which gradually weakens and destroys Dick Turner. But Jeannie Gunn rises above even this tragedy with an affirmation of life and love which, although secular in nature, are almost religious in nature at the conclusion of her autobiographical report.

How very different from Jeannie Gunn, Karen Blixen and Doris Lessing are the interracial experiences and artistic outpour of Ruth Prawer Jhabvala in India from 1951 to 1975. The poverty and quasi-miscegenation which lead to insanity, murder and tragedy in the Rhodesia depicted by Doris Lessing in *The Grass is Singing*, lead rather to a rich social and philosophical humour in the sexually and racially liberated stories of Ruth Prawer Jhabvala.

Karen Blixen, Doris Lessing and Jeannie Gunn are all quite certain what overall view they wish to project in their work about colonial Africa and Australia. Ruth Prawer Jhabvala—as befits a cultural polyglot who was born of Polish parents, spent her childhood in Germany, lived two decades in England and over two decades in India, but now divides her time between Delhi, New York and London—is quite incapable of committing herself to any one view of post-colonial India.

In her *Introduction: Myself in India*, Jhabvala uses images of mutilated lepers, a boy being hacked to pieces as a sacrifice to the Gods and "old, half-starved widows who skip and dance about . . . because they are Krishna's milkmaids" (20) in order to express "how intolerable India—the idea, the sensation of it—can become." (20) Her ambiguity is expressed in her confession that she needs to escape from India, but she always gets bored with Europe and wants to come back to India.

Jhabvala's cultural ambivalence results in philosophical irony, but it also gives her a range of empathy and imagination which empower her to assume so many different points of view in her stories. She herself best expresses her cultural ambivalence which could act as the key to understanding her stories in the following image:

> Once somebody said to me: "Just see, how sweet is the Indian soul that can see God in a cow!" But when I try to assume this sweetness, it turns sour; for, however much I may try to fool myself, whatever veils I may try, for the sake of peace of mind, to draw over my eyes, it is soon clear to me that the cow is a cow, and a very scrawny, underfed, diseased one at that. And then I feel that I want to keep this knowledge, however painful it is, and not exchange it for some other that may be true for an Indian but can never quite become that for me. (21)

It is this painful knowledge, this compulsive insistence on finding a personal path through the maze of Anglo-Indian culture-clashes, that result in the ironic perspectives of Jhabvala's stories. Irony is two-sided. That is, Jhabvala is always aware of the two, or more, sides to an issue. She works in terms of binary opposites, with each opposite position having its own solid rationale. Nevertheless, she loads the dice both for the reader and for her protagonist in making the choice between these opposites. When we, or the protagonists, think about it, there really is no choice at all. But there is often a painfulness about the choice because the protagonist knows what she or he is giving up. There is also an ironic awareness of the rightness of both sides, or at least the inevitability that there will always be at least two sides, two opposing ways of life.

The binary opposites in terms of which Ruth Prawer Jhabvala depicts post-independence, inter-racial India are grouped around the following themes: destructive but fulfilling passion versus respectability; the lure and fear of the unknown as way of truly exploring the real India versus the security and the luxury of English conventionality; the irresistible love of Indian art or Indian religion versus English, expatriate clubbiness and exclusivity; the English protagonist's quest for tranquillity of soul and spirituality versus a resignation to unimaginative conformism and mediocrity; the notion of individual equality versus the submissive devotion of the foreign disciples to the Indian gurus or swamis; Indians who proudly keep away from Europeans and Europeans who proudly keep away from Indians and numerous anarchists who provocatively bridge the gap through miscegenation, art or religion.

There is no false drama about the clash between these binary opposites in Jhabvala's stories. It is more that each character gradually and inobtrusively gains in depth and commitment and we the readers gradually grow in intimate understanding of his/her lifestyle. The stories are therefore about slow, organic change or gradual coming to full awareness of self and this awareness is inevitably tinged with quiet irony or a not always explained sadness about other, lost possibilities.

Ruth Prawer Jhabvala's sympathetic and mildly ironic insights into her mainly upper class characters win our empathy and our curiosity about the solutions they will find for their problems. Sometimes the solutions are drastic because the opposites are culturally so far apart. But even then there is no false melodrama or overstatement. People often change their whole way of life in the last sentence of Jhabvala's stories. This change has usually been smouldering on since the very opening sentences of the story, however. The change involves a compulsive and romantic burning of bridges by the main character and the making of an irrevocable step.

This irrevocable step is often an artistic or religious or erotic step which leads the character away from bourgeois order and Apollonian self-control. There is a corresponding move towards Dionysian ecstasy and self-fulfilment, but not in any overstated way or with false optimism. There is more a mood of relief that a false charade of social pretence is now over, that a genuine, private need is being met. In middle age the characters discover what has been troubling them for years and years and they turn their back on prestige, socio-political status, security, convention, wealth and commonplace order. Instead they choose a private-spiritual sphere where they feel intuitively that they will find elusive self-fulfilment. This existential choice often involves an upper class woman seeking sexual liberation. The question which we readers must sometimes ask ourselves is this: are the closures of these stories a romantic and not quite plausible wish-fulfilment?

Let us now illustrate some of these generalizations by examining specific stories in the collection *Out of India*. In the story *The Housewife*, Shakuntala is a conventional, upper middle class matron with one dubious weakness. She is prepared to carry out all of her domestic and familial duties tirelessly, provided that she is permitted to meet her singing instructor on the roof of the house at dawn and learn to develop her singing. At first this seems a harmless enough hobby, it is an all-consuming passion which is the only meaningful thing in her whole life. Gradually the contrasts between the binary opposites are built up and intensified. Shakuntala is trapped by her respectability of her twenty-five-year-old marriage and her husband's enduring love for her and the tyrannical expectations of her in-laws. By contrast the teacher is a poor vagabond. He has given up all domestic commitments in order to devote himself solely to the passion of music. Of him and the other musicians it is said:

> They ate when they liked, slept when they liked, chewed opium in their betel, loved and formed friendships. (151)

Not that the reader should form sentimental daydream notions of this artistic freedom. The teachers are subject to the tyranny of their musical guru who beats them and uses them as servants for his every whim. But so in love with music is Shakuntala that she regards this as "a reasonable price to pay for the privilege of being near so great and blessed a man." (152) Gradually the shame of Shakuntala's passion for music grips her, leaving her in the pain of unfulfilment. Her teacher treats her with contempt because she is nothing more than a housewife. Finally Shakuntala leaves her bourgeois home, searches for her teacher in the cheap restaurants of Bombay and submits to his musical and sexual inspiration.

> There was no going back from here, she knew. But who would want to go back, who would exchange this blessed state for any other? (163)

The middle class English woman in *An Experience of India* likewise gives herself over to a shameful passion. This passion is not so much her adulterous miscegenation and promiscuity with the Indians whom she meets on her aimless travels, but rather her desire to become genuinely Indian. She hates the "tastefully appointed air-conditioned apartments" (126) of the English expatriates who despise filthy Indians in the same way that Doris Lessing's English characters loathe the kaffirs of Rhodesia and Zambesia. She says: "I had come to India to *be* in India. I wanted to be changed." (126)

She therefore experiments sexually with Ahmed the musician and with a very unspiritual, bullying swami in a saffron robe. But she doesn't find any utopian submission or bliss; instead she gets jaundice. She has nightmares about drinking water from a well in a Rajasthan fort with a corpse at the bottom of it. She begs the help of her husband—the effete, pedantic, frigid Henry—to get her out of India to somewhere clean and safe like Geneva. But no soon does the hapless Henry accomplish this than she knows she will have to leave him and stay, in dire poverty, to experience the "freedom and adventure" of travelling, once again, third class and aimlessly through India.

In a similar vein the rather unattractive Betsy in *Passion* allows herself to be sexually used and despised by her adulterous and impoverished civil servant Indian lover. Har Gopal yearns for the middle class comfort of Betsy's apartment and her well-paying job as secretary. But Betsy yearns for the masochistic abasement of her passion and throws away her job and her apartment so that she can receive Har Gopal "somewhere very cheap, very Indian." (105) Ironically, Har Gopal is disgusted and dismayed by Betsy's disrespectful contempt for her nice job and her nice apartment. Such is the impossibility of understanding between the binary opposites of the two cultures.

There is a similar, shameful passion in the story *The Man with the Dog*. Here a well-to-do Indian grandmother neglects her familial duties because of her passion for a European foreigner, a cranky, finicky old man who dislikes India intensely and only socializes with fellow Europeans. Even though she detests the smell of his dog, she is consumed by passion for the dog's master, living for the times when he allows her "to come into his rooms and stay there with him the whole night." As she says:

> He is usually asleep before me, and then I sit up in bed beside him and look and look my eyes out at him. I can't describe how I feel. I have been a married woman, but I have never known such joy as I have in being there alone with him in bed and looking at him: at this old man who has taken his front teeth out so that his upper lip sags over his gums, his skin is grey and loose, he makes ugly sounds out of his mouth and nose as he sleeps. It is rapture for me to be there with him. (115)

Jhabvala deliberately exaggerates to the point of humour and grotesqueness the objective unattractiveness of the old man in order to stress the inexplicability of passion. Even when this conceited old man insults India and all Indians in front of her scandalized family, she cannot bring herself to give him up. She cannot be what her respectable and proud children want her to be, "an old widowed mother . . . devoted entirely to prayer and self-sacrifice." (123) In the end she begs him to continue to stay on in her home, even though she knows that he has nowhere to go in his comparative poverty and that he is dependent on her. It is as though her strength as a female and her happiness come from not needing to posture or indulge in self-deception for the sake of a false dignity. Instead she is not afraid to pretend to submit to his frail majesty in order to manipulate him into staying on with her. She experiences a wholeness and a fulfilment, even in her scandalous old age, which is denied to the male characters whom Jhabvala creates because they are obsessed with their dignity.

A related story about an elderly female defying convention and respectability is *The Widow* in which middle-aged Durga refuses to be stripped of her "silken colored clothes and of her golden ornaments" just because she had "committed the sin of outliving her husband and was consequently to be numbered among the outcasts." (40) Durga too finds her own "painful" "knowledge" and risks being "crushed by (her) environment" in a defiant "attempt to remain standing," (21) as Jhabvala says of herself in the introduction to these stories.

But Durga covets independence and power and even tries to buy herself a young lover and no good can come of it. She is trapped by her yearning for a son (her elder husband had been impotent) and when this yearning is defeated, she abruptly gives away her wealth and power, having realized paradoxically that the only way in which she can experience divine love is to give up all earthly trappings and submit to humility. Her relatives self-righteously accept her wealth in wonderfully ironic concluding passage in which they disguise their greed and their triumph with a pseudo-pious appeal to the God-inspired rightness of tradition:

> They were glad for her sake. There was no other way for widows to lead humble, bare lives; it was for their own good. For if they were allowed to feed themselves on the pleasures of the world, then they fed their own passions too, and that which should have died in them with the death of their husbands

> would fester and boil and overflow into sinful channels. (56)

And so the relatives generously agree to take Durga's place and let themselves "overflow into [their own] sinful channels." What greater family love could one hope for? If Jhabvala is ironical here about Indian traditions and about the hypocrisy of the religious renunciation of worldly pleasures, she is openly satirical about ashrams and swamis in the story *How I Became a Holy Mother*. The sceptical narrator, Katie, describes the ashrams as "dust bowls . . . in the dirtier parts of very dirty holy cities or even cities that aren't holy at all but just dirty." (252) Katie also despises the tasteless, cheap linoleum and the gawdy calendar pictures of the fat saints inside the ashrams and the jealous, harem-like atmosphere in which all the female disciples fight over the Master's favours. Particularly biting is the description of the Meditation Hall, which "was repainted salmon pink and the huge holy OM sign at one end of it was lit up all around with coloured bulbs that flashed on and off." (266)

This story thus features the usual binary opposition between proud scepticism and faithful submission. The irony of the ending, however, is that Katie in spite of herself falls in love with the Master's disciple, Vishwa, and erotically competes with the Countess for his sexual favours. Bitchily she enjoys her triumph when she allows the Countess to find them in flagranti and she masks her sexual satisfaction with a lazy pseudo-religious yearning for the sacred mountains and temples of Northern India. (268) In this story Jhabvala ironically reveals sacred religiosity to be tasteless theatre and hokus-pokus and piety to be a cover for power-struggles and sexual jealousy.

There is decidedly less scepticism and irony, however, when Pritam withdraws in the bloom of her youth into hermit-like isolation and shabby self-sufficiency in the northern hills of India. She becomes gruff, manly and shabby as she self-consciously defies the respectability of her family. As a compensation, perhaps, there is a great deal of satirical humour about the fact that she maintains a non-sexual but very intimate relationship with Doctor Sahib, a weak, incompetent little man who lives alone further down the hill and who talks to her endlessly about historical romances and the divine retribution or rewards of reincarnation. "Even his cardboard lens seem(s) radiant" when he cries:

> Yes I too, though not a saint, struggle and battle here alone in

> my small hut. I cry out in anguish and the suffering endured in terrible but also—oh, Madam—glorious! A privilege. (242)

Jhabvala may make fun of Doctor Sahib's harmless self-glorification, but she nevertheless slants the characterization against Pritam's relatives who are rich, pampered and superficial and in favour of Pritam who is seen as an iconoclast, sceptical but sensitive, suffering but silent, and determined to be her unconventional self in her quiet communion with pure nature. Pritam has found her very own "painful" "knowledge."

The intellectually unequal but genuine friendship between Pritam and Doctor Sahib is similar to the unconventional friendship between Nargis the niece who is mistress of a well-to-do household in Bombay and an anti-bourgeois uncle. Their dreamy friendship is also based on a withdrawal from society and a cultivation of moody reflectiveness or spiritual serenity. This serenity of the uncle, however, is not achieved in some bogus ashram, but rather through music, Persian poetry and in his beloved bazaar. Jhabvala appears to be making a romantic, philosophical and artistic glorification of the esoteric bazäars of India as property, luxury, hard work, conventionality, hard common sense, making money and regular schedules for daily life. Here is a description of the uncle in his beloved bazaar:

> He walked up and down in the bazaar, looking at the stalls and the people, and then he sat outside the sweetmeat seller's and had tea and milk sweets and read out of his little volume of Sufi poetry. Sometimes he was so stirred that he read out loud for the benefit of the other customers and passersby, even though they couldn't understand Persian. . . . Then it seemed to him that everything had become suffused in purity and brightness—yes, even this bazaar where people haggled and made money and passed away the time in idle, worldly pursuits. (204)

In terms of the themes in which I have been analyzing Jhabvala's art, that is in terms of binary oppositions and multiple ironies, perhaps the most successful story is *Two More under the Indian Sun*. As with most of Jhabvala's stories there is little plot and little drama; there is more a gradual deepening of long existent contrasts between two English friends, Margaret and Elizabeth. These contrasts are developed around a wonderfully Indian theme of "the relative merits of the three ways towards realization . . . the way of knowledge, the way of action, and that of love." (188)

Margaret embodies "the way of action." She is a dynamo of energy, organizing activities "of a charitable or spiritual nature" for "holy men from the Himalayas, village welfare workers, organizers of conferences on spiritual welfare." (183) Ironically, however, all of her charitable actions are tainted by her bullying interference in other people's lives.

Margaret's semi-permanent visitor, Babaji, from the holy mountains at Almora, has cast "anger and all other bitter passions out of his heart and was consequently always smiling and serene." (183) He represents "the way of knowledge." But, ironically, his total wisdom consists of "rocking and smiling and looking with tender love at two birds pecking at something on the lawn" (184) and parroting the cliched, pseudo-moral principles of bossy Margaret. In fact, as a man of knowledge, the Babaji is really more like a spaced-out idiot with a lobotomy. Nevertheless, unobtrusively, he is a passive catalyst inspiring people around him to show their better side and inspiring them with a vision of his beautiful mountains.

There remains Elizabeth who is married to a fairly tyrannical Indian. She embodies "the way of love." Margaret is not slow to tell Elizabeth that she is disappointed in her because she hasn't thrown herself into political and religious activism the way that Margaret herself has. Margaret also tells Elizabeth that if she would just stand up to her husband Raju's bullying a bit, they would not be happier. But Elizabeth knows an ecstatic love which Margaret will never feel. She remembers the makeshift games of cricket she has played with Raju in their bedroom and her delight in his triumph at winning. She remembers the bliss of turning on the bedroom light "just for the pleasure of looking at Raju lying beside her." (193)

And so it is that all three friends, in spite of their manifest inadequacies, paradoxically embody the three Indian sacred ways to realization. The consciousness of the ideal and the ironies about human inadequacies are quintessentially Ruth Prawer Jhabvala at her best.

In this paper I have attempted to compare the perspectives of four female European intruders in the farflung tropical colonies of the once glorious British Empire. It seems that we may characterize Baroness Karen Blixen as an aristocratic adventuress in her feudal empire in Kenya, given in her leisure to mystic musing about true aristocracy and humans as the idea of God. Doris Lessing creates a woman who is a frigid, perverted racist trapped in a satiric tragedy about the social effects of the British colonial presence in Rhodesia and South Africa. Jeannie Gunn creates an image for herself in her autobiography as a loyal, plucky, middle class wife who will follow her husband like Biblical Ruth even to the tropical ends of the world, or in this case the Antipodean extremes of the British Empire. With Ruth Prawer Jhabvala we have found an ironic philosopher who is capable of protean metamorphosis in the most varied guises in order to express her ambivalent love-hatred for India.

C.J. Koch's Feminine Perspective

F.A. INAMDAR

None of the critics on C.J. Koch has ever thought about his feminine perspective.[1] My aim in this paper is to study this aspect by taking into consideration his four novels: *The Boys in the Island* (1958), *Across the Sea Wall* (1965), *The Year of Living Dangerously* (1978) and *The Doubleman* (1985).

Koch's feminine perspective raises a few questions, such as: is Koch primarily interested in masculine creation? Does he dismiss his feminine creation as secondary and ineffective, or does he judge his women by masculine standards? Does he idealize his women, consequently is he able to portray "real" men only? Is his masculine creation, one of disillusioned idealists? Whether they help each other in attaining their aims? Or, do they destroy each other by their egoism and self-involvement?

I

In *The Boys in the Island* Francis comes in contact with three women: Heather, Keeva and Betty. Koch's overall interest is in masculine creation. These women get involved with Francis in his search for a dreamland: the futility of seeking such a dreamland and his struggle to live by and within illusions. The romantic idealism and enlightened realism inform Koch's major fictional men and women, and form themselves into a unified artistic perspective.

Francis's attraction for Heather is spoken in terms of his search for the dreamland. He is attracted by her eyes "as blue as hills." Initially, Francis-Heather relationship develops on physical attraction which forms a general pattern in Koch's novels. Their bodies "wriggle closer" (61) during their ride on the Ferris wheel, and Francis feels "something quivered in him in a new way." (61) Consequently, he thinks that he had entered Heather's life. Koch ominously predicts that their relationship is dogged with failure. This is done through "the fierce bake of the sun" which "withered the few flowers growing sadly there," (76) and through Heather as a deceitful entity with: "so much a woman's, beneath a girl's face." (79) Their future failure in love is even prefigured by "Anne's pile of bowls had slipped from her hands and broken on the floor." (87) But all this is developed through Francis's concern for Heather. His relationship of dedication for her, to suffer for her: "he wanted to protect her from the father, and from the land which wrung her tears. Worship and pity swung him on their tide, and he wanted her." (90) His delight in the presence of Heather, and their mutual affirming of each other's value shows a development of love from both the sides. Born out of such a concern Heather says, "I've never known a boy like you. You're my first real boy-friend." (83) But Koch's treatment of this episode heavily leans on Francis's display of iove. All along, Heather appears a passive receptacle of Francis's love: "he began whispering to her the words he had heard too many times in bad films and on the radio, but now found he had to say himself—they were like three pebbles dropped in a pool." (93) Their love does not go beyond stolen kisses and their intensely desired consummation is symbolically foiled by Heather's Aunt Cecily. Koch, through Francis, conceives Heather as a girl evoking the landscape. Her calf-love for Francis cools down. She settles down to marry Donnie.

This is prefigured through what Francis sees: "She was mildly remote from him as the paper-yellow hills of dry grass." (114) And it is her dry concern that makes her blind to Francis's feelings. Thus, Koch shows the commercial attitude in man-woman relationship. Born out of this attitude, she says, "Donnie'll be good to me." "He's doing real well with his father's farm. It's been nice with you, Frank—but I wouldn't know where I was with you. You don't know *what* you're going to do, do you? You said so." (117) Heather is seen as a lifeless doll in the presence of her father's will: "She seemed to have become a doll." (118) Koch's attitude towards Heather is one of a mechanical entity in the hands of the parents. Koch, at this stage, is not able to develop either the complexity arising out of love, or portray the full-blooded character in Heather.

Koch leaves behind the portrait of Heather along with Francis's tryst with the mainland. The two women he encounters in Melbourne are Keeva and Betty. Heather is "Daddy's daughter"—whose image is broken, and out of which are born Keeva and Betty. Both are representatives of social forces. They possess sufficient autonomy to shape their fate. Keeva is not concerned with social mores and is totally occupied with her own existential problems to work for self-fulfilment. She subjugates men just as men pretend to subjugate her. She is incapable of giving herself in love like Heather. Lewie lies helpless in the clutches of a powerful Keeva. She belongs to thieves's literature, notably written in the tradition of *Moll Flanders*. Koch has not made vice seductive, though Keeva's antics frighten us out of our wits. She does not have any regard for her physical well-being, nor any scruples in instigating Lewie to rob their old neighbour, Athol. She takes pleasure in her craft. Her satisfaction for mischief arises out of making fun of others. We never see her attempt at self-recognition, but at master-minding mugging, thugging and stealing: "She's nice an' nasty for *no reason*—just to keep you on y' toes!" (148) Lewie, Francis and Jake are small, weak and helpless and they are at her mercy. Her deadly weapon is "her sex-appeal," (153) with two half-moons of her breasts. But Betty is a shadowy figure and would have been left out of the novel without any loss.

II

The feminine perspective in *The Boys in the Island* is sketchy and raw as Koch is hampered by the thematic context of the novel. In the other novels, he reveals himself as one who has a perfect control over his thematic intent. His men and women are displaced persons. These expatriates share their common lot and try to understand each other to settle down in life. But often, his men tend to be afraid of settling down in life with their sweethearts because of their "messed-up" past. As Francis fancies for a dreamland, so does O'Brien. The former wants to fulfill it through his love for Heather; for the latter, Ilsa is "a strange country."[2] This is a recurring paradigm. We see it in the portraits of Hamilton and Richard. In each case, the attainment of the dreamland is what defines reality; like O'Brien, Hamilton, "through her, looked for an England that had never been his and had never, in fact, existed."[3] Koch's feeling about the Australians's rootless lives applies to his feminine and masculine portraits: "one had the feeling that everything was somewhere else."[4] In O'Brien's decision to go his own way and wash his hands off Ilsa, there is a distinctive quality that characterizes the majority of Koch's masculine idealists: a preoccupation with fidelity that takes precedence over commitment to their beloveds who have led a life of social butterflies.

Koch's portrait of Ilsa shows opposite tendency. Ilsa, unlike O'Brien, reveals her selfless love for and complete trust in him. Her dream, like O'Brien's, is for a personal betterment to raise a happy home. Her impulses, like those of Katrin Vilde, are as romantic and idealistic as O'Brien's, but they are altogether of a different quality: they are clearly of belief and love rather than of jealousy and fear for the uncertainty of their future life. Her mind fastens on her love for O'Brien. Hers is a realistic portrait. She represents, perhaps, the sole gleam of real love in a world dark with lust and torn by the conflicting interests of those who are politically self-serving like Vera. And, as Koch suggests through Ilsa's effect of love on O'Brien, it is this kind of guiding ideal that mankind needs in order to transcend distrust and uncertainty for one's future. But O'Brien is weak to overcome his limitations. As a result, he vacillates between distrust and uncertainty. Through her love and trust he does not sense the importance of union. While we may criticize O'Brien for his ultimate rejection of Ilsa for "the idea of the *mess* that worries you, isn't it?" (140) and judge his lack of charity and "largeness of heart," Koch's focus remains clearly on Ilsa's capacity for trust and love. These capacities identify distinctly feminine qualities in Koch's fiction, except *The Boys*, and offer a necessary balance for masculine self-centredness, and fear for the scandal. Between them, Ilsa and O'Brien represent two extremes in the spectrum of human relationship and demonstrate how even the noblest impulses, when pushed to the extreme, can be disastrous.

In the end, Koch adds a tragic dimension to Ilsa's character. Just as O'Brien's character leads to lack of trust and want of charity, so Ilsa's portrait is projected as one who "moved indifferent as a saint to possessions or permanence her face having a saint's pious blankness." (141)

In *Across the Sea Wall*, Koch describes the kind of idealism that leads to disintegration of the union between lovers, but he hints through Ilsa's portrait that commitment to trust and love and a quest for one's own home is what distinguishes the feminine attitude from the masculine impulse. It is a similar contrast that Koch underscores in the characterization of Jill and Hamilton. While both aspire to reach their dreamland through each other, Jill, unlike her lover is never distracted from her concern to love him and attain her motherhood through him. She wants to escape from "being on display all the time." (114) Her friendship-deal with Kwan springs from her desire to ward off men from racing her into bed in five minutes. Hamilton's attitude towards this union is one of "suffocation." As a foreign correspondent he can hardly combine "job with domesticity." (141)

Indeed, despite its deeply pessimistic tone, *The Year of Living Dangerously* brings to light a notion that Koch explores throughout his writings, that in feminine hands love itself can be a powerful ideal which, despite its illusions, inspires acts of courage and heightens sympathetic understanding of others. In addition, he seeks to demonstrate that love offers a valid means of exploring life because it can serve both to define the self and to foster solidarity with others. Although its illusions can indeed be destructive, as Koch details in *The Boys in the Island, Across the Sea Wall, The Year of Living Dangerously* and *The Doubleman,* love is an emotion capable of expanding consciousness and enlightening our vision.

In *Across the Sea Wall* Koch places in opposition the revelation of Ilsa's love for O'Brien and the decay of Michael, who is selfish and egoistic: "He has no feelings; lives inside himself; and loves only himself." (52) Michael's actions are predominantly self-serving, like those of their former husband, Eddie, who wanted only to "work, save and buy things." (53) Michael's sights are fastened on money-making through Ilsa's success as a dancer girl in Singapore. Her glory will be his success, and it is generally on his eagerness to earn money—not her happiness—that his aims rest. Ilsa's love for O'Brien, while not altogether selfish, we might conjecture (he will marry her, he will give her life meaning, happiness), yet embodies an element of honesty, practicality, and commitment. She tells O'Brien: "The man who holds me will have to be a man I love and admire." (53) Her commitment to O'Brien comes out clearly when she says, "I am in love with you. Do not care what money you have or have not." (67) As a token of her belief in O'Brien, she shows her belongings about which he thinks that she is showing "the pieces of her soul." (68) During their first love encounter, she presents herself not as "a sexually easy show-girl" but "a mournful and dignified woman disconcerted at his callow assault." (49) Though to instil confidence in O'Brien she tells about her dislike for lecherous life; he says, "men are fools and bastards" and "they care nothing for you as a person, want only sex," (77) yet Ilsa recognizes instinctively that there is no real possibility for fulfillment in his attitude towards her. She tells O'Brien clearly, "what a fool, to bet everything on you. . . . You are empty. *Nothing*. Empty shop." (140)

Whereas O'Brien's dream tends toward a vague, self-centred illusion, Ilsa's relationship with him embodies not only a commitment of love, but also an opportunity for both personal growth and happiness. It is life-seeking as opposed to O'Brien's life shunning dream.

But nowhere does Koch offer a more searching analysis of the feminine ideal of love than in *The Doubleman*,[5] where masculine jealousy and suspicion of fidelity contrast sharply with the feminine devotion, which for Katrin Vilde represents a vehicle for marital amity. In attempting to overcome her self-interest for conjugal sanctity, Katrin develops not only a sense of purpose and identity but also the means to transcend her initially limited outlook to fulfill Richard's expectations of her sacrifice. Koch presents a predicament for his women either to choose career or a spouse. This problem of choice spells disaster in Ilsa's life. She joins dancing club only because she needs to express herself. This aspect makes her a Kali figure, fit only for O'Brien's worship. For him, loving her was ridiculous. Therefore, he says, "she was beautiful yet grotesque; dignified yet alarming." (*Across the Sea Wall*, 50) Similar predicament is with Katrin Vilde. Richard's jealousy springs from her singing career with Brian. He discovers that it was not her hobby but her "central passion." For her, Brian is "Geza Lukacs come back in a new guise." (318) Therefore, Richard's sweet home is on the brink of destruction. But Katrin chooses to stay with her husband by sacrificing her singing career. Her portrait excels that of Heather, Ilsa, and Jill by opting for family happiness at the cost of her passionate career. This is not to say that Koch has idealized his women and is only interested in masculine portraits. Though his women portraits are called, for instance, Ilsa for O'Brien, "an unknown deity, waiting, for him in the Asiatic evening" (*Across the Sea Wall*, 51); Jill for Hamilton is "some waif or nymph" (*The Year of Living Dangerously*, 120); Richard's union with Katrin takes on a metaphysical dimension: "the desire for God. Being united with Him," (120) yet they have talents for reaching toward others. For instance, Katrin gives Richard the supreme proof of her love, stronger than mere passion. Her sacrifice brings a deepening of character, an increase in perspective. She is for Richard an ideal that threatens to destroy, while paradoxically enriching his life, by taking to her singing career. But again it is Ilsa who recognizes the social and moral impossibility of a permanent attachment, and consequently makes the necessary sacrifice to be "forever displaced." (*Across the Sea Wall*, 140) Her ideal love offers a means of creative self discovery. Moreover, it is the life-affirming force that enables Jill and Hamilton to solemnize their union. And it is Katrin who transcends her selfish desire through an heroic act of sacrifice. Throughout Koch's novels, it is this feminine perspective, this life-affirming force that serves to counter the destructive elements found in masculine nihilism, withdrawal and lascivious behaviour.

NOTES

1. C.J. Koch, *The Boys in the Island* (Australia: Sirius, 1987), p. 60.
2. C.J. Koch, *Across the Sea Wall* (Australia: Angus and Robertson, 1982), p. 59.
3. C.J. Koch, *The Year of Living Dangerously* (London: Grafton Books, 1986), p. 139.
4. C.J. Koch, *Kunapipi*, VIII, I, 1986, p. 21.
5. C.J. Koch, *The Doubleman* (London: Grafton Books, 1986).

"Am I Not a Person?": Character and Narrative in Patrick White's *The Aunt's Story*

GLEN THOMAS

Texts are often the site of an attempt to discover the figure of the author. The author becomes a means of interpreting the texts to explicate the characters and their depictions. To date, much of the criticism of the texts of Patrick White has been dominated by the figure of the author White was at pains to construct. Reading the texts through the author is an attempt to totalize the text and impose a point of origin or terminus upon the writing. "The author is . . . the principle of a certain unity of writing—all differences have to be resolved, at least in part, by the principles of evolution, maturation and influence."[1] The author becomes "a final signified . . . [which] suits criticism very well, the latter then allotting itself the important task of discovering the Author . . . beneath the work: when the author has been found, the text is 'explained'—victory to the critic."[2] White, as the constructed "paper author," becomes the touchstone of criticism, the autobiographical details of the life of the writer becoming the keys to explicate the texts which appear under her/his name.

The Aunt's Story occupies something of a watershed within the White criticism, signifying the arrival of White as a writer. Walsh sees *The Aunt's Story* as "many-layered, finely organised . . . rich in material and clean in design,"[3] (18) a text which shows "new maturity of thought and style." (19) Argyle refers to *The Aunt's Story* as an extension of White's vision and accomplishment, (21) reminiscent of Lawrence. (22) Herring singles out *The Aunt's Story* from the previous two novels, in that *Happy Valley* and *The Living and the Dead* reveal that White had not yet fully assimilated the techniques of Joyce and Woolf, (4) in contrast to the discipline of style of *The*

Aunt's Story. (8) McKernan identifies the text as modernist, springing from White's "concern about disorder." (171)

The Aunt's Story is thus often regarded as White's first mature work. There are exceptions: Edgecombe for instance regards *The Aunt's Story* as lacking the clarity of vision of *The Tree of Man*, which he sees as the point of White's maturation.[4] Classifications of influence, development and maturity carry within them the implication of unity and coherence. In positing *The Aunt's Story* as the work of a mature author such criticism seeks to resolve textual difficulties (such as the "Jardin Exotique" section). For example, Colmer anchors the identification the reader makes in the form of the author whose "self is reflected and refracted in each novel as a whole, not in a single figure." (27) This form of interpretation relies upon the Jamesian theory of the subject within fiction where the author-subject provides the

> definite origin and centre of the novel outside or behind the novel. . . . He will not speak with his own voice, or see with his own eyes—but his voice and his eyes will be there behind the consciousness and voice of the fictional subject he has constructed.[5]

In positing the figure of Patrick White as the resolution of all textual inconsistencies criticism is attempting to move outside the text. "Patrick White" has become the transcendental signifier, the origin or terminus of writing and contradiction.

The central section of the text, "Jardin Exotique," has been explained as "modernism,"[6] "stream of consciousness" writing,[7] "Joycean" in tone.[8] These terms are used without interrogating the text to discover whose "consciousness" has begun to stream and without any precise definition of "modernism." Attempts have also been made to explain the "Jardin Exotique" away as the manifestation of a disturbed mind, as in Walsh's reading: the central section as partly a narrative of "personal collapse." (15) Such readings rely upon theories of realism and mimeticism, in that the character upon the page supposed has some form of existence outside the text. Barthes regards it as an error to attempt to lift a character from the page and submit him/her to psychoanalysis.[9] Further, there is no evidence within the text of "Jardin Exotique" that Theodora is indeed mad. The text does not argue either way for the putative madness of

Theodora. When Sokolnikov's wife accuses him of madness he tells her that "[w]henever the answer is not in bronze, that is the cry of the middle classes." (181) Theodora's sister Fanny, an exemplar of the middle class, (17) also thinks Theodora to be "quite mad." (17; 256) Certain characters are thus used to qualify the judgements of other characters. In questioning these judgements the text would not appear to endorse the suggestion that Theodora is mad; nor does it deny it, thus disrupting categories into which characters are placed. The text thus refuses to negotiate the argument; this works to displace the logocentric discourse of truth as the basis of the text.

The textual status of Theodora Goodman is an ambivalent one. She is an aunt, a spinster, (12) a position the text regards with amibiguity. To be an aunt is "at best" that which a spinster may become: "at most, but also at least, an aunt." (12) In terms of binary constructs she is, at the opening of the narrative, deficient in complements. There is no uncle for her as aunt; and with the death of her mother, no parent for her as child. She occupies a position of textual slippage, which is "at most" but also "at least"; a textual lacuna that in the second section of the novel the text attempts to fill with the narratives of other characters.

Lou may seem to occupy a position of complement for Theodora as aunt, yet when the text suggests such a relationship it is undermined. To Theodora, Lou is "like some dark and secret place in one's own body." (13) Thus she becomes appropriated and assimilated within the character of Theodora. The text seeks to connect Theodora and Lou by initially demonstrating the distance between Lou and her parents: "Lou had no obvious connection either with Frank or with Fanny," (13) then drawing a physical connection with Theodora. Lou is again linked physically with Theodora at the close of the first section, where Lou's breath is "almost her own." (131) This suggests that the text is attempting to fill the space Theodora represents through her lack of complements. Yet these alliances are then displaced, as in the conclusion to the first section where Theodora feels unable to reach Lou across "the distance that separates." (132) This repeated alliance and displacement would indicate that lacunae within the text are not easily filled; hence the necessity of repeating the process of suggesting alliances with other characters and then displacing them, usually with further alliances (such as with Sokolnikov, Zack, Katina).

Theodora is a site of textual contestation, a locus of shifting attributes and interpretative discourses. A similar argument can be made for Theodora's home, Meroe. Two Meroes contest the discursive space of the text: the Meroe of Australia and that of Ethiopia. The "skeleton trees" of the Australian Meroe are said to have their roots in Ethiopia. (20) The hills surrounding the house had "conspired with the name," (20) a name which is thus being doubly occupied. Meroe is also associated with George Goodman, and upon his death is said to dissolve. (85) The text thus contains slippage in the signifier, in that there is not a clear and unambiguous relationship between the signifier and the signified: the Meroe referred to may be the Australian or Ethiopian referent, a doubling of the signified.

The narrative Theodora relates of Meroe to Lou would seek to resurrect this "dissolved" entity. At first the text suggests, "there is very little to tell." (19) The next one hundred pages are devoted to this "very little." The text then returns to Theodora's remark about "very little to tell." In addition to these points the text reveals that Theodora has told the story of Meroe before. (19) The narrative that follows therefore constitutes an analeptic retelling of an earlier narrative.[10] There is a pattern of displacement and return evident in the remarks Theodora addresses to Lou ("[b]ut my darling . . . there is very little to tell"). They repeat her earlier comments and in turn are followed by a displacement to the narrative of Meroe, then a return to the textual present. At the close of the first section Theodora again makes reference to individuals who "do not have many stories to tell." (131) This is juxtaposed with the image of the filigree ball which would "fill at times with a sudden fire." (131) In such an image the narrative alludes to the following section of the text wherein Theodora Goodman, a character with little to tell, is filled with the narratives of other characters, although these are not narratives which are wholly her own.[11] This is reinforced by the reference to Theodora as "hollowed out" (132) like the filigree ball. The suggestion of little to tell recalls the title of the novel. *The Aunt's Story* may refer to the story of an aunt, or a story told by an aunt. And if there is little to tell, what would the story of the title refer to? It is reported that Theodora tells stories to Lou and her brothers, (13) while the title of the text suggests the narrative of Theodora. This indicates that there is no single narrative of or by an aunt but, rather, a multiplicity of narratives which in often tenuous ways involve Theodora.

The narrative fragments which "fill" Theodora in the "Jardin Exotique" section are reiteration of prior events. The first of these, the narrative of the earthquake, is prefaced (and completed) by the words, "do you remember." (142, 144) Thus, the narrative of the earthquake in which Theodora plays a vicarious role is posited as belonging to the past. The more developed narratives of the section, such as the Ludmilla narrative, may be understood as pursuing intermittent development throughout the section. The distinction between *fabula* and *sjuzet* operates in both examples. The *fabula* (the total of the events presented in the narrative, "what really happened,")[12] is extracted from the *sjuzet* (the narrative construction, presentation or order of events in the text.)[13] Through re-reading, the reader extrapolates the story and narrative pattern from the discourse, thus producing the plot, the "interpretative activity elicited by the distinction between *sjuzet* and *fabula*, the way we use the one against the other."[14] An example of this process is the reference Sokolnikov makes to being shot in the left buttock while running away in the dark. (219) This is a reiteration of the scene of Ludmilla's death and the wound the General receives when fleeing. (204-9) The General's *fabula* is extrapolated from the *sjuzet* and the plot is produced. The reader presumes the General was shot on this occasion and not another.

The narrative pattern of the text involves Theodora vicariously in the narratives which are transferred or projected to or upon her. These narratives in which Theodora takes part are not new, in the sense that each of the fragments of the "Jardin Exotique" section are referred to as belonging to the past. These narrative fragments may be read as projections from Theodora's deranged psyche:[15] an insane Theodora has a series of delusions regarding the history of the lives of those she meets in an European hotel. "Jardin Exotique," however, makes problematic the question of narrative boundaries and disrupts the notion of linear, unified consciousness as concomitant with narrative by not providing a fixed subject. This is done through the conflicting narratives, all of which feature Theodora (although significantly, they do not consistently name her as Theodora). As a subject Theodora is constituted in and by language and the act of naming. It is in these shifting names that the fragmentation of the subject occurs. Theodora is not a stable character, but a shifting locus within the text, without some form of personal core.

The narratives of the characters of the Jardin are structured as syllepses, "numerous insertions of 'stories' justified by relations of analogy or contrast."[16] The syllepses of *The Aunt's Story* offer information on the construction of the other characters within the text, referring to textual past events which are related in the text for the first time. These syllepses are again filling a locus in the text occupied by Theodora who shifts among the different syllepses. One reservation is that the syllepses are contradictory: for example Theodora becomes Ludmilla and is killed, yet survives the earthquake in another form. The subject of the text is therefore not a stable entity, but a contradictory site within the text, a grouping of conflicting expectations and discursive placements. Lawson has noted the high incidence of rhetorical syllepsis in White's work on the descriptive level, a "yoking of mental, emotional or spiritual quality with a physical one." (291) That there should also be this amount of narratological syllepsis suggests that an obsession with opposites and binaries is operating on a macro-level of the text. Although there is a distinct difference in the narratological and rhetorical use of the term there is a similarity in technique in the coupling of (often unsettling) narratives or qualities. Narrative syllepsis further disrupts the linear narrative of the subject, as there is narrative transference to other narratives which involve a series of shifting subjects rather than a stable centre within the text. The motivating factor in narrative transference in Brooks's model is the desire of the subject to simultaneously make the past the present and the "history of this past definitively past: to make an end to its reproductive insistence in the present." (228) Brooks uses the Freudian model of the analysand narrating her/his case history, but this model may be applied on a narrative level in the desire of the discourse to compartmentalize the past and the present of subjects constructed. The narratives of the characters of the "Jardin" are thus reworked so that "affect, repeated from the past, is acted out as if it were present, yet eventually in the knowledge that the relations involved are surrogates."[11] Theodora thus becomes a surrogate in a series of different narratives in the desire of the discourse to order past and present.

Derrida disrupts the notion of a stable centre in "Structure Sign and Play." He argues that the centre "could not be thought in the form of a present-being, that the centre had no natural site, that it was not a fixed locus but a function, a sort of non-locus in which an infinite number of sign-substitutions came into play." (280) The centre exists as a construct which has no absolute point of origin within a "process of signification which orders the displacements and substitutions for this law of central presence—but a central presence which has never been itself, has always already been exiled from its own substitute." (280) This substitute "does not substitute itself for anything which has somehow existed before it." (280) There is always-already a shifting locus within the text and not an absolute centre or place of origin or terminus, which would become the transcendental signifier. Derrida's description is a map of the central section of *The Aunt's Story*. Theodora is a subject which refuses to act as the centre of the text; she functions instead within a series of substitutions which do not have explicit origin or telos.

A model for the reading of *The Aunt's Story* is the reading process of Flaubert's *L'Education sentimentale* as outlined by Brooks. Brooks regards the Flaubert text as refuting attempts of the reader to identify with central character(s). *L'Education sentimentale* has as its basis the Balzacian novel. This model, however, is only present in an "as-if" form against which the novel plays.[18] A textual model for *The Aunt's Story* is the *Bildungsroman*, yet the text does not provide a linear analysis of the life of its subject, putatively Theodora Goodman. The irruption of narratives of what the text refers to as "other lives" disrupts the conventional structure of the linear narrative. The central section of novel becomes

> an uncertain vacillation of meaning and its impossibility, a troubled search, through inadequate systems of meaning, for a decision about whether any order of signs and sense could create a significant version of life and history.[18]

Brooks relates the progress of the narrative to the desire of the subject as orienting the narrative. In the text of *The Aunt's Story* the desire of the subject can no longer maintain the divisions between past, present and future,[19] and act as a point of orientation for the linear progression of the narrative. The demarcations between past and present blur so that there is a continual shifting across the temporal zones of the text.

As the site of re-enactment of the narratives of other subjects Theodora Goodman does not provide the impetus for the progress of the narratives of the "Jardin Exotique." "No longer can the reader espouse the protagonist's desire, no longer can he read in the forward-moving expectation created by the force of that desire."[20] As suggested earlier, *The Aunt's Story* functions through displacement and return, not a linear narrative. This displacement, in the transference of narratives of "other lives" to the character of Theodora, is related to the loss of temporal organization Brooks sees the subject as imposing upon the narrative. In "Jardin Exotique" a split develops between the *fabula* and *sjuzet* in that the "Jardin Exotique" is not "the aunt's story," but the narrative of other characters within the text. There is thus no *sjuzet* for the *fabula* posited in the title. The reader cannot identify with the desires of Theodora, particularly in "Jardin Exotique," because she is the focalizer for the narrative while the discourse presents the narratives of other characters.

An example of this is Theodora's conversation with Sokolnikov. At this point she is Ludmilla, the General's sister. The General makes reference to "something which has got to happen." (174) Unsure as to "whose corpse had been prepared" upon the "amateur stage" Theodora "knew that the *guignol* must not begin." (175) Within this short passage a number of significant points emerge. Theodora, as Ludmilla, is recalled to the moment when "then showed you the gun," (174) which may be a reference to the conclusion of the Ludmilla narrative whereby Ludmilla is shot in a clearing in a forest. (208)[21] This may link with the reference to the corpse in the clearing, the identity of which Theodora and the reader are uncertain. The "amateur stage" emphasizes the fictionality of the narrative. There is also Theodora's belief that the "*guignol* must not begin." (175) Theodora thus attempts to exercise control over the narrative in this instance, yet the *guignol* does begin, and ends (I use this with reservations, in that an ending is not absolute, as the text shows) with the death of Ludmilla. That the episode should be referred to as a *guignol* is another indication of the fictionality of the narrative, which may further suggest that the text is to be read in the genre of the comic.

The stress upon the narrative as fiction problematizes the notion of the reader identifying with the subject of the novel or reading the novel as a realist text. Theodora functions as the site of a series of conflicting generic expectations, in the way in which the narratives of her "other lives" interrupt the linear narrative of the text. The interest in these other lives is that they are essentially the narration of earlier events, re-enactments of what is said to have already occurred. Brooks argues that repetition in narratives is bound with the distribution of textual energies, the manifestations which are linked with his discussion of desire in narrative. These desires are closely linked with the act of reading; repetition in the text functions to conserve textual energies so that "energies released around the text . . . will not be lost."[22] The recurrence of character traits in *The Aunt's Story* is an example, although associated across different characters. Theodora, Lou and Katina Pavlou all share character traits, such as their inability to know what to do with their hands. Lou and Katina share a relationship with Theodora, as a kind of Aunt. (12, 143) Ludmilla and Theodora share attributes in their sallowness, spinsterhood, slender build and moustache. This constitutes a distribution of narrative energy. The discourse will ensure that it continues and will thus preserve narrative energy. The connections between characters thus exist on the level of discourse, as the discourse and the characters are each other's accomplices.[23] Characters are thus not the creation of an author but of the discourse, which creates characters to "play with them, to obtain from them a complicity which assures the uninterrupted exchange of the codes."[24] The discourse will ensure its continuation, and to do so will distribute the narrative energy through the text so that none is lost.

The final image of the novel, that of the "doubtful rose [which] trembled and glittered, leading a life of its own" (287) constitutes an enigmatic culmination to the text. This final image is one which returns the reader to the text, to the "Jardin Exotique" section, and the description of Mrs. Rapallo's cape which, as Theodora and Ṣokolnikov watch, "was leading a life of its own." (182) The final image is thus a repetition of an earlier one, which forms a loop in the text. The discussion which follows the sighting of the cape is also illuminating in this context. Theodora tells Mrs. Rapallo that she and Sokolnikov

> ". . . were playing a tragedy of which I have not heard the end."
>
> "The end?" Mrs. Rapallo screamed.
>
> So that Theodora laughed too. (183)

The narrative is drawing attention to itself as a work of fiction, writing of itself as a "tragedy." Theodora also realizes her position as one upon which others project the narratives of lives, to rework these narratives of personal history. The laughter with which Mrs. Rapallo greets Theodora's mention of the end may imply an ironic comment on the belief that the end is actually attainable. Theodora laughs as well, which is an ambiguous response. This scene when read in conjunction with the final image complicates the definition of the end of the narrative. That the "doubtful rose" should have the same status as Mrs. Rapallo's cape, and that the conversation revealing the complexity and amibiguity of closure occur here suggests a reading of the text that would make the final image problematic and not simply an image of personal unity or freedom. The enigmatic final image of the rose is testimony to the earlier laughter of these characters. The end, as Mrs. Rapallo and Theodora realize, is undecidable, "always provisional."[25]

The discourse accords with the narratives of the characters of the "Jardin Exotique" section as reiterations of events. The Anna Stepanovna narrative recognizes its status as a re-working of textual history; Varvara points out at the commencement of the narrative that "we have begun again." (169) Varvara is said to be representative of a beginning; Ludmilla/ Theodora, however, is left to "take over . . . right at the end." (169) Yet Theodora does not ever "take over" the narrative of "Jardin Exotique"; she remains produced by the narratives of the other characters. If the end is merely an illusion, then Theodora/Ludmilla would not ever be able to "take over" the narrative. As previously mentioned, Theodora has no *fabula* of her own and therefore her "taking over" the narrative is made virtually impossible.

The most developed (if such a term may be used) of the narratives in which Theodora functions, that of Sokolnikov and Ludmilla, is of some interest. It relates the series of events that apparently led to Ludmilla's death. (208)) In narrating Ludmilla's death her narrative thus seems to have a form of terminus. Theodora can then say, "then I am dead." (208) Theodora had also wanted to say "I am dead" upon the death of her father. (85) Yet it is impossible to make such a statement in the present tense if it is to be true. Through reference to statements such as these, the text again stresses its fictionality. These statements also bring out the split in the subject of the discourse, the difference in the subject who speaks and the subject spoken about. Theodora, however, is not dead, in that her narrative continues beyond this textual point. Yet if Ludmilla is dead, then the narrative the General transfers to Theodora is past, a history. Ludmilla has been resurrected in order to replay her own death. Immediately after her death, however, Ludmilla again lives. Sokolnikov refers to Theodora as Ludmilla during the incident of the nautilus (209-15) and other subsequent episodes.

These examples reveal the unwillingness of the text to reach any form of narrative ending. The "deathless" Sokolnikov continues to refer to Theodora as Ludmilla until the end of the "Jardin Exotique" section, (250) after the fire.[26] Those who die in the fire are said to "destroy each other," in an image of energies cancelling each other out in a balanced equation. The occupants of the Hotel, in their transference to Theodora of narrative energies and repetition, serve to blur the distinction between past and present. Through their narratives the past and the present merge, disrupting the linear progression of the narrative. These narratives share a common concern, however, in that they all involve an attempt to relate a narrative of the individual. Brooks argues that "[i]t is of overwhelming importance to us that life still be narratable."[27] Thus, in an attempt to facilitate the narration of the various lives of the novel, the linear plot has to a large extent been disposed of. *The Aunt's Story* is illustrative of the difficulty of the attempt to arrive at a point of terminus of the subject. The narrative of the text cannot arrive (within Brooks's model) at a final point of affirmation of the self; instead the narrative concludes with a repeated image, which denies the drive to enclose and resolve the narrative. After her mother's death Theodora is unable to say "I am I." (11) As Mrs. Goodman's death opens the text of the novel, and thus prompts Theodora's inability to affirm "I am I," the novel constitutes the narrative of a subject (Theodora) under erasure. The text acknowledges that the "only certainty is death" (150) and then demonstrates in Ludmilla's narrative that death is not an easy state to reach. Like Mrs. Goodman, Ludmilla is resurrected within the narrative in order to replay her death in the patterns of analepsis and syllepsis.

This ontological and epistemological uncertainty is evident in Holstius's disclaimer that "there is little to choose from, between the reality of illusion and the illusion of reality." (278) The text has consistently undermined these categories in the "unreal" narratives of the "Jardin Exotique" and the problematization of their textual status. This textual difficulty is evident in the attempts to read the "Jardin" narratives as the product of a disturbed mind, and therefore dismiss them as unreal, whereas the first and third sections of the text are constructed as the "real" sections. Holstius is dismissed by Dutton as non-existent, (27) yet he appears in the text in the same way that other characters do. The realist reading would therefore inhibit the complexity of the text, in this division between characters which are real and those which are not. This is similar to the limits placed upon the text by referring the signifying elements back to the author, in the imposition of certain set boundaries to the text such as the relation of the characters to the life of the author or the delineation between the real and unreal characters.

The Aunt's Story is therefore a plural text, one which would resist the efforts to totalize the range of signification within its systems. A point about the "Jardin" section is that the narrative of Theodora, which the text used as impetus for the progress of the "Meroe" section, is arrested in the "Jardin Exotique" where the narratives of the other characters hold sway. Theodora is displaced as the focus of the narrative in the second section and returns as the subject in the third. The text presents on a macro-level the same structure which characterizes the narratives of the "Jardin": displacement and return. In the "Jardin" Theodora does not function as the subject of the narrative, but as the focalizer of the conflicting narratives of the characters of the text.

This form of focalization is unusual, as a character is used to focus the narrative of other characters, accompanied by constant shifts in the name of the focalizer. The narrated episode of the death of Ludmilla is an example, where the character is referred to as "Ludmilla" (within the micro-narrative) and "Theodora" within the space of a single passage:

> "Am I not a person?" asked Theodora.
> "That is not for you to decide."
> "Who are you anyway?" someone else asked.
> "I am Ludmilla Sokolnikov, and I keep house for my brother in St. Petersburg." (208)

The focus is difficult to determine as there will be a continual return to the character of Theodora but not to her narrative. Theodora's narrative is returned as the focus of the discourse in the third section of the text, but with reservations. Theodora becomes Miss Pilkington, and the discourse refers to her as a "blank." (267) When asked by Eunice to relate some of her travels to the Johnsons, Theodora does not oblige. The text is now unable to narrate.

The irony of this is brought out in the last conversation with Holstius, who tells Theodora that the people who take her away will encourage her "to relax in a white room and tell [her] life," (283) to narrate what the text has shown to be non-narratable. The supposed aim of the text has been to "tell the life" of Theodora, yet the text has shown that this is problematic in that it presumes a concrete and stable subject of discourse. The qualification Holstius adds is in this light: "[o]f course you will not be taken in by any of this." (283) Characters are aware that the subject cannot be narrated in the way the "telling of the self" would suggest. Those who believe so are described as "admirable people really, although limited." (283) Limited and limiting, in the attempt to reduce the plurality of the text to the humanist narrative of the self, to seek the concrete core of the individual, whereas the text has emphasized the lacunae within the discourse and the fragmented nature of the subject. The subject of the text will be structured by and in language. The attempt to narrate the subject would constitute an attempt to totalize the language, to draw a finite conclusion to the systems of meaning; to discover the origin or terminus of the writing. As the discussion of the novel has shown, this desire to totalize the language is resisted by the text. To posit a single meaning of the text is to close off the writing, to totalize the text in one statement. If texts are shifting and contradictory then this desire for totality is an ideal. Any ending is, as Brooks suggested, "always provisional."[28]

NOTES

1. Michel Foucault, "What is an Author? *Textual Strategies: Perspectives in Post-Structuralist Criticism*, ed. Josue V. Harari (London: Methuen, 1980), p. 151.
2. Roland Barthes, "The Death of the Author," *Image Music Text*, trans. Stephen Heath (London: Flamingo-Fontana, 1984), p. 147.
3. Patrick White, *The Aunt's Story* (1948, Harmondsworth: Penguin, 1968).
4. Rodney Stenning Edgecombe, *Vision and Style in Patrick White: A Study of Five Novels* (Tuscaloosa: Univ. of Alabama Press, 1989), pp. 148, 150.
5. David Carroll, *The Subject in Question: The Languages of Theory and the Strategies of Fiction* (Chicago: Univ. of Chicago Press, 1982), p. 56.
6. Susan McKernan, "A New Kind of Novel: The Work of Patrick White," *A Question of Commitment: Australian Literature in the Twenty Years After the War* (Sydney: Allen, 1989), pp. 166-88.
7. Barry Argyle, *Patrick White* (Writers and Critics, Edinburgh: Oliver, 1967).

8. Thelma Herring, "Odyssey of a Spinster: A Study of *The Aunt's Story*," *Ten Essays on Patrick White*, ed. G. A. Wilkes (Sydney: Angus, 1970), pp. 3-20.
9. Roland Barthes, *S/Z: An Essay*, trans. Richard Miller (New York: Hill, 1974), p. 178.
10. Shlomith Rimmon-Kenan, *Narrative Fiction: Contemporary Poetics* (New Accents, London: Methuen, 1983), p. 47.
11. This is partly the case with the narrative of Meroe, which involves Theodora yet is not wholly her narrative either.
12. Peter Brooks, *Reading for the Plot: Design and Intention in Narrative* (Oxford: Clarendon OUP, 1984), p. 13.
13. Ned Lukacher, *Primal Scenes: Literature, Philosophy, Psychoanalysis* (Ithaca: Cornell UP, 1986), p. 37. This is again not unique to *The Aunt's Story*. This distinction operates in all narratives, although in simpler narrative there may not be so great a disjunction between the *fabula* and the *sjuzet*.
14. Brooks, p.13.
15. Ingmar Bjorksten, *Patrick White: A General Introduction*, trans. Stanley Gerson (St. Lucia: Univ. of Queensland Press, 1976), p. 45.
16. Gerard Genette, *Narrative Discourse: An Essay in Method* (1972), trans. Jane E. Lewin (Ithaca: Cornell Univ. Press, 1980), p. 85.
17. Brooks, pp. 234-35.
18. Ibid., p. 177.
19. *Ibid.*, p. 178.
20. *Loc. cit.*
21. This is linked with the earlier distinction made between the *fabula* and the *sjuzet:* from the *sjuzet*, the reader (after re-reading) extracts the *fabula* and the links between the narratives are explicated.
22. Brooks, p. 123.
23 Barthes, *S/Z*, p. 178.
24. *Ibid.*, pp. 178-79.
25. Brooks, p. 281.
26. The General's escape from the fire is another instance of the recall of the past. He immediately embarks upon a recitation of history— "it reminds me. . . ." (p. 249)
27. Brooks, p. 285.
28. *Ibid.*, p. 281.

The Artist and Society: Jung and Patrick White

CYNTHIA VANDEN DRIESEN

This study falls neither into the category of literary criticism nor into the field of psychology, but into the nebulous field that appears to lie somewhere in between the two. It is proffered in the spirit in which Graham Hough contends all criticism should be advanced, that is, a kind of discourse in which "finally all conclusions are of a kind that could never finally be proved as true or false," a discourse which does not attempt to be more than "suggestive" and "persuasive, in the manner of good conversation."[1]

Sometime ago the *National Times* spotlighted what is called, "The Puzzling Case of Patrick White": the peculiar mixture of fascination and respect, of hostility and dislike which his work evokes amongst his countrymen; his own peculiar love-hate relationship with his native Australia, the undoubted quality of genius in his work, and its marked religious character which appears to go so much against the grain of the contemporary outlook.[2] All this seems less puzzling, becomes in fact highly meaningful, when considered within the context of Jung's theories of the great artist and his role in society.

Artistic inspiration

For Jung it was a deeply significant fact that about the same time that the Goddess of Reason was enthroned at Notre Dame, Anquetil de Perron brought back to the West the translation of the Upanishads, which was to be Europe's first contact with Eastern religious thought and mysticism. He felt it illustrated strikingly the rule that "For every piece of conscious life that loses its value—so runs the law—there arises a compensation in the unconscious . . . no psychic value can disappear without being replaced by another of equal intensity."[3] Jung felt that the contact with Eastern thought would have far-reaching effects in waking Western man to a realization of the psychic depth of his own nature. Through this he could hope to repair the damage wrought in his own spirit through the stultification of the religious and spiritual instincts which the uninhibited growth of rationalism and materialism in the West has brought about. In Jung's view, disruption in the psychic life of the community follows the same pattern as that within the individual: as soon as one of the channels of psychic energy is blocked, like a stream that is dammed, an upheaval becomes inevitable, but as long as the individual psyche functions undisturbed within a recognized system of belief, no problem is experienced. As soon as the system is found inadequate, as soon as a person outgrows it as it were, neurosis results. In the medieval world, people believed positively in a God who was their loving father, but today, "Modern man has lost all the metaphysical certainties of his medieval brother and set up in their place the ideals of material security, general welfare and humaneness."[4] Jung incisively analyzed what he sees as the present impasse of humanity. Apart from the rapid march of science and technology, the experience of two world wars and the threat of nuclear holocaust have radically shaken complacency. Modern man has begun to realize that every apparent advance adds to the threat of catastrophe, so that perhaps the worship of reason and materialism has reached its final stage of development. The inherent tendency towards the balancing of psychic energy results therefore in a compensating movement. Jung felt he already observed signs of a forthcoming change in the rapid growth of interest in psychology, showing that "modern man has to some extent turned his attention from material things to his own subjective processes."[5] He cites also a new interest in spiritualism, astrology, even witchcraft, and all kinds of psychic phenomena. In the context of the present study, one remark of Jung is of particular significance— "At any rate art has a way of anticipating future changes in man's fundamental outlook."[6]

Jung provides a far more meaningful interpretation of artistic inspiration and activity than does Freud. While both Jung and Freud held that the driving force behind artistic creation was rooted in the unconscious, for Freud art was no more than a substitute gratification, an expression neurosis, while for Jung art was one of man's most important intuitive and exploratory activities.[7] This difference follows inevitably from the difference in their concepts of the unconscious.[8]

For Freud, the id represented all that was dark and diseased, all that was suppressed from the conscious life of the intellect. For Jung, it was also the source of primal psychic energy, and could also therefore be the source of sustaining curative powers. As a result they also differed strongly in their attitude to the symbol which is largely the product of unconscious processes, and also inevitably in their approach to art and its meaning. For Freud the symbol represented a means of defence for the ego against the inadmissible contents of the unconscious. For Jung it was the natural language of the unconscious through which some complex and urgent meaning could be conveyed to consciousness. As Jung has pointed out, to reduce the work of art to something which should be analyzed in terms of the artist's repressions is to reduce it to the status of a neurotic symptom.[9] It is its quality of universality which makes art great, the personal idiosyncrasies of the artist is the least important factor. So he proceeded to his conclusion—if the work of artist is not compensatory to the artist's own conscious attitude, "the question we must answer is this: in what relation does it stand to the conscious attitude of his time?" Jung's own explanation is that "An epoch is like an individual, when conscious life is characterized by one-sidedness and by a false attitude, a compensating movement in the unconscious activates those archetypes necessary for bringing about psychic equilibrium. This is effected by the collective unconscious in that poets, seers, or leaders allow themselves, as it were, to be guided by the unexpressed need of their time, and point the way to fulfilment through word or deed. It is thus the work of great artists comes to fulfil a definite need of the society in which they live.

Erich Neumann, who elaborated on this theory of Jung to provide an illuminating commentary on the relation of art to its epoch, describes what this entails for the artist. It is a description which appears strikingly to fit the case of such a writer as Patrick White: "Compensation for the cultural canon means opposition to it—that is opposition to the epoch's consciousness and sense of values. The creative artist whose mission is to compensate for consciousness and the cultural canon is usually an isolated individual who must destroy the older order to make possible the dawn of the new."[11] The position of the great artist then presents a curious paradox. He appears to be sharply divided from the life of his contemporaries, but is in fact responding to their deepest need. As Neumann puts it, "When the unconscious forces break through in the artist, when the achetype striving to be born into the light of the world takes form in him, he is as far from the men around him as he is close to their destiny. For he expresses and gives form to the future of his epoch.'' What occurred in the Renaissance was the reappearance of the earth-archetype, and the dislodgment of the heaven-archetype which had in the name of religion, led to the denigration of the beauty of the natural world, and the life of the senses. Today we are again in the throes of the disintegration of the existing canon, and this is reflected in the sense of disorientation in much modern art. However, alongside the disintegration is evidence of the shaping of a new canon. As though to redress the balance of the modern tendency to over-emphasize the material and the physical, there are signs of a new movement towards re-emphasizing the spiritual and religious factors of experience. It could be held then that the emphasis on these aspects of experience in the work of such writers as Patrick White (who, as shall be seen, is no isolated figure from this point of view in the larger context of world literature) is evidence of the workings of a new zeitgeist. According to Jungian theory, it is the common openness to the promptings of the unconscious in a particular period which alone can explain the mysterious force which has been designated the ''zeitgeist'' of an age. It is the common force that seeks to drive all those who ever compensated for the cultural canon at a given time or shaped a new one.

Religion and the writer

Although a recent article by Dorothy Green attempted to prove that Australian literature has in fact a much more religious character than is generally recognized, the work of Patrick White is generally accepted as marking a new departure in its concentration on the inner spiritual crisis and the individual religious experience.[12] It shows rather an affinity with an important trend in the larger context of writing in the West. Here, as several critics have remarked, there has been a noticeable movement towards the rediscovery of the religious and spiritual dimensions of experience, and recognition of the validity of a transcendent order in the artist containing attempt to impose meaning and order on his experience.[13] Often, as in the case of White himself, though these writers may not themselves subscribe specifically to orthodox Christian doctrines, their works are pervaded by Christian imagery, and explore basically Christian themes of grace and salvation. While these elements in the work of such eminent figures as Faulkner, Steinbeck and Robert Penn Warren have been frequently commented, the trend is also apparent in the work of several other younger writers. Without wishing to imply that a new religious awareness affects all American fiction, in an interesting study of works by William Styron, John Updike, Philip Roth and J.D. Salinger, each of which has at its centre "the experience that is the apex of religious striving: the individual spiritual crisis that leads to the acceptance or rejection of God," Robert Detweiler convincingly makes his point that "a new attitude to religious in fiction . . . does in fact exist."[14] In England, writers like Graham Greene, Evelyn Waugh and Muriel Spark have all long established reputations which ensure that the label "Catholic Novelist," need not necessarily be a derogatory one. Anthony Burgess is of the opinion that "In cases where we least expect it, the elements of religion are accorded as much interest as the machinery of adultery or intrigue."[15] In the field of poetry particularly, it is a striking fact that the work of many of the great figures of the age have a markedly religious character. Apart from the giants like T.S. Eliot and Yeats, and also the later Auden and Hopkins, the stream of religious poetry continues in the work of Edwin Muir, Elizabeth Jennings, David Jones and others.

One needs, however, only to glance at the work of these poets and novelists to realize that the trend towards religion by no means represents a simple return to the doctrines of orthodoxy. Rather, what the contemporary religious artist seems most concerned to dramatize are the difficulties of a settled faith. Along with this there is a recognition of the fact that to be meaningful and relevant in the context of the contemporary world, the religious stance must necessitate an involvement with, not a withdrawal from, the realities of ordinary human existence.[16] These tendencies appear even in the work of frankly committed writers such as the French Catholic novelists Mautriac and Bernados, or the work of Graham Greene. Although these artists formally admit their adherence to the Roman Catholic faith, in their best work the bounds of Catholic orthodoxy are often stretched to the utmost.

Patrick White then shows himself very much as a man of his age, when, despite his explicitly avowed concern with religion and "the relationship between the blundering human being and God," he also declares, "I belong to no church but I have a religious faith."[17] His novels do not set forth any coherent set of orthodox doctrines. Rather, religion in his work must be defined broadly as a belief in the existence of a transcendental order which impinges directly on the life and destiny of the individual human being who must therefore work out a satisfactory relationship with, and adjustment to that order. He does not set out to celebrate settled stages of untroubled belief. Rather, as he depicts it, the inevitable condition of human existence seems to be that spiritual vision and understanding is always fleeting and transient. Laura Trevelyan's difficult avowal could be placed appropriately in the mouths of any one of White's central character's "I do believe, even if it is not all the time." Moreover, White's work constantly emphasizes that the transcendental world is best approached through the things and events of the actual phenomenal world. The religious spirit, as this is exemplified through the attitudes of the central characters of the novels, is shown to be intensely responsive to this world, the natural world of bird, beast and flower as to the world of their fellow human beings. The highly complex webs of imagery drawn from the natural world through which White dramatizes his transcendental themes reinforces this sense of its significance to the religious spirit.

In analyzing this trend towards religion, observers usually attribute it to the artist's conscious recognition of the fact that it was impossible to draw continued inspiration from the sterile idea of a negative universe. Negative nihilistic philosophies of existence are not conducive to continued creativity. This conscious deliberate decision does not negate Jung's idea that in compensating for the onesidedness of the life of the community, the artist is essentially obeying the dictates of the unconscious. Rather, it gives added emphasis and direction to these promptings. Patrick White, for instance, has repeatedly elucidated the nature of his aims—to create here in Australia, "a race possessed of understanding."[18] In an interview with Craig MacGregor, having admitted his own belief in God and concern for religion, he avers, "Now as the world grows more pagan, one has to lead people in the same direction in a different way."[19] His most unequivocal pronouncement in this regard has been perhaps his words to Clement Semmler, "What I am increasingly intent on trying to do in my books is to give professed unbelievers glimpses of their own unprofessed factor. I think that most people have a religious factor, but are afraid that by admitting it they will forfeit their right to be considered intellectuals."[20]

Yet frequently, also from White's own accounts, it appears that in the actual processes of composition, the influence of the unconscious is a factor of the first importance. In fact his first published poem was something he had dreamed of and written down on waking.[21] He has described his procedures to Craig MacGregor, "When you first write down the narrative it might be unconscious, but when you come to work it over you do it more consciously."[22] On the same occasion he stated, "I always like to write three versions of a book. The first is agony and no one would understand it. With the second you get the shape, it's more or less all right. . . . They are largely something that arise out of my unconscious. . . . I rewrite endlessly, it's more like oxywelding than writing." It is not surprising that he should place a particular value on intuition, declaring, "Practically anything which I have done of any worth, I feel I have done through my intuition, not my mind." Questioned as to why he appeared to disparage the intellect, he says, "I don't reject reason, but I think intuition is more important creatively in the beginning . . . everything I write has to be dredged up from the unconscious which is what makes it such an exhausting and perhaps finally such a destructive process."[23] He confessed to Elizabeth Riddell that he couldn't write a novel on some "sure fire subject"— "I couldn't do it. I can only write the way it comes out. Or rather it half comes out. The rest is dragged out with forceps. I don't write with pleasure."[24] One recalls Jung's description of how on occasion the unconscious holds the artist almost helpless in its grip: "Art is a kind of innate drive that seizes the human being and makes him its instrument . . . it is something necessary for him to sacrifice happiness and everything that makes life worth living for the ordinary human being."[25] White's description of the genesis of *The Tree of Man* to Kylie Tennant could be proffered as an illustration. Having settled in Australia, he had not done any new work, till, "down by the cow-bails one evening, *The Tree of Man* began to shape and whether I liked it or not I was beginning another book."[26] When he remarks "I have writing, I can't explain why I do write, except by saying that I seem to suffer from a kind of disease which can only be eased by writing."[27] One recalls the artist-figure he portrayed in *The Vivesector* driven to create on occasion, almost in spite of himself. Nor does it seem that over a writing career that now spans decades, he has begun to find the processes of creation any easier. Very recently, he told David Leitch, "Each novel is a torment that has to be gone through. The one I'm writing now more than any. . . . I work so slowly. . . . You've got to dig yourself in and get on with your work."[28]

Against the current

Erich Neumann emphasizes that, although at a superficial level he might appear to be working against the grain of the contemporary outlook, the creative man is actually deeply bound up with the life of his time, "more deeply than the common man who lives in the security of the cultural shell."[29] To the most superficial observer, it is apparent that White's education and background was such as must have brought him into contact with the liveliest intellectual and cultural crosscurrents of his time. Educated abroad, first at an English public school (an experience he heartily detested), he went on to read modern languages at Cambridge, and travelled widely in Europe and the United States. Subsequently, he led the life of a young London intellectual until his experience of the Second World War and its aftermath in England triggered his decision to return to his native Australia. Although he had throughout this youthful period remained hardheadedly independent of coteries in the intellectual and cultural environment in which he had moved, as David Leitch remarked, "White had been observing the process of decay. . . and missed nothing."[30] *The Living and the Dead* records his reaction to the sterility of English upper middle class culture, as *The Aunt's Story* glances briefly but evocatively at the chaos of Europe on the brink of war. For White, as for so many intellectuals and artists of the time, the experience of war was deeply traumatic. He told Elizabeth Riddell, "Anybody who has been in a war and who thinks, will know that it has been the most horrifying and wasteful period of their lives."[31] It seems that this experience of global cataclysm impelled a kind of spiritual stock-taking that culminated in White's return to Australia, and "the scenes of childhood, which is, after all, the purest well from which the creative artist draws."[32] Neumann emphasizes that "Only by suffering perhaps unconsciously under the power of his culture and his time can he (the artist) arrive at the freshly opening source which is destined to quench the thirst of his time."[33]

It was not that White found in his native Australia a haven from the "distressingly parastitic and pointless existence" he had observed elsewhere. In his analysis of "the Great Australian Emptiness" he mercilessly castigated aspects of Australian life which seemed to stand out particularly sharply to the eyes of the returned exile. His gibes at the "blind blue eyes" of the youths and girls, the predominance of the muscles, the addiction to cake and steak protested against a way of life that seemed to him simply physical and shallowly hedonistic.[34] It seems that the years have brought no softening of attitude. Recently, he has referred again publicly to Australia as "The country of my fate which in recent years has become increasingly abhorrent to me, which I believe it has to all men of good will engaged in a search for something more than a material solution."[35] Apart from such pronouncements is the testimony of the novels, which has led several Australian critics to castigate White for what they see as his contemptuous and unfair portrayal of Australian life. Yet as Elizabeth Salter points out, White's work is "the pearl that results from the irritation of its surroundings." After the war, White's surroundings were his native Australia.[36] Yet one has only to recollect the dreary frivolity of English middle class life in *The Living and the Dead*, or the glimpse of Europe on the eve of the war, and the American who "scrabbled on the surface of life," in *The Aunt's Story*, the restless perverted Greek hero Pavloussiss in *The Vivesector*, or in *The Eye of the Storm* the emotionally dessicated "French" princess de Lascabanes, to realize that for White, spiritual malaise, and the need to struggle against superficiality and purely materialistic values, is far from being a purely Australian dilemma. After all, the decision to return to Australia had been taken as a result of his feeling that England had become "an intellectual and spiritual graveyard," and he has more recently reaffirmed his decision to return to Australia had been taken as result of his feeling that England had become "an intellectual and spiritual graveyard," and he has more recently reaffirmed his decision not to return because "It has been ruined." After a recent visit to America, he declared the people were "quite vegetable . . . one never caught sight of anyone you could imagine reading any book." New Yorkers seemed "like a herd of dark distracted animals miling through the streets."[37] The truth seems rather that White's own temperament and outlook is such as to set him strongly at odds with the currents of philistinism and materialism as he finds these manifested everywhere in contemporary life. His spiritual affinity is with Blake, Yeats and Eliot, who see the malaise of the modern world as deriving from its gross materialism, its extreme rationalism and mechanization leaving no room for mystery, reverence and worship. The Australian scene provides White with a microcosm through which he dramatizes a vision universal in its implications.

A deeper empathy

Jung's theory of the artist and his relation to society, however, also implies that despite the apparent opposition of values, there does also exist a deeper empathy. In the case of such an artist as White, how widely is his desire to find "more than a material solution" shared by his contemporaries?

A definite answer is hardly possible. I said at the outset that this study does not set out to be more than suggestive and persuasive. In that spirit I shall merely indicate very broadly certain contemporary developments, signs of which Jung himself felt he discerned years ago, which seem to point to considerable changes in the spiritual climate of our time.[38] Neumann, looking at modern art, observed alongside the evidence of disorientation, signs of new possibilities of harmony: "The art of our time inclines towards a radical spiritualism . . . which surges up from within and compensates for the materialism dominating the outward picture of our time."[39] The interest of the ordinary person in things psychological, mystical and spiritual has grown. Interest in psychic phenomena, in astrology, and even witchcraft are all features of the contemporary scene. Courses in transcendental meditation are advertised, and responded to by housewives, business executives and pop stars.

The Jesus movement was certainly symptomatic of a new interest in religion in some sections of the youth of the community, while the growth of hippie communes and the fascination with the religions of the East testifies at least to an attempt to seek after "more than a material solution." Interestingly, in the 1970s Australia, whose youth Patrick White had himself bluntly condemned some years earlier for their propensity to "stare at life through blind eyes" provided two striking instances of what could be interpreted as evidence of the workings of a new spirit. Drawn from the field that White referred to as the "Australian Moloch," sport, Margaret Court and Shane Gould felt moved to affirm publicly that they had both found something lacking in their lives even after they had attained the pinnacles of success, and that "only religion had filled the void."[40]

It could well be maintained today that the religious stance is no longer regarded as intellectually inadmissible as it once was, when it seemed that the march of science would reveal all truth. The writings of Popper and Bronowski have emphasized the fact that the claims of science are neither absolute nor infallible.[41] A dialogue is now recognized as possible between people of science and people of religion. The career of Teilhard de Chardin, an eminent scientist and devout Jesuit priest, is highly instructive in this regard. The theory of evolution, once regarded as having dealt the death-blow to religion, forms the cornerstone of his thought.[42] Julian Huxley paid handsome tribute to him, for having "Through his combination of wide scientific knowledge with deep religious feeling and a rigorous sense of value . . . forced theologians to view their ideas in the new perspective of evolution and scientists to see the spiritual implications of their knowledge."[43] In fact a measure of the change in intellectual circles with regard to the acceptability of the religious experience is exemplified in a comparison between the attitudes of Julian Huxley with that of his equally celebrated grandfather, T.H. Huxley. Where Huxley senior could declare quite unequivocally, "I do not very much care to speak of anything (as) unknowable," and dismiss religion and the efficacy of prayer and miracles as valueless "because of the inadequacy of the evidence to prove any given case,"[44] his grandson was willing to admit, "Religious experiences are . . . ineffable, in the literal sense of the word which makes their discussion difficult. But their significance is both high and deep (as I am in all humility aware) and they certainly need re-examination and re-appraisal if their great potential value is to be recognized."[45]

All this, however, is but the signs of the stirring of a new spirit. John Wren-Lewis remarked that despite the large number of books written to demonstrate that religious belief need not be destroyed by science, "the general public continue resolutely to believe that science has disproved religion,"[46] and so our age continued to be characterized as a secular age. While the debate must remain inconclusive, I would like to conclude this section of my discussion with a quotation from Ronald Gross (Professor of Social Thought at New York University) on Humanist Manifesto II: "There is more in heaven and earth Horatio than is dreamed of in your philosopy—Hamlet's gentle admonition to his friend is echoed, it seems to me by the widespread reaction to Humanist Manifesto II. Many intellectuals, artists and social activists . . . find this document insufficient in response to today's widespread and palpable hunger for transcendence." He cites the example of people "too important to the humanist cause because their sympathies lie with the progressive approach to world problems," and quotes one of them (Leda le Shan) on "the crippling of our psyches by our over-committment to scientific thought and the atrophy of our equally important potentialities for transcendent experience.''[47]

David Leitch's article on White was accompanied by two sketches by artist Coopes. One of these especially seemed to me to convey particularly eloquently something of White's grandeur and importance in his Australian context, and even in the world at large.[48] It depicts tiny human figures atop a craggy peak into which the stern, accusing features of the artist are embedded. His massive strength renders the indifference of the little group insignificant, yet his strength supports them, giving them indeed the vantage point from which to view their world. Whether disliked or admired the great artist cannot be really ignored because his work, in Jung's words, ''comes to meet the spiritual needs of the society in which he lives.''[49]

NOTES

1. Graham Hough, ''The Function of Criticism, *Listener*, 25 April 1962, p. 709.
2. See *National Times*, 27 March-1April 1978, p. 1.
3. C.G. Jung, ''The Spiritual Problem of Modern Man,'' *Modern Man in Search of a Soul* (London: Kegan Paul Trench, Trubner, 1941), pp. 241-42.
4. *Ibid.*, p. 235.
5. *Ibid.*, p. 237.
6. *Loc. cit.*
7. C.G. Jung, ''Psychology and Literature,'' *Modern Man in Search of a Soul*, pp. 175-99. See also Jung's essays in *The Spirit on Man, Art and Literature*, Collected Works, Vol. 15, trans. R.F.C. Hull (London: Routledge and Kegan Paul, 1966).
8. For a useful discussion see Morris Phillipson, *Outline of Jungian Aesthetics* (North-Western University Press, 1963).
9. C.G. Jung, ''Psychology and Literature,'' p. 191.
10. *Ibid.*, pp. 191-92.
11. Erich Neumann, *Art and the Creative Unconscious*, trans. Ralph Mannheim (London: Routledge and Kegan Paul), p. 94.
12. Dorothy Green, ''Sheep or Goats? Some Religious Ideas in Australian Literature,'' *St. Mark's Review*, No. 6, June 1976, pp. 3-29.

13. Robert Detweiler writes, "the teleological dimension has returned in the form of the individual religious experience so that the critic must approach the novel embodying that dimension with a seriousness and objectivity." He also notes that a large number of inter-disciplinary studies published as evidence of "the intensity of the current dialogue between literature and religion." See his monograph, "Religion in Post-War American Fiction: Four Spiritual Crisis," University of Florida Monographs in the Humanities, No. 14 (Fall 1963), pp. 50-52. Ignatio Silone feels "the discovery of the Christian tradition remains the most important gain that has been made in these last years for the conscience of our generation," Quoted in Amos Wilder, *Modern Poetry and the Christian Tradition: A Study in the Relation of a Religion to Culture* (New York: Charles Scribner, 1952), p. 219.
14. Detwiler, p. 4.
15. Anthony Burgess, "The Manichaeans," *TLS*, 3 March 1966, p. 154.
16. In their studies of the religious trend in contemporary literature, both Amos Wilder and Charles Glicksburgh note this fact. See Amos Wilder, *Modern Poetry and the Christian Tradition,* p. 46. Also, Charles Glicksburgh, *Literature and Religion: A Study in Conflict* (Dallas: Southern Methodist University Press, 1962), p. 54.
17. Craig MacGregor, *In the Making* (Melbourne: Nelson, 1969), p. 218.
18. Patrick White, "The Prodigal Son," *Australian Letters*, I, 3, April 1958, p. 40.
19. See MacGregor, p. 219.
20. Quoted in Peter Beatson, *The Eye in the Mandala Patrick White: Vision of Man and God* (A. H. and A. W. Reed, 1977), p. 167.
21. See Barry Argyle, *Patrick White* (London: Oliver and Boyd, 1967), p. 4.
22. MacGregor, pp. 219-20.
23. G.A. Wilkes and Thelma Herring, "A Conversation with Patrick White," *Southerly,* XXXIII, 2 (June 1973), p.139.
24. Elizabeth Riddell, "White," *Australian*, 7, August 1970, p. 33.
25. Jung, "Psychology and Literature," p. 195.
26. Kylie Tennant, "Writer in Stained Glass," *Sydney Morning Herald*, 22 September 1956, p. 10.

27. Pat Griffith, "Famous Author Hates Writing," *Advertiser*, 18 November 1961, p. 17.
28. David Leitch, "Patrick White: A Revealing Profile," *National Times,* 27 March-1 April 1978, p. 33.
29. Neumann, pp. 98-99
30. Leitch, p. 34.
31. Riddell, p. 15.
32. Patrick White, "The Prodigal Son," pp. 38-39.
33. Neumann, p.99.
34. Patrick White, "The Pradigal Son," pp. 38-39.
35. Leitch, p. 32.
36. Elizabeth Salter, "The Australianism of Patrick White," in *The Commonwealth Writer Overseas: Themes of Exile and Expatriation*, ed. Alastair Niven (Liege: Revue des Langues Vivantes, 1976), p. 232.
37. Leitch, p. 35.
38. This "Evidence" is not cited here as necessarily implying a return to religion as such, but as broadly indicating a new value for the things of the spirit and the rejection of a purely materialistic approach to existence.
39. Neumann, p. 127.
40. "Religion Fills a Void," *West Australian*, 7 June 1976.
41. See Karl Popper, *Conjectures and Refutations: The Growth of Science* (London: Routledge and Kegan Paul, 1965). Also, J. Bronowski, *The Commonsense of Science* (London: Heineman, 1951).
42. Teilhard de Chardin, *The Phenomenon of Man* (2nd edn, New York: Harper and Row, 1965).
43. Julian Huxley, "Teilhard de Chardin," *Essays of a Humanist*, p. 112.
44. See *The Essence of T.H. Huxley*, ed. Cyril Bibby (New York: Macmillan, 1967), p. 114.
45. Julian Huxley, "The Humanist Frame," *Essays of a Humanist*, p. 112.
46. John Wren-Lewis, "Science and Religion," *Twentieth Century*, No. 1036, 1968, p. 54.
47. Ronald Gross, "The Hunger for the Transcendent," *Humanist*, XXXIV, 36, September 1974, p. 36.
48. Leitch, p. 39.
49. C.G. Jung, "Psychology and Literature," p. 198.

In the Distillery

CHRIS WALLACE-CRABBE

The making of poetry is a dramatic thing.

Peter Steele

Peering back, way back, into the soft green years before World War II, I can still discern or recall signs of the first magic: the magic of language. My family was strong on tales, rhymes, jokes, riddles and all manner of ways of condensing the kernel of some truth in words. My garrulous aunt Violante (born 1891), mingled romantic tales of our Highland family with songs like "Maresy Doats," and riddles and nonsense verses, like this one which puzzled me for quite a while because the final rhyme was cut off, snub-nosed:

In Parliament House when a motion is made
Each member stands up and uncovers his head,
But in *this* little house it is just the reverse.

Other nursery rhymes and nonsense poems laid down their materials in little Christopher's consciousness, alongside the incomparable legerdemain of Kipling.

Kipling fitted into the imprecise oral history we had of our family—on the paternal side—as a crookedly Celtic line of soldiers, pirates and swashbucklers. All this exotic side of things was reinforced by my Dad being away for four-and-a-half years during the War, doing fascinating things in the Far East, the Straight East and the Middle East, storybook regions that were represented by his lively letters and drawing, along with the strange objects he would send home to us in Melbourne: wolfskins and lengths of silk, red lacquer pots and Benares brassware, ivory and jade, kukri and kris.

I didn't write poetry as a kid but was fascinated by books as containers of the exotic, as lamps which emitted strange genies when rubbed. And I sipped my history from stories, whether fictitious or embroidered-factual. To Kipling, Stevenson, Jeffrey Farnol and such-like jaunty, faraway writers I added a favourite poem at the age of ten, or thereabouts. It was James Elroy Flecker's gilded piece, "The Old Ships," which begins,

> I have seen the old ships sail like swans asleep
> Beyond the village which men still call Tyre,
> With leaden age o'ercargoed, dipping deep
> For Famagusta and the hidden sun
> That rings black Cyprus with a lake of fire.

There was an absolute distillation of historical romance; the poem was charged with incantation.

Maybe the fact that Dad was away at the War for such a long time already encouraged me to see small things as symbolic of later ones. Souvenirs, bric-a-brac, airletters, I had to read them all as symbolic of a missing parent—and of the vast continent of Asia. Could this have disposed me towards the condensed quality of lyric poetry? Ah yes, condensation can be seen as the nitty-gritty of verse, as the young Gwen Harwood was told when she was a girl: concentration, as with Bonox, a whole ox in one small bottle. Maybe, too, the fact that my father was a professional journalist, interested in everything but not for too long, played its part.

Not that I wrote poetry as a boy, or no more than my classmates. One of them actually wrote a good poem at the age of ten. My friend Peter Taylor, now a lawyer, wrote this inspired piece of verse:

> Dentist's room.
> Much gloom
> And fear;
> The fatal hour is near.
> Nurse comes,
> Sore gums.
> In I go.
> Come out.
> Hurt?
>   No.

From this peak of inspiration Peter descended and became a solicitor.

But the mysteries of our lives during World War II have kept coming back to haunt me. Two or three years ago I came up with a poem called "East," in which I tried to distil some essence from those distorted, colourful and incomprehensible years:

When he came back from War
he still wore the soft
greyesh blue of the British
air force, not our dark blue
(he had been too old for ours)

and my little brother whispered,
"That man's still here," in the cold
morning, unable to
assimilate this return
from the fabulous, curried East,

far to our north, far up
the eurocentric map
which Dad had fought to maintain
in face of the sweat and sprawl
of Japanese incursions.

When Dad flew in from the War
our world was perfectly
old, traditional, dinkum,
the iceman's weeping truck
still dawdling down warm streets

and a Chinese greengrocer
obscurely urging his horse
another few short yards.

After VE Day I drowsed my way through a desperately normal adolescence, my thoughts much taken up by the leg break, the square cut, the backhand return of service (very tricky to control) and the stab-kick. To the best of my knowledge I wrote only one poem in my years of secondary schooling and that was so bad that it was rejected by the school magazine.

Let us forget about sport and Second World War, returning to early influences and familiar objects. My imagination had a flying start. My family rented a house or a flat, rather than buying a home. They did, however, surround themselves with books, pictures, objects. So I was brought up in a world lightly saturated with writing and art. Beyond his journalism, my father was an illustrator, cartoonist, printmaker; my younger brother picked up the threads, becoming a profoundly original painter, before his second blossoming as a writer of detective novels in recent years.

So for me poetry has always had more in common with the visual arts than with other word-games, for all that I'm also interested in it as drama. It seems that a short poem is like a picture representing some dramatic moment, some distillation, some instant of immense potential. It reveals the world as *charged* with some energy, somewhat like an oiled spring waiting to be released. Often the poem is based on an eloquent sense of absence, implying the presence that should be there, or is about to return. Take "December," for example, which is also a Victoria Market poem, a poem about Christmas turning up amid the resinous airs of summer:

> I came at random
> To a papery wind blowing
> And rivers of darkness flowing through the market
> Between deserted stalls,
> And I turned at a random scent
> To see the trucks that loomed along the kerb
> Each in turn heavy with Christmas trees
>
> And no one around to buy
> Nobody here to sell,
> But a resinous wind blowing.

This lyric has a point-of-view, much as a painting done on the spot might have, but it also alludes to absences and implications. Paintings don't often do that: they find it difficult.

Of course, poetry deals with the visual in a quite distinct way. When you look at, say, an Arthur Boyd painting you actually see trees or lovers or water delineated in oils: when you look at any text you only see print on a white page. It is the imaginary artist in the attic of your skull who has to visualize the written experience.

I was having dinner with friends a few years ago and we were having a discussion that I found very interesting. We started talking about the clear images one can get from writing or poetry, and as a consequence, asking ourselves just how clear are those images? Do you actually see, in every detail, what happens when Tennyson writes, "The splendour falls on castle walls," or when Hopkins says, "Glory be to God for dappled things." or when Browning writes, "That's my last duchess hanging on the wall/looking as if she were alive"? Do you really see that, in the kind detail that you would on a film screen or a television screen, in a picture or in a painting? Or do you get an impression on the mind's visual screen that is still somehow general and mainly verbal, not fully fleshed out in detail. A line we chose was Thomas Hardy's "The rotten rose is ripped from the wall," and I said, is the rose on the top right-hand corner of the picture, or in the middle of the picture, or the top left? Is it a red rose? A pink rose, a white one? Confusion reigned, and yet we all found that the "The rotten rose is ripped from the wall" was an extremely powerful visual image of a storm tearing a climbing rose bush off a wall. In the end we agreed that, although it had such power, it wasn't particular like a picture, in that you didn't know where the rose was on the wall or what kind of wall it was, stone or stucco; yet it still retained the immediacy and power of a visual image.

What does the mind's eye see, then, when it responds to my poems? To exemplify this question, let me offer two examples of my wares; both are poems from the 1970s, both are short, but they stand at different angles to the world. The former is an impressionistic piece, maybe painterly (a bit like Clarice Beckett, you might think), while the second has a narrative galumph to it, creating a figure who is both comical and mythic (it had an effect: someone took up my notion of Captain Melbourne and turned him into a comic strip). But it might be interesting to consider how far these two poems generate visual effects. And another thing: in attending to the former poem, how much previous cultural baggage does a listener or reader bring along from his or her prior knowledge of the Latrobe Valley? Similarly, how much of the playful impact of the latter poem derives from those hoary old jokes about Melbourne versus Sydney?

The Empty Mask

In all the Gippsland sky

no fleece of cloud
to muffle this dewy brightness

Only one tuft
snagged low down
on a dwarf power station

Tall gums
are standing on the toes of their shadows
and the hills dream

The Collective Invention

Wanting a myth for blowing up the gods,
In his flowing silver cape and plastic wings
Captain Melbourne zooms over Lonsdale Street.

His faithful girl assistants screech below
In their custom runabout:
Their T-Shirts bear the sweet inscription JUSTICE
And they wear it well.

Admiringly, the crimes and their dwarf henchmnen
Hustle away,
Skulk underneath overpasses,
Terrified of the sterling Captain
And those just bosoms busy on their trail.

Glancing up from our sandwiches, if we're lucky
We might spot him gliding overhead
In his line of business,
Doing the common good all day long,
A handful of thunderbolts in his shoulder holster.

O Captain Melbourne, man of the wind and rain,
You are our hero,
Save us from northern weakness,
Continue still to zap and biff and pow.

It could be said that "The Empty Mask" aspires to be pure gist, while

"The Collective Invention" is largely jest. But then, I've always thought that high spirits were one of the things that poetry should go after, as much as the apprehension of essences. If we compare poetry to prose, it is not only the case that poetry should be more musical and evocative, it should also be more concentrated in its effect: full of beans; a ball of muscle; or, to put it another way, an enchanted contraption in which the language has been wound up tight.

Oh yes, alas, and oh, dear me, poems are written in language, the very same medium in which we speak, and in which we discuss them. It is a medium which can be abstract or generalized, jokey or discursive. But it is not tangible in the way paint is, or a sculptor's bronze or steel. Poems, then, discuss their own aims, their own methods, their own innards. But if that's what a poem is up to, the poet has to keep the whole caboodle interesting: has to infect the language used with all the kinds of verbal play and colourful figuration that it is possible to drum up.

But what is the language *doing* there, in its poem? In as much as the aim of the poem in question is the crystallization of wisdom, the language is there to represent speech frozen in mid-gesture. But in so far as the poem is mimetic, the language functions to set down a series—or a congeries, more precisely—of impressions, like those in "December"; the words and phrases, by way of a long tradition of agreed verbal conventions, function as a series of impressionistics brush-strokes, so that we have with "each—in turn—heavy—with Christmas trees," a pictorial sequence.

Something is still being left out in this duality between wisdom and mimesis. It is the energy displayed by poetry as sheer making, the poet as maker, daring to offend both God and Plato. Thus Wallace Stevens writes in his "Adagia" that "The poem is a nature created by the poet," and again, "The poet makes silk dresses out of worms." With my own predilections, I should prefer to say that the poet works like Robert Klippel, elaborating new creations out of worn-out materials. A strong new poem is a jigger, a lovely whatsit which has never been seen before.

Writing and art abstract in such different ways that you might say they go the same distance out from the actual thing, but in different directions. For instance a painting or drawing of a table might give an impression of what's on top, what's on the bottom, and maybe an idea of what it's made of, what sort of colour it is, what its proportions are, etcetera; on the other hand, a written text gives you a feeling of causation in time. A painting can't show you, except by oblique suggestion, a series of events. Even a very simple text can tell you, "She walks through the door, she pauses in the middle of the room, she stops to tap her cigarette in the ashtray, she eats an apple and then walks into the back garden." Even the lowest level of fiction can do that at the drop of a hat. Art just can't get that particularity in time, it can only give you particularity in space.

But it was writing verses that I went on with, persisting through such jobs as being a true journalist, a Gas & Fuel clerk, a maltster's labourer in Richmond, a sleeper-driller in the Morwell Open Cut and—like other writers—a schoolteacher. At Haileybury College, for two years after graduating from a part-time degree, I wore my patience to the bone teaching English, French, maths, history and with great pains, geography—I even taught eleven-year-olds a whole year of Scottish history: it was just like "The Seven Samurai"! But the poems kept bubbling up and at twenty-five I published my first collection, *The Music of Divison*.

That slim volume came out in 1959, in a biscuit-coloured dustjacket which Jack Hibberd later suggested was most appropriate because it matched my biscuit-coloured complexion. Forget the colour; it is, however, intriguing at first to find a book which has come out with your name on the cover. It is as though you suddenly have another self, a secret sharer, a public name, an authorial double.

So there I was: a poet of sorts, the fellow behind the book. I have already tried to define some of the ways in which poetry, and particularly my own poetry, resembles the visual arts: what the seeing in poetry sees. Another question which raises its wordy head is this: just how does the impulse to poetry differ from the writing of prose? That's a curly one, but also a familiar one, because a great many people want to ask it, particularly in an age of prose like our own (or is this the Post-Prose age?). The French poet, Paul Valery, has this to say about the distinction:

> Those ideas which cannot be put into prose are put into verse. If one finds them in prose, they demand verse and have the air of verse that has not yet been able to take shape. What ideas are these?
>
> They are the ideas that are possible only in very lively, rhythmic, or spontaneous movements of thought.

"The Thing Itself" is an example of the kind of thinking, or leaping, or condensing, that I could never have managed to do in prose.

Let me make some observations about my own career; that is to say, about my own development as a poet—not exactly a mainstream career pattern in our century. It was not the poets who went yachting with Alan Bond, rode to polo with Packer or sipped French champagne on the terrace with Lady Mary Fairfax. No, the poets went on getting fifty bucks a throw for their best poems and teaching for a living wage. Still, the slow curve of a literary life has its diverisfied satisfactions—and it lasts longer than being a swimmer or a tennis player.

Having decided at the end of my adolescence that I was going to be a writer and not an industrial chemist (despite Mendeleef's enchanting periodic table of the elements, and the wonderful colours which the salts of copper, iron and chromium displayed) I got on with reading and writing poetry, as well as working by day to earn an honest penny. Why write poetry at all? Eliot called it a mug's game. it is certainly not the filthy lucre, not the circulation (a book of mine is very lucky if it reaches 2000 copies) and not the diminutive fame, but the fact that I have let myself sink too deep in this language art to get out again. Being a language person, a wordsmith, I am bound to live by the stuff, seeking out its gists and piths, moulding its dips and ridges, orchestrating its charms. There is a deep, almost incomparable joy in getting a poem to work out; pressing through its various colourations until it works: making the whole contraption hum.

But where did the poems come from? What did (or do) they have to do with raw life and death, with my home or washing the dishes or a cocky statement by Paul Keating or a small flight of brilliant lorikeets heading over the Melbourne General Cemetery? There are more answers to that question than you could shake a stick at.

When I was scribbling my early poems I believed two contradictory things about what I was writing: that it was my own sincere personal utterance, and that it was capable of representing the external world accurately. If I had thought more strenuously about musical examples, like Vivaldi's "The Four Seasons" or Vaughan Williams's "London Symphony," my naivete would have been as clear as day.

As to my first, innocent notion that I was presenting my own, unique experience, squeaking from the heart, time has disabused me of that. When I look back through the psychic telescope at poems I wrote in the 1950s, it is perfectly clear that they are poems written by the 1950s rather than by any CWC that I can recognize: not only the verse-forms, but the phrasing, images, rhythms and even the range of permisisble ideas, all have been produced for me by an age that now seems remote enough to boast the stegosarus and the hideous triceratops. As Valery once remarked: "We have no means of getting exactly what we want from ourselves"; of course we don't, because external systems have already written too much of the programme. Maybe it was the Life Force that done it: or the Cold War; or the Banksia Men.

At the hot moment of writing, though, it feels utterly different. Like an actor or a spy, one feels free to act out one of a host of posisble identities. Godlike, you feel free to invent alternative selves, or roles that are momentarily real. I even have a recent poem in which I speak as God the Creator himself.

Garrulous, long-nosed William Wordsworth claimed that poetry was "emotion recollected in tranquillity" and Thurber capped this by saying that humour was "emotional chaos recollected in tranquillity." Good phrases these, but in each case that lovely noun, tranquillity, strikes me as off the mark. What is the poem actually bespeaking after the strange crystallization (Stendhal's word) has taken place? The universe distilled in its diversity?

How different the possible answers to what the stuff of poetry is can be shown by three of my poems. The first, tiny, one is a happy accident, a *poeme trouve*; I got it, intact, over the loudspeaker at Adelaide airport:

> Excuse me please
> would passenger Death
> travelling to Melbourne
> on Flight 219
> please call at the front counter?
> Passenger Death.
> Thank you.

Of course, public address systems are never entirely frank, so that it does remain open to question whether there was a traveller called Death on that flight, or whether my subconscious got to work on the raw materials and produced what is needed. (There were four deaths in the Melbourne phone book, if you count the one spelt De'ath).

This aspect of my writing has affinities with surrealism, or at least with the modernist art of collage, as practised by Kurt Schwitters, who first stuck tram tickets onto his canvases, and more recently by a swarm of street poets, Merseyside poets and such. It keeps you on your toes, having your eyes wide open and plucking random notions off the smoggy vine of dailiness. But it is not typical of my poetry at large.

In another kind of poem the germ is not something given, or accidental, but the product of thought. An imaginative argument has been conceived and followed through. The Muse knows in this case that one thing leads to another, that a vividly coherent world picture can be argued into being. Such a poem is my re-writing of prehistory, "The Evolution of Tears." I had been thinking about human evolution before and after the last two ice-ages when this theme began to swim into my consciousness and distil its version of history. The plangent retelling of our species pleased me:

> I wonder whether grief was already invented
> as far back as the Mindel and Wurm glaciations,
> some rogue gene having tipped the scale.
>   I wonder
> whether the human creature was chosen by grief
> as much as by stone tools or opposable thumb.
> Did our hopeless remote forebear sit blubbing his eyes out
> (her eyes?) by gunyah or cave? We cannot know.
> Tears leave no grooves in archaeological sites,
> a broken heart has never been trowelled up;
> the lacrimae rerum do not resemble objects
> though misery be as hard as a stone in your hand.
>
>   A long way down the line were those other properties,
> the lily of logic with a rose between her teeth,
> rationalization, debt, the barque of state,
> but darker human traits had crept in first
> teaching the dread monosyllables, lost and gone.
> One, more obscene, begins with a capital D.
>
> Chemical? We comprehend grief, but not always.
> A burial rips the guts out of everyone close.
> We fail. We suffer. One slides into the ground
> who had been a spirit, horsed round and laughed as we do

and now joins the majority. . . .
  the tacit ones . . .
in a horizontal kingdom underfoot.
We do not understand.
  Together we rise,
feather, turn and fly away.

The third brand of distillation is what might be called the Pure or Symbolist poem. This is the lyric that is all music, like a Chopin Prelude. Often it arrives unannounced, like a thief in the night with a silver balaclava over her head. It comes as a rhythm, a verbal tune, a beguiling form, and virtually dances its way into being. With such a pure lyric, the poet may well find that the component parts are only recognizable well after the poem has been completed. Such a visitation was the small lyric, "Sand in my Shoes":

Dreams of the dour and winsome,
a world for ransom
and a stammering impresario
by the piano.

Ah, the American magazines,
the flagon red after light toil
and summer's fading masterpieces
cool as coconut oil.

Where do the raw materials of this poem come from? It was written at the seaside, near Mossy Point, a rather dreary holiday resort on the New South Wales south coast. The stammering may come from Patrick McCaughey, former Director of the National Gallery of Victoria, and a man who would certainly be associated in my mind with American tastes or fashions. His fierce modernism might well be contrasted with "fading masterpieces." And so on. But these are not the *meanings* of the poem as it stands: a little song about sand and summer bearing the title of and old beach song of Al Bowlly's. It is what it is, all gist or all image. This is the kind of poetry which is not reducible to prose, not paraphrasable.

But there one is, in what Henry James rather optimistically called the Middle Years, with a recognizable name, perhaps with a certain reputation. But who *is* the me whose name appears on the cover of my books? It might be the snapper up of unconsidered trifles; or the thinker; or the secular preacher; or the creator of pure symbolist music in verse. The self that I am depends on what needs to be said. Keats, who died at twenty-five, knew all this when he wrote in a letter,

> As to the poetical Character itself . . . it is not itself—it has no self—it is everything and nothing—It has character—it enjoys light and shade; it lives in gusto, be it foul or fair, high or low, rich or poor, mean or elevated. . . . A poet is the most unpoetical of any thing in existence; because he has no Identity—he is continually informing and filling some other Body—The Sun, the Moon, the Sea and Men and Women who are creatures of impulse are poetical and have about them an unchangeable attribute—the poet has none; no identity—he is certainly the most unpoetical of all God's creatures.

The poet is much more like a novelist and a dramatist than we often suppose, except that the entities he or she characterizes, brings to life, are rarely characters in the ordinary sense of the term: but they inhale a life of their own, if the poem is to convince. The poet comes upon some concatenation of scene and mood, some webby complex of emotions and gives it the greatest degree of life. The self dissolves as far as possible into what Keats called "some other Body," trying to present the *inscape* of the situation. It seems to me that a poet should be able to respond to Cezanne's marvellous admisison, "I sometimes imagine colours as great noumenal entities, living ideas, beings of pure reason."

Some poets, Browninglike, literally seek to create characters. I have tried myself to invent political and other figures caught at some moment of crisis, from God to a Cold War spy, to the Aboriginal emigrant, Bennelong, brooding amid the lush green hatefulness of Europe. Many poets, though, invent and present characters who would seem closely to resemble themselves. Think of Gwen Harwood, of Dorothy Hewett, of Robert Adamson: all three follow in the romantic convention of pasisonately dramatizing a being whose biography resembles the poet's own. In such poetry as theirs the private and the articulated stand in a very complicated relationship, as Harwood admitted in a witty article in *Southerly*, cunningly saying, "I see myself behaving like a mother duck feigning a broken wing to draw enemies away from my secret nest,'' and ''I often wish now that I had kept right behind the curtain and never revealed who wrote the poetry (maybe I could have had a front man with flashing eyes and floating hair).''

I take her point. There are so many selves to try and make sense of, to try and hang onto, even. There is the one who gets up in the morning and takes the kids down to the kitchen; the one who works at Melbourne University; the one I remember from thirty years ago; the one who dreams; and lastly the one who seems to speak out of that poem. How hard it is to keep the team playing together! Some of my poems are explicitly about relation between members of this interior family, this psychological zoo. I love to ask how the internal creatures get on and what sort of noises they make together.

Of all those selves the most mysterious is, of course, the one who dreams and comes back from voyages hauling after him some odd creature glittering and dripping from the deeps. I think the most interesting part of Alec Hope's zigzag book, *The New Cratylus*, is the chapter in which he talks about dreams and their ambiguous dealings with the poetic imagination. What is the possible commerce between those vivid, evocative, deeply visual experiences and that which can be communicated in words? Usually, very little, I believe. But I have on a number of occasions tried to make my way across that difficult rope bridge and make the experiences of my dream-self over into poetry, either by transcribing whole or part-dreams into language, or, on very rare occasions, bringing back a dreamed poem. The openings of several of my poems have been in brute fact dreamed, but my best trophy was incredibly dreamed in French and in an elaborately neat verse-form:

> Mais les reves
> Sont vraiment
> Toute la vie
> De ma vie
> En petit,
> On dit.

What that little freak has to do with anything I do not know, especially since I cannot even speak French with any competence. The subconscious is a funny Christmas stocking. And its eloquent symbols can feed those of poetry.

It would be nice if a poetic career confirmed you in a lucid self. Unfortunately, two things happen at once: your style hardens and narrows yet you somehow become aware of how multifarious identity is, how undisciplined. As the old, blind writer Borges nicely said, "we swim in mystery and ignorance." But out of that flux, through words, we try to distil meaningful symbols. We firm up the provisonal, dividual self, over and over again, like a coach whipping a footy team into shape. We catch the good moment, briefly, and rejoice in its luminosity. Another poem has been distilled.

Christopher Brennan: The Man and the Poet

ROBERT ADAMSON

> Born November 1 1870, in Harbour Street off Hay Street as one turns down from the old Haymarket. My father was brewer at the Castlemaine Brewery in Hay Street and built his house where he could be near his work: he had at critical moments to visit it at night. . . . While the house was building we lived in Quay Street just behind and beneath the brewery.
>
> Christopher Brennan, Curriculum Vitae[1]

Brennan began his formal education at St. Aloysius School in Bourke Street but later attended St. Ignatius College (Riverview) on a scholarship founded by Cardinal Moran. After finishing school, Brennan was expected to go to Rome with the Cardinal and study for the priesthood. Brennan decided not to do this and instead enrolled in Arts at the University of Sydney in 1888. He explained in his curriculum vitae that religion had begun to worry him by his nineteenth year. "It seemed to me that I lacked fervour, that I was mechanically repeating a dull exercise." By the time he began studying philosophy in 1890, Brennan described himself as "a ripe agnostic, already beginning to elaborate a special epistemology of the Unknowable, which was the Absolute."

Brennan's crisis of faith in 1889 went very deep, and having abandoned his vocation for the priesthood, he tried to internalize it, transferring its expression to metaphysics and poetry. He found later in Novalis a justification for this enterprise: "Who but a poet may dare to undertake to define the metaphysical totality of life."[2]

In 1892 Brennan gained his Master's degree with honours in philosophy. He was awarded the James King of Irrawang Travelling Scholarship and left for Germany in June 1892. He made for Berlin, where he was attracted by the University's reputation for classical studies. He boarded with Frau Werth, who was eventually to become his mother-in-law, in lodgings opposite the State Opera House. Brennan was always deeply interested in music and sometimes visited the State Opera House with an American musician friend.

Besides courting Frau Werth's daughter, Anna Elisabeth, Brennan spent much of his time in Berlin reading Flaubert. He did not take the University very seriously and seems to have done little there, returning to Sydney without any new academic titles. He did, however, discover some articles dealing with the French Symbolist poets and on 13 September 1893, he bought a copy of Stephane Mallarme's *Vers et Prose* from a bookseller in Berlin. Brennan became a great admirer of Mallarme and later had his edition of *Vers et Prose* interleaved, copying into it all Mallarme's other poetry that he could trace. By the time he left Berlin, Brennan had read practically all of Mallarme's more important poems. Mallarme had cast his spell and his poetry was to influence most of Brennan's later work.[3]

Brennan returned to Sydney in August 1894 in the middle of the Depression and was unable to find work for some months. His friend, A.B. Piddington (then member for Tamworth), eventually secured him temporary work in the public service and this was followed in 1895 by a permanent position in Sydney's Public Library. Brennan was particularly sensitive to cold weather and during winters working in the library he would wear a heavy overcoat over his shoulders with the sleeves hanging loose while he worked. Even when he went outside he did not bother to put his arms into the sleeves and adopted the habit of carrying books beneath the coat. Right through the winter, with his long black sleek hair drawn back from his great forehead and the great coat with his books underneath, he would swoop about like a huge black rifle-bird.

While Brennan waited for his lover Elisabeth Werth to arrive from Germany he read Keats. This not only guided his poetic development, it also strengthened his belief in the kind of love he felt for Elisabeth. He wrote love poems to her—poems of separation. He was a "dreamer in love with something greater than love."[4] In August 1896, two of his poems were published in the *Bulletin*, marking a significant advance in Brennan's literary career. Another important thing happened to Brennan in 1896: he received his first letter from Mallarmé.[5]

In 1897 Brennan's first important volume of poetry, *XXI Poems: Towards the Source* was published by Angus & Robertson, who printed 200 copies. The book was given a mixed reception by reviewers. But before Brennan saw any of the French and English reactions to *Towards the Source*, he received a much more important communication from Germany: Elisabeth Werth would soon arrive in Sydney to marry him, her decision evidently facilitated by Brennan's improved income that year. Six days after her arrival they were married in a Roman Catholic cathedral. Their European romance, interrupted by a separation of four years, had become an Australian marriage. "They began to live together in Sydney, to test their love, their vows, and their different romantic dreams."

The five years following Brennan's marriage to Elisabeth Werth were perhaps the most important in his spiritual and creative life. It was during this time he wrote more poetry than at any other time in his life. By July 1902 more than half of "The Wanderer" was completed and Brennan had also written more than eighty of the poems published a decade later as *Poems* (1913).

In 1901, after several knockbacks, Brennan was given a permanent lecturing position at the University of Sydney as an associate professor of German and comparative literature. One of his contemporaries, John le Gay Brereton, a poet and also the professor of English, paid tribute to Brennan's brilliance when he said that he "could have filled with distinction any one of the University chairs in philosophy, classics, literature or languages."

During the period from 1897 to 1902, Brennan's marriage was severely tested and although there were brief periods of happiness, quite soon after he moved to Mosman in 1902, Brennan's marriage and family life began to disintegrate visibly. The process was slow and uneven and he did not actually leave his wife until 1923. Many factors combined to drive Brennan and Elisabeth apart. They argued increasingly about money, and hostility between Brennan and Elisabeth's mother had become another source of conflict. It was also becoming increasingly obvious that Brennan had a drinking problem, culminating in his making a drunken exhibition of himself in public. At a Town Hall recital by the organist Lemare, Brennan arrived during a Wagner piece and commenced droning the melody in a voice gradually approaching a roar. He then stood up from his seat, still droning, and waving his hand in time with the music, looking like some fantastic abominable red snowman, his large head flapping its feathery black hair and emitting strange sounds. Eventually he collapsed onto the floor and the police were called.

By 1922, family life had become unbearable for Brennan and he had met somebody who offered him hope. In the summer of 1922 Vie (Violet Leonie Singer or "Bird") offered herself to Brennan. She did not say, "I love you: I want you" but rather "Do you want me? You can have me." Very small, and unusually beautiful, Vie had exquisite taste in clothing, and according to Jack Lindsay had a "bright quality." Early in 1923 Brennan and Vie took rooms in a terrace house in Paddington. Brennan must have known he was courting disaster.

Brennan wrote a poem to Vie "Because she would ask me why I loved her"

> seek not, sweet, the *If* and *Why*
> I love you now until I die:
> For I must love because I live
> And life in me is what you give.

These lines reveal all. When Brennan was not at the University, he was with Vie constantly. He loved the "dear companionship of day after day, the sweet foolish trifles of domesticity." He and Vie went everywhere together and spent time walking in places Brennan loved—the Lane Cove River area, by creeks and inlets, and on picnics with friends to Balmoral and Manly.

In March 1925 Vie was walking along a tram track in Brookvale at one in the morning when a tram returning to Manly ran her down and killed her. Brennan was inconsolable. Three months later, a report in the *Evening News* of 2 June contained the following: "Paragraph 4 of the wife's petition, alleging adultery by her husband, was admitted by the respondent [Brennan]." Brennan later said "From the first moment that I saw the *Sydney Morning Herald* report of my lawyer's action I recognized that without the cement of hypocrisy the state of Denmark must fall asunder."

Despite his wonderful lectures on Symbolism "with knowledge and understanding unparalleled in some respects even in Europe," Brennan's achievements as scholar, poet and critic had won him very little recognition and no academic advancement. After the *Evening News* report of Elisabeth's divorce petition the feeling at Sydney University was unanimous: "Professor Brennan must go."

II

You look into a dark room, a slum in Woolloomooloo, notice the whitewashed walls, low ceiling and small window through which there is a view of a brick wall and clothes hanging on a line. Road-pecking pigeons have built shaggy nests in the gutters. In the room are a cane chair, a bed, lino on the floor, and a strip of dead carpet. There is a plank of wood used as a bookshelf, with two empty bottles of whisky, manuscripts, Greek texts and a set of Grenfell and Hunt's *Oxyrhyncus Papyri* on it. Pick up a book and there are annotations written in Brennan's fine italic script. On one page there are a few lines of poetry, including "I am so deep in day": the first line of the last lyric Brennan wrote.

Brennan is down the road in the Prince Albert having "breakfast." Nobody wants to know about him. Some say he is probably dead by now. His landlady has noticed that the local doctor has a handsome edition of Brennan's last book. It is such a limited edition that Brennan himself does not even have a copy.

Brennan sits at the bar having a conversation with an invisible friend. Beside his glass of cool ale are works by Aeschylus and Pindar that he translates each morning in his special corner bar-study. An old fellow drinker has accepted Brennan's imaginary friend and butts in to cadge a drink. "Here's one on Pindar," Brennan says to the barmaid. Suddenly there is a loud disagreement. The invisible one doubts the authenticity of the wine label Brennan reads aloud. He answers himself, "Let us be charitable, as good drinkers should be, and accept the label; and try to imagine what a Roman magistrate of Dijon or of Beaune—for there were Roman vineyards on these slopes—would have said if someone had prophesied that seventeen centuries later a bottle of Pommard would have found its way beyond the edge of the habitable world and be drunk by barbarians in the middle of the outer ocean." Then interrupting himself in his invisible persona, "But Ptolemy had said there was land at the antipodes," Brennan corrects the interjection, "It was Strabo. But I doubt if anyone believed him."[6] Brennan then stands, waving his arms in the pungent air, and brushes the scene away with a stroke from his right hand. The only Symbolist in Australia is a tall, solid figure, his greasy hair raked back like a mane. His eyes, black with alcohol, scan the bar. He pulls the remnants of his collarless shirt together, bunching it under as he buttons his tight coat.

He considers the years. His wife is gone and his lover, Violet Singer, has been killed by a tram and cheap gin. the University of Sydney has forced him to resign. A few friends pay his rent. One of them, Richard Pennington, is waiting for him back at his flat. Pennington has just returned from London and knows Brennan has written the only book of poetry in English that compares and corresponds with the work of the French Symbolists. One of the most influential French Symbolists, Stephane Mallarme, has written to Brennan saying:

> Wonderful poet, yet this letter is to say I feel your work implies that there is between you and me some affinity in a dream-world, we are kindred spirits, I keep your book within reach—*Towards the Source* is no empty title: you surge back wildly, powerfully, limpidly, up the everyday current of poetry towards its rarest source. Words, such choice words, used only when they are needed, and tempered in the life-stream that purifies, they are washed in essential inspiration, and although your language is totally English, I can truly sense that your song has passed through ours, yet it gives the feeling that you have made it, and it is, distinctly yours. Thank you dear reader, as a friend or, since this name is, from afar, dear to you, *Stephane Mallarmé.*[7]

Brennen carries Mallarme's letters in his head, the originals having been exchanged for two bottles of whisky. When he gave away or swapped his last copy of *XXI Poems: Towards the Source*, Tennyson and Swinburne were spinning out the last of their poems. It was before the Modernist movement in England. In Paris two poets had noticed the astonishing poet writing Symbolist poetry in Australia. A letter to Brennan from the French poet Sebastien-Charles says of Mallarmé: "He often speaks of you, and holds you in very high regard."[8] A letter from the Orientalist Gustave-Charles Toussaint after Mallarme's death also gives an indication of Mallarme's interest: "I had spoken to him of you, and he used to like to think that you were reading him down there, under the fourfold constellation."

In his book *Some Recollections*, Richard Pennington described the literary mood in Australia at this time:

> Poetry under the Southern Cross was expected to be bush-

> whacking balladry or Moorish serenades to ladies in tropical groves but here in the paper-covered pamphlet (*XXI Poems: Towards the Source*) was an English Symbolist flourishing, impossible thought, under Queen Victoria.

When you are drinking in the light, when the lucidity of your vision is so sharp it starts to cut, some of the things happening around you become unbearable. You drink and you are in a limbo between life and death. There is around you a bell jar of thin, slightly fogged glass. Outside that is a barbarous place where cruel and narrow minds float before you. You drink and some of the light fades. It becomes for a while a world of books you have read. You shuffle through their pages until you find one that is blank, the white abyss. It's a hospital sheet. A priest from St. Ignatius materializes, Aeschylus reads like your "stiff" translation. The "chemic art" floats up from his *Poems*, he remembers the raft of Swedenborg, then throws the mystics overboard. The mystical doctrines of Gnosticism can turn to pathways leading back to your first memories of Christ. Maybe in the long run we do find what we threw away.[9] Just slip aside and recall those lines:

> I am so deep in day
> the antient woe may sleep
> and not a cark or care can creep
> where I am sunk in day
> So sunk and drown'd in day
> the antient woe may sleep
> nor hint of harm nor hate may seep
> where I am lost in day
> And yet 'tis good to know
> tho' I be lost in day
> the antient woe may wake and keep
> its watch so far away.

Axel Clark looks into Brennan's being during his last few terrible years through his reading of this poem:

> There is a poignant simplicity—perhaps one may call it finality—in Brennan's use of the word "good": he could now accept "the antient woe" as a cardinal fact in his life, and even welcome it as a kind of guardian angel. The poem is one of his

> few successful lyrics: the serenity it achieves is not a gesture, but a profound reflection from the heart of Brennan's experience.

What rocked me when I read these lines of Clark's was that he noticed, like Charles Buckmaster, the use of the word "good." In 1971 I published Buckmaster's book *The Lost Forest*[10] in which he quotes six lines from Brennan's poem *The Wanderer*. I clearly remember reading Brennan with Charles, and can still hear him saying "I am so deep in day." He quoted that line often. He also emphasized the word good in "and yet 'tis *good* to know/tho' I be lost in day/the antient woe may wake." I now understand bleakly the reason Charles found these lines a comfort. It was the last conversation I had with him and in it he emphasized his love of Brennan's poetry.

III

Politicians and academics, the Attorney General, the Deputy Chancellor of Sydney University, a large congregation of family, friends and foes—people who had helped him when he needed help and others who had done nothing or had assisted in his downfall—were at Brennan's funeral at St. Canice's Church, Darlinghurst on Friday 7 October 1932. The *Sydney Morning Herald* said it was a large congregation. Axel Clark, Brennan's biographer, said it was a funeral like Henry Lawson's ten years before, with many people of consequence attending.[11]

By all accounts, the graveside service for Brennan was a disappointment. John Le Gay Brereton delivered the oration saying, "All the poets of Australia honour Christopher Brennan, and recognize him as a prince of their order." Editor and critic, A.G. Stephens, saved the day with an infamous outburst from the sideline:

> Why the hell can't he say what a man he was what a man? Just that. And how the Senate kicked his teeth in just to sate Mungo Maccallum's (sic) senile respectability. To hell with this burble! Jack Brereton's dropped his pants.

I understood more fully the implications of Stephen's outburst the first time I stood outside the Christopher Brennan Building at Sydney University one cold night. Not even a full building, but a stuck-on continuation of the Mungo MacCallum Building. I considered the irony of this and its bizarre symbolism. Axel Clark alludes to this discreetly in his biography, saying the effect is "strange."

IV

In 1970 I was fortunate enough to work with Terry Sturm. He was co-editing *New Poetry* with me and through him I discovered Brennan's prose. At the time of discovering Brennan I was intrigued by a statement A.R. Chisholm made in his introduction to *The Prose of Christopher Brennan* that "Brennan was one of the world's greatest scholars and a poet whose reputation has been largely confined within the bounds of his native country only by the lack of a complete edition." It was only after reading Brennan's prose that I began to understand his poetry—his theory is fundamental to his poetry. He wrote of symbolism:

> Now our life consists not merely of high movements and hours of insight, such as give birth to poetry, it consists also of days, weeks and calendar months of dullness and mediocrity, that outer weariness which made Baudelaire a maniac. There are, as most of us keenly feel, two lives: that lies in the brightness of truth, this stumbles in error; that is radiant with love and beauty, this is vexed with its own littleness and meanness, that is unfettered, lying beyond good and evil, this is caught in the quagmire.[12]

V

Australia had no Pound or Whitman, but we had Brennan. He was a precursor to Modernism in this country and without him our poetry would have taken much longer to get out from the ghost-woods of England and the dells and trills—the cutout culture of the warbling Victorians. He dealt with the poetry of the broken, "The voyage through self to self,"[13] and was a poet who knew: "He who seeks the beautiful must investigate the ugly."

G..A. Wilkes, in his introduction to the facsimile edition of *Poems* (1913) quotes Brennan's description of this book as "the sublimation of a whole imaginative life and experience into a subtly ordered series of poems, where each piece has, of course, its individual value, and yet cannot be interpreted save in its relation to the whole."[14]

NOTES

1. Christopher Brennan, Curriculum Vitae, Brennan Papers, Mitchell Library, State Library of New South Wales.
2. Dorothy Green, "Towards the Source," *Southerly*, No. 4, 1977.
3. Perrin, 3rd edition 1893, see *The Verse of Christopher Brennan*, edited by A.R. Chisholm and J.J. Quinn, (Angus & Robertson, 1960).
4. Axel Clark, *Christopher Brennan: A Critical Biography* (Melbourne University Press, 1980).
5. *Ibid.*, p. 97.
6. Richard Pennington, *Christopher Brennan: Some Recollections*, with a foreword by G.A. Wilkes (Angus & Robertson, 1970).
7. Christopher Brennan, *Christopher Brennan: Portable Australian Authors*, ed. Terry Sturm (University of Queensland Press, 1984).
8. *Loc. cit.*
9. Dorothy Green.
10. Charles Buckmaster, *The Lost Forest* (4: Prism Poets, 1971).
11. Christopher Brennan, *The Verse of Christopher Brennan*, ed. and intro. A.R. Chisholm (Angus & Robertson, 1960).
12. Christopher Brennan, *The Prose of Christopher Brennan*, ed. A.R. Chisholm and J.J. Quinn (Angus & Robertson, 1960).
13. Dorothy Green.
14. G.A. Wilkes, *Poems*: 1913, Facsimile edition with an Introduction (Sydney University Press, 1972).

Vincent Buckley: Tracing Personality

PETER STEELE

Hoping for objectivity about those we have loved and then lost to death is not the same as hoping for impersonality: indeed, to be left with impersonality is to be left with a double loss. When they have been artists of any stature, the same goes for their art. Whatever Eliot may have meant by his praise of impersonality in poetry, and whatever more recent interpreters may hope to gain in losing the self for art's sake, I cannot doubt that the tracing of personality is at the heart of certain kinds of writing. The project engaged in would be unintelligible if this were not so, and the project, though often subtle, never looks like being unintelligible. Thinking now about the presence of Vincent Buckley's writing, I realize that this conviction of mine has been underwritten more by knowing this man in the writing, the writing in this man, than by any other circumstance. Even when I am "writing myself" in poetry or in prose, the sense of tracing personality is no stronger than it is when I am reading Buckley's work again. What follows here must be influenced by that fact.

Words, our treasure, may be our deluders, and fools will find more fools's gold in them than others. "Personality" comes to us inflected in a variety of ways, from its potent theological sense of that which is definitively the self to an otherwise invisible identity which is surrounded by hope and flim-flam. Somewhere between these two poles is personality as that which is our distinctive endowment, a kind of cast, colouration, or timbre. It is that in which we both know and proffer ourselves. We get it when we come to be selves, and there is nothing which we can ever say or do or undergo which is not in virtue of it. Still, its being given is not the end of the story. That we can contrast personality with character may tend to sell personality short, but at least it makes the point that we have it in us to resolve and to resile, to do as well as to do distinctively. It has been said that our eyes show what we are, our mouths what we have become: personality and character do their making together.[1]

And "tracing"? I have in mind among other things the preoccupations of two utterly different writers, Henri de Lubac and Jacques Derrida. De Lubac is a theologian of such formidable learning as to daunt even his admirers, and Derrida is—well, Derrida, and no friend of the theological. Amongst De Lubac's works is one called *Sur les chemins de Dieu*, translated as *The Discovery of God*.[2] It studies the longstanding Christian tradition that in one way or another the world offers vestiges or traces of the divine, and it tries to do justice to the twin senses of those footprints, however they may be made—that they attest presence, and also attest absence. The notion is not of course peculiar to theologians; in fact the whole history of the Christian project is a history of its exploration in thought and experiment, and perhaps the same may be said of other religious traditions. Christianity, in the course of its self-articulation, has come frequently to acknowledge an interplay between the given and the withheld both in word and in deed. It finds itself saying with Aquinas and with much earlier writers that we know of God rather what He is not than what He is. When it has had both its wits and its guts in order, it has also found itself saying that we know of the human rather what it is not than what it is. "The best in this kind are but shadows" may have been conceived by Shakespeare in dismissive vein, but it has many traditional Christian versions. We trace God, trace the world, trace ourselves: we do not encompass any of them. "If a lion could speak, we could not understand it," said Wittgenstein: the leonine within and without us speaks, and we do not understand it.

The tradition of which De Lubac writes is one which frequently alludes to our frustrations, but its dismay is not terminal. Aquinas believed that the human intellect could not exhaust the essence of a single fly, but that was not in his view ultimately dismaying. The trouble came not from being constitutively dysfunctional, but from the fact that the infinite creative power of God was deployed upon any and every fly, so that to encounter one exiguous creature was to be impinged upon by the boundlessly divine. The fly, as it were, itself became one trace of God. Knowledge, in this tradition, has a vertiginous element to it, from which necessarily and understandably we usually flinch, but for which provision can be made in other ways, whether in prayer or in the deeds of love, even if it is not for that reason that these are entered into. One can live the tracing, as it were.

In turn, the intellectual or the artist will carry the living of the trace back into reflection on God, self, or world, where it shows itself as the mind's acknowledging anew spoor, trace, or vestigia.

Of the making of articles about Derrida there is no end, and this is not one of them. But what is clear is that, with much deliberation, he has organized all his endeavours around the sense of fugitivity in language and thought. And whereas in the tradition which De Lubac addresses the venture of understanding, though incessantly humbled, as in principle sanguine—the traces, after all, are *real* traces—for Derrida and his trailsmen this is not so. What is on offer is at best a quest without a grail, a game in which the goalposts keep moving themselves. As one summary of his position puts it, "Derrida refuses the primacy of a past that is not necessarily mediated by the present, refuses a privileging of an origin, and refuses the possibility of a return and a restoration. Just as for Nietzsche 'the truth is that there is no truth,' for Derrida, the 'origin of origin is a non-origin' and the 'trace of the trace is itself a trace.'" What all this will lead to, apart from either logogriphics or silence, is not yet clear: as for the spirit in which it is offered, I am reminded of the thirties saying, "The situation in Berlin is serious but not desperate; the situation in Vienna is desperate—but not serious." But like deconstruction or not, it has certainly brought into high relief what every thoughtful writer knows: that language, idolized, turns to dust: that the traffic between articulation and what we articulate is stranger than has yet been said.

Aquinas never bulked large in Buckley's pantheon, and Derrida would at best have had a seat near the door. Most of the time, even in his earlier years, he was not very interested either in theologians or in anti-theologians. But since I believe that the tracing of personality exercised his mind instinctively, and since that tracing was rarely unambiguous, it helps to have some of the possibilities in view. He wrote a good deal, though nowhere near as much as he wanted to write. Some of this was occasional, and was meant to be purely so. He had a pronounced and developed sense of distinctive moments, and he did not wish them to be confused in his own or in anyone else's mind: so what he had to say, however exactly phrased, could be intended for transient purposes. Much of what he wrote, though, whether in poetry or in prose, was couched in such a way that one could not doubt the intention: to have, if not the last word, at least a lastingly memorable word. These two ways of writing were not always dissevered by program; one could find either element predominate for a while, especially in writing of any length. And, of course, as usually happens when a person is a writer through and through, smeared with words as the painter's shirt is smeared with paint, things are always being reworked, consciously or otherwise. The notion of the "holy places" keeps coming up, for instance, in talk or essay or poem. To read much in these is to find the preoccupation tinctured differently not only because the purpose varies but because one accomplishment or failure in penetration affects what happens next. But when he settled to his work what always emerged was a concern with personality. The topics changed: this was the topos.

I do not mean by this that he always wrote about persons—though perhaps, implicitly, he did. Rather, as is clear in everything he wrote and said about the English Romantics, about Yeats, and about many other poets, it was both the prospect of personal engagement with nature and the world of action, and the ability of nature and that world to elicit distinctive attention, that engrossed him. Like most of us, he had heard enough about the so-called "bathetic fallacy"—the supposing that we conduct our affairs, think our thoughts, or write our words in a world merely antiseptic or merely septic to the human aliens. Having a notable capacity for compassion, he would never have condescended to the many for whom the final *donné* is that impersonality is the bitter truth: and in fact among his own afflictive demons was one which plied that view of affairs. But it was against almost everything in his nature to turn away from the personal, or from that which, for whatever reason, could claim intent personal alertness. I cannot imagine his not wanting to write poetry; but to be attempting a kind of poetry which, with aloofness or resolution or desperation, eschewed as far as possible the personal would for him have been an act of self-mutilation.

A good place to begin in thinking further about these matters is with a passage from *Cutting Green Hay*. In a chapter entitled "Prince-Bishop," he writes this:

> When I was a child, his portrait hung in my parents' house, in the front parlour, next to those of my grandparents. When I was in my teens, I often slept beneath those three enigmatic gazes, each of them carefully not regarding the other two, and wondered about each of them in turn. I must say that the Archbishop looked the most whimsical, the most gamey of the three. The feelings he commanded were unique not only in their intensity

> but in their kind. Not even the most sanctimonious place-seeker could feel for Cardinal Gilroy, or Archibishop Duhig, what many felt for Mannix: it was an amalgam of reverence, love, and fierce approval. He stood for law and order and also for rebellion; he represented the untamed part of the Irish in its effective and socially visible aspect. And he was a man of slow, biting, courtly eloquence, far more eloquent than any barrister or statesman, whose message was never concealed by terminology, though it might sometimes be made oblique by tone.
>
> When I came to "know" him, at the end of the forties, it seemed to me straight away that, while his ironic wit was his most obvious trait, it was a wit of a peculiar kind; there was something undisclosed about its sources. It was the tone of an old man, of course, it testified to an old man's cynicism or disillusionment, but there was some emptiness to which it pointed, some metaphysical "black hole" beyond his interlocutor, and his rooms, and his own mind. It was marked by loneliness and a tortured quality against which his dignity, his princely bearing, his anecdotes and his silences, protected his visitors. I have spoken of this quality before and can find no one who agrees with me; one or two people who met him more often than I have suggested that mine is a melodramatic account. I offer it not as "explaining" anything but as the merest intuition or guess. I experienced it every time I saw him.[4]

It is worth lingering on this portrayal of Mannix—which might incidentally be read with profit before Clifton Pugh's literal portrait. First of all, what Buckley gives us is a study of the Archbishop, to be fleshed out certainly in the rest of his chapter and at other points in his book, but here instructive in its own right. If all portraits are interpretations, that is a fact of which he made the most. Face, figure and mind are read into and read off, with a sense that both the subject and the engaged intelligence demand this. There is a difference between a spectatorial and a contemplative gaze, and Buckley found it impossible to be, in that sense, merely a spectator. "Character isolated by a deed/To engross the present and dominate memory": Yeats thought this a fine, an indispensable thing, whereas Buckley would to a degree have fought shy of its theatricality, certainly in his later years. But its summoning quality, its bidding for attention if not for allegiance, was something to which he responded instinctively. Studies come of studiousness, though not of pedantry: and Buckley is habitually studious of the selves on whom he dwells. The most unmistakable of personalities may still make for mistake not as to identity but as to contour, and to avoid this is part of the study. In practice, the avoiding is done by making more than one attempt at the representation, and in *Cutting Green Hay* these repeated forays are frequent.

It is not only with Mannix that one might refer to three ways of focusing attention: upon the figure cut, the meaning sought, and the vanishing point. It does not always have to be a picture seen in childhood, teens, and twenties that frames the man considered, but the device is nonetheless characteristic: it wards off distraction, sets the terms of attention, and in effect says "Go!" to the gaze. And although in this passage Buckley says little about Mannix's literal bearing, the way his presence might bear upon the attention is conveyed everywhere. Elsewhere in the same book, as in *Memory Ireland* and in many places in the poetry, he is reaching for the same thing. Of James McAuley, for instance, he reports, "Our first meeting is vividly memorable in gesture, demeanour, movement, the mental apparatus of rapport; but I can remember little of what was said, beyond 'The name's Jim,' as he turned on his heel to say farewell at the stop for his bus or ferry."[5] In verse and prose the distinctive figure cut by McAuley in public or in private emerges with vivacity. That it should do so is influenced by the somewhat guarded comradeship which Buckley often found elicited from him, but the account is more than *pietas*. A way of standing, literally or metaphorically, is a way of saying: and Buckley always wanted to know not only where someone stood, but how.

With that goes the seeking for meaning. Buckley's mind, which could be formidably dialectical, was not basically philosophical, if by that is meant one which seeks formal congruences, formal resolutions of meaning. He liked these things, as he liked aphorism, in its place: but recurrence to the particular, not for illustration but for animation, was a natural gesture of his intelligence and sensibility. Fittingly, then, he was a good man with an adjective: look, for instance, at "enigmatic," "whimsical," "gamey," "sanctimonious," "untamed," "slow," "biting," "courtly," "oblique," "undisclosed," "tortured," "melodramatic." (I remember his writing in the margin of an undergraduate essay on the *Portrait of the Artist as a Young Man*, in the early sixties, "What do you make of that beautifully placed 'fowlwise'?": he was teaching me to watch and to listen, both.) All this gave him a love for the graphic and the vivid, and plainly that is part of the attraction for him of figures who, well-known or not, have a gift for seizing the imagination, part of the attraction of Mannix. But the attraction is not merely planar, so to speak: the planes are of interest because they divulge, much as in Leonard French's *The Bargeman*, which long hung in Buckley's room at the University of Melbourne, and which is now reproduced on the cover of the *Last Poems*. Buckley would often, in prose or verse or anecdote, manoeuvre around his subject, getting a better perspective on him or her, but always with the assumption that at the critical point the presented self would make a telling disclosure. It was in a way the quest for the epiphanic, and like Joyce he was ready to assume that epiphany made its own laws, chose its own occasions. He brought to his attention a politician or a taxidriver, a spiritual counsellor or a barfly, things which he had learned from Coleridge, Blake, Eliade: delivery *delivered*, sweat *showed*, a voice *selved*. One of the things he saw with fascination in Mannix was a man who meant, as an actor acts or a nurse heals.

But it is equally characteristic that he should find in Mannix's wit "something undisclosed about its sources." Others, he tells us, doubt his estimation, but that does not raise doubts for him. In the terms which I am using here, in tracing Mannix's personality he finds that there is a point at which the trace fades. Not surprisingly, he finds this in the realm of wit, which so often does have the double effect of yielding and withholding meaning—of ringing like true coin, but of signifying a wealth beyond itself. Buckley himself had a deep need for privacy, which was almost matched by need for a convivium, whether domestic or social. His quoting, as the final words of *Cutting Green Hay* Yeats's "And say my glory was I had such friends" points, when one thinks about it, in a couple of directions, and one of them is towards privacy. When he is delineating others, the working assumption is often that there is something cavernous about them, whether this be agreeable or disagreeable. At one stage he was much taken with the writings, and perhaps the example, of Emmanuel Mounier, and I do not think it accidental that Mounier wrote both with subtlety and with passion about the varieties of personality.[6] Even of people whose behaviour he found odious, Buckley wrote and spoke in considering moments as if there was always more to be said—not only more to be found out about the ramifications of personality, but more to be divined of its roots. And if this was true of those he found inimical, it was more strongly true of those found sympathetic. In neither case did he suppose that to understand all is to forgive all: in fact he may often have wondered, "After such knowledge, what forgiveness?" The governing supposition was that what was bodied forth in one word or deed or another was a telling but inadequate index of the personal. Perhaps what this amounts to is that he found various strategies for saying that we can, sometimes very finely, know what to make of another, but we cannot ultimately know who they are. This though would not prevent the persistence in refning the "what to make": it merely involved acknowledging the vanishing point. He probably never put it more poignantly or more exactly than in the last words of "Stroke," written on the death of his father.

> Dying, he grows more tender, learns to teach
> Himself the mysteries I am left to trace.
> As I bend to say "Till next time," I search
> For signs of resurrection in his face.[7]

Whatever one makes of Buckley's sense of Daniel Mannix, for many people Mannix became monumental, even mythopoeic: he was, as it were, Britannia's potent rival in this remote place. Buckley could find such reared presences gripping, but he could never take them entirely seriously. I think that this was because his interest lay, first and last, with continuities between the representative and the common, even the commonplace. Revealingly, in an interview with Paul Kavanagh and Peter Kuch, when speaking of Lowell's influence on his poetry, he says:

> *Golden Builders* was very influenced by *Life Studies*. But the sorts of people who appear in *Golden Builders* are quite different from the sorts of people who appear in *Life Studies*. They are foreigners. It is a poem about emigres. I dislike Lowell's people in *Life Studies*, in so far as I have any feeling for them. They are all elitists, all big names, or failed members of the Imperial General Staff. The people in *Golden Builders* are not like that. They are people who have had to leave their own countries, and who own nothing. I like them. I wish I could have presented their speech better, but I simply didn't have the technique. Although I admire *Life Studies* enormously, where

> are the poor? Where are the exiles in *Life Studies*, or in Lowell's work at all? He mixed in his imagination with the people he mixed with in life, namely the privileged. It is a big shot culture. My work has nothing to do with that.[8]

There is more at issue here than a choice of subject. He found the privileged condition not only alien, but unreal. Whether it came of money, of consensual applause, or of cultural inheritance, it seemed to have smack of self-idolatry about it for him: stocks and stones, cut off from natural context, were taking themselves seriously while not noticing that they were dead. The dedication of *Cutting Green Hay*, "For Solidarity," (in 1983) had a more than political resonance to it; it was a broadly social, almost an anthropological, gesture.

I never heard him suggest that he had, like some other poets, been drawn to write fictional prose. He would probably have chafed under the constraints of ordonnance in a novel of any length. His gift was for life in its fluidity, its labile character, though he could be stern about the necessity of taking stands, and a moral spinal column ran firmly through the body of his work. At all events, he did have a novelist's eye, or perhaps a short-story writer's, a Mary Lavin's, a Frank O'Connor's, for distinctive behaviour within small but suggestive compass: and the attention most of the time was on the personal as that which solicits respectful if sometimes perplexed attention—which offers traces, and invites tracing. Here are two passages from *Memory Ireland*, both from the chapter called "Lasting a Winter":

> It was then we started learning about the Kildare personality under stress. It had two keen symptoms. First, no one "knew" anything, and it seemed that poeple preferred to be confused about what was happening, preferred not to know. Only one man in Naraghmore "knew"; he was the president of the water co-operative, he had no phone, and the messages he delivered standing by Mrs. Hickey's store and sub post-office were so long and circumstantial that one had to misunderstand them. For the others, it seemed that there was a lesser burden, a lesser obligation, in being uninformed and confused, that indeed the best wisdom was not to know. That is, the command mood, need, spirit, was to endure together, not to act together. The second symptom became visible as the icy conditions contin-

ued, and people passed from mouth to mouth the wisdom that the next danger was from freezing pipes, and the best way to avoid this was to leave your taps open, so that whenever the water came into them from the replenishing pump, the pipes would have water running through them all their length. The only, or the main, trouble was that the water-level was always lower anyway when the electricity was restored, and this practice lowered it still further; there might be pumps, but there was no weather, and there wouldn't be any until the taps were turned off. . . . But the symptoms themselves were clear: fear of being implicated, and fear of being left behind, the two incipiently neurotic symptoms of a society which, however homogeneous it may be, is deeply non-communal, frightened to cohere, and frightened to provide the conditions which might enable it and call on it to cohere.[9]

The profound ambivalene which can arise in a sane and intelligent person immobilized within this constricting world-system can be seen in the case of Mrs. B, a woman well into her eighties, who cared for herself, tended her habitat very watchfully, and kept a weather eye on the world from the door of her cottage. She was a cheerful and lovable person, by no means a melancholic or any other sort of neurotic, yet the world mystified her into an extreme of indecisiveness in the dozens of conversations I had with her.

Is the climate good or bad? The weather is (usually) baddish, but can be apologized for one way or another. Who will win the election? Is Charlie smart or is he a rogue? Rascally, it may be. But he's smart too. Is he unique to Ireland? Both yes and no lead to some consternation. She will vote Labour, but will not say so, and if she mentions the Labour candidate at all, it will be to say that he's a hardworking man, a schoolteacher. Will an Irish horse win the Derby? Probably not, but then again. . . . All of these uncertainties, concealed, feigned, rhetoricized, or flirty, have to do with Ireland itself. What is one to think of Ireland? That in turn has to do with the contradictory facts, that Ireland is said on all sides to be grand in all sorts of ways, but that it is experienced as dissatisfying and full of woe, so that the most anyone can do is wait and watch and crack a joke and be too hard on the neighbour. . . . What is a body to think? She keeps deep within herself her capacity to feel, until it is, as it were, a

> way of thinking. But, as to human contact and disclosure on the great human issues, whatever you say say nothing.[10]

Learning about "the Kildare personality under stress" came about because Buckley and his family were in the midst of vexing situation; what came to be said of the practices and habits of mind of the local people was always associable with moments of immediate need. As he says at the end of this chapter, "I do not pretend to sociology, or any other kind of sanctity subtitute": like the Wordsworth whose poetry he found treasurable, he was interested in what came home to him palpably. But he kept tracing the behaviour of the people of Kildare, or the styles of Mrs B, in hopes of finding out what they meant. This was normal for him. Naturally, he did not always succeed, either because the situation was too intricate to be knotted, or because the explanations themselves raised further questions: he certainly mistrusted too-ready conclusions himself. (He was fundamentally out of sympathy with Chesterton, but he would have relished Chesterton's story about Edgar Jepson who, at a club in which an old man "would hold up a large hand at intervals and preface some fairly ordinary observation by saying, 'A Thought' . . . goaded beyond endurance is said to have exploded with the words, 'But, good God man, you don't call that a *thought*, do you?'"[11] Buckley's standards of what counted as a thought could be disconcertingly high.) And once again, as with his contemplation of Mannix, there is the mingling of clues, but little more than clues, being given by events and their estimation.

Many years before, in the opening essay of *Essays in Poetry Mainly Australian*, "The Image of Man in Australian Poetry," he had written:

> Poetry deals with man at a metaphysical level—but with man's metaphysical status reflected in his actual state, localized in his actual physical surroundings, embodied in his sensuous and spiritual reactions to his world. It strikes to the meaning and not the detail of man's life. The complex of signs which we find in any really fine poem is a symbol of man's metaphysical state presented through whatever in fact is most real to him as a suffering and diurnal being.[12]

He changed his mind about many things in the more than 30 years that remained to him after writing that, but that formulation would do not only for the poetry he wrote to the end, but for much of what he wrote in prose. The way the problem of the water was addressed or evaded in Kildare, the way Mrs. B engaged with and disengaged from a world too much with her—these he found symptomatic of a specifically Irish predicament; but the intellectual disposition, and the weave of sensibility, which he brought by choice to Irish affairs were those which, often in conversation, touched on most things that came up. To go for the "actual physical surroundings" and at the same time "the meaning and not the detail of man's life" is not having five bob each way: it is making a claim for the import of the physical, and the import is not merely physical.

There is an evident urgency in the passage from "The Image of Man in Australian Poetry." Many people who were taught by Buckley or who heard him speak, and many who read the literary essays which he most cared about, would immediately identify that note of urgency. It was magnetic, though as magnets can do in some circumstances, it could repel: it would be very unfashionable in academic literary circles nowadays, being doubly damned in its humanistic enthusiasm. And it had its problems for Buckley himself—those of the gifted democratic leader. In his later years he came to believe that life in the academy disenfranchized poets from what they most wanted to do, and he ached to get away from all that. At an earlier stage, when he was teaching literature to small or large groups, or when (for instance) he was generating insights for himself and his audience in the Newman Society, anyone at all sympathetic with his venture could not miss the note of drama and often dramatic urgency, in his presentation. It was not that the occasions were in the conventional sense theatrical: certainly not florid. The manner was sometimes grave, sometimes relaxed. Through it, there pressed a sense that visionary attention was often called for, that this had a bearing on the daily conduct of affairs, that the momentous was not esoteric but could be elusive, and that there would ordinarily be both demands and joy in the search. It was in fact, in Walt Whitman's phrase, a "democratic vista," though it could still frighten off or reduce to reverential awe those whom it was intended to enable.

The devil of it for a person with charismatic gifts whose intention it is to liberate others into an enhanced sense of their own freedom is that singularity may tell against the theme. Others may conspire with this preclusion: Mrs. Wordsworth told the eager Keats that

"Mr. Wordsworth is never interrupted." Buckley would have found this farcical, the more so in that two of his mentors were thus displayed in different forms of helplessness, but he himself suffered the humiliations of singularity, as well as cruder ones which he shared with many. What is at issue in this is far more than questions of social dexterity or magisterial felicity. Once again the matter of personality in action is inescapable, and the interest it holds is not only the aesthetic one of the stylishness, but the ethical one of how claims on attention are being established, and to what end, and with what provisionality, absoluteness, and genuine authority. The world of the teacher, *viva voce* or on paper, can be one of pomposity or urbanity, of diktat or delicacy. These alternative styles, though, may themselves be diversions from the moral and indeed spiritual question of how that flame, the life of the mind, is to be kindled, hearthed, torched, and wielded. Buckley was certainly one of the two most determining teachers I have had. He taught me various particular things, but essentially he taught me that you do not mess with the mind unless you are prepared to find that you are thereupon messing with sensibility, imagination, will: and that to back off from what all that may entail can have explicable circumstances but cannot have any excuse. Not surprisingly perhaps, when he was being watched or listened to by less engaged persons, while they found the spectacle emotionally gripping, they often wondered what in God's name was going on. A mystagogue would love this, of course: it is his *metier*. Buckley sensed it sometimes and hated it. Prestidigitation was, so far as he was concerned, an art for the imaginatively, and probably the morally, retarded. Teaching, ideally speaking, was the place where you facilitated animation, and by that very face became redundant. Most of us who are teachers will from time to time give lip-service to such a model: but the lips are at best dubious moral agents, and the test is what happens when the matching of minds begins.

His teaching changed, as did that of some of his colleagues. The change was analogous with that of many American poets, from tense would-be-definitive formulation, to something more hospitable, open-textured, broadly responsive. He became, not more easy-going, but more easily-carried, as a teacher in the middle years. He was differently attuned, differently keyed; talk of poetry became not more genial exactly, but more patiently generative. He ceased to care about writing appraisals, however insightful, of the work of individual poets. The matter of Wyatt or Yeats, like the matter of any closely defined cultural or ethnic or religious community, ceased to engage him much. Something, to which I shall refer when speaking about his poetry, offered to engage him more imperatively. But before I turn to that, I would like to say something about the fashion of his critical writing.

There were times when he wrote criticism, just as there were times when he lectured, when all but the most alienated of auditors or readers knew that here was someone who was genuinely in the grip of the material, and as genuinely drawn beyond the material. The manner had its provenance, and begot its imitations, but its character was its own, and its points of impingement decisive. Here for instance are two passages from *Poetry and the Sacred:*

> In a sense, then, Blake at his best is not only a prophetic, but also a fleshly, an incarnational poet. Poets often represent qualities antithetical to those they claim to admire. Yeats too thought of himself as an esoteric poet, representing both ancient insights into experience and the ancient myths which express them, but he was in fact a poet of dramatic situations, in which a modern world is brought to its apotheosis. One of the striking things about Blake's great lyrics is the strength and humanness of the feeling expressed in them. It is only in his poems of the second class that he is a calm, limpid poet who has won beyond (or has not yet managed to attain) strength of feeling. Nor does his greatest poetry have the transparency we might expect; it has an unusual density of texture, and an unusually dramatic structure. This is as true of "the Tiger" and "The Sick Rose" as it is of "London." Their power comes from the dramatic starkness with which conflicting tendencies are brought into relationship.[13]

After a passage from *Four Quartets*, in which the speaker has articulated some bitter moral distress, to do not with one lapse but with the contemplation of an established policy:

> If ever there was a great passage of explicit moral wisdom in modern poetry, here it is; the gravity of the speaking voice is too exalted for us to use the word "didactic": the impersonality is almost that of some annunciation. Yet it is an impersonality won from grappling with the obviously tormenting elements in

> the poet's personal situation; a note of fierce pain persists, a note almost of violence, perfectly controlled by the conventions of meditation which Eliot has himself created. The meditative conventions which can contain such a fruitful and exalted ambiguity are flexible ones indeed, and the intensely close relation which is established between Eliot and a compound ghost so familiar as to be almost an *alter ego* shows that it is not merely the renunciation of a world-view that is in question.[14]

Both passages gain some of their force from what has preceded them, the arguments which they summarize, but to a degree they stand in their own right. Randall Jarrell said once that poetry has "and . . . and . . . and" meanings: not all agree with him, but Buckley certainly would. It is not a question of ferreting out more and more allusions, or making the grid finer so that no witticism can fall through and be lost: there is a place for that, though most of us who think about poetry have made too big a place for it. The "and-ing" of meaning usually has to do with a heightening of ambition with the course of a poem, or a set of poems, and a lowering of agitation: it is an ambit of alertness, not an avidity for collectibles, that does the work. Comparisons with the other arts are natural; when they are well made one sees more clearly that great proficiency, while an admirable and sometimes an indispensable thing, is not enough for great accomplishment. One has to sense as well a press of personality in which something like gentleness and something like inexorability are combined: industry does not bring magic. What Buckley was about as a critic was isolating that press of personality in action. Like everybody else, he saw in part what he went to see: but unlike many other critics, even very good ones, he went on seeing with pertinacity and with patience. Nobody could think him slow-minded; but he knew, and taught others to know, that one has to be paced by other minds, other sensibilities, if one is to see what they have to say. It may not seem much to ask of a serious reader, but even serious readers find it a lot to give. No doubt many of Buckley's students were aided in the pursuit by his own manner, in which calmness and passion could alternate, but in which concentration was of the essence.

There is another point to be made in this context. Both passages assume that the making of poetry is a dramatic thing, and assume that life's venture is a dramatic thing. I doubt whether there was any single conviction which was of more importance than this to Buckley. It is far from being a universal sentiment, and it may not even be a frequent one. My own strong sense is that for many people such a view is to be resisted or resented, whether for honorable or for other reasons. To perceive life projectively, to embrace not as vexatious necessity but as natural and opportune the fact that one is riddled with temporality and orientated towards lifelong growth—this is a hard saying, easily dismissed as one of the weeds which accompany adolescent flowering, and to be got rid of as soon as possible. For Buckley, the naming of human reality was the naming of drama, and the making of poetry and quasi-poetical literature was both a participation in and a heightening of that drama. Hence, when as in the couple of passages I have cited he named that which he most valued in reading Blake or Eliot, he was bound to allude to endeavour, mutation, and arrival as vindication of what preceded it.

The other side of the drama, of course, is its fugitivity. Blake was not a precision-tool for producing excellence, and neither was Eliot; good things, and even more the best, were retrieved against the odds, and were told against by what James called "the perpetual force that makes for muddle." By the same token, their accomplishment being taken for what it was is not self-guaranteeing; if Homer nods, his readers often seem to have sleeping-sickness. Buckley was alert to this infuriating fact, and it made for an increased sense of urgency in his teaching and his critical and other writing. He had high hopes and low expectations, as a *confrere* of mine puts it, about people's response to the life of the mind, and especially to that part of it which is also a life of the heart. He did not imagine that he was himself immune from the temptations of triviality, intellectual sloth, arrogance, and he could acknowledge this, often with charm: to describe oneself as "bravely fighting off attacks of false modesty" has its own winning way. What he did not do in general was either to assume that those with whom he was concerned were incorrigibly inept at reading to the degree that he thought called for, or to assume that they must go about it in his own way. Hopkins said that his reaction to great literature was to admire and do otherwise: Buckley made that disposition seem the obviously desirable one.

In his introduction to *Cutting Green Hay*, Buckley wrote, "It is a book about the society, the habitat constituted by human beings and their doings. The self of the narrator does not need stressing, for it can be deduced, or seen in silhouette as the light falls on the places where he lived with others."[15] In large measure this could have prefaced his poetry. To trace the habitat—concessive and inclusive word as that is—of the self and the others was a way of disclosing or divining the self. This project is not in itself unusual. It may be thought classically Romantic, and to have been given new modalities by Yeats and later Irish writers in particular, as well as by some of the best of Australian poets, especially when they were writing at the top of their forms. But Buckley was after something more than many of those—more, and harder to denominate, so that the very terms of success or failure at any moment cannot easily be specified. If one had to have a mantra for all his poems it might be that from *Golden Builders*, "And you say/Over and over/ As if paying tribute money/ 'The environment is within me.'" This poem is full of sorrowful, even terrible moments, and it is called "Practising Not Dying (ii)": but even in drastic circumstances what is intoned or incanted is Buckley's singular and peculiarly demanding sense that the trace of the self is the trace of the world. This, above all, was the matter of his poetry; it was where he started, where he finished, and what he cared about all the way through.

Had he no other concerns, occasions, topics as a poet? In one way, yes. There are the riven and rapt poems of love, especially in the later books. There are the explicitly or implicitly political poems, always cast with the doubleness of attitude which Buckley felt about the political—that it was inevitable, ubiquitous, serviceable, and often ridiculous. There are the poems of frolic, or relish, or checking. Almost everywhere, bidden or unbidden, there is our guest, death, hoarsely saluted in the title *Arcady and Other Places*. If anybody had asked for it, he could have done you a poem in all sorts of manners, or to all sorts of easily designable ends: the *Last Poems* alone are evidence for this. But the reason why people will continue to read his poems is that he really did suppose that to write the self was to write the world, both of them in their fluxions as well as in their stabilities. He became if anything more aggressive, in the good sense, about this: he had the actor's "attack" in the poetry. He had been known to mock those who would rather "be poets" than write poetry, but in a sense for him as for some others it was a false dichotomy. The borders between sensibility, the palpable or comprehensible, and articulation, seemed to be permeable, and necessarily permeable, for him. It is not that he was naive about the recalcitrance of either word or world—in fact his poetry bears witness to those recalcitrances to an uncommon degree: in the end, he had nothing more to learn from either the

Thomistic or the Derridaean stress. But he believed through and through that what his first book called "the world's flesh" is our flesh too, and not unfleshed by being thought, felt and named, but more fleshed in the intensity of its animation.

Hearing that, someone who did not know how the game went in practice might suppose that it was all good news. There is in *The Pattern* a prose fragment calculated to revise any such easy supposition. It is called "Pen-sickness":

> Pen-sickness; when you remember the poem waiting, perhaps liquid and infinitely yielding to each touch, or leaning back, resistant, towards its original spare shape, or dense and featureless as ice: then every gesture the world has made in it, every evening perception, every sip of speech, every word, comes back as bile, running perception into the throat hot as gruel from the long canals of the belly: in your own body, as in your language, there is something wanting to refuse you: you have proved your words indigestible: what was to have been the equable completed form takes on the thin consistency of vomit: you look at the paper with retching eyes. You are reminded, are you, of what it means to finish, to be finished, to be sent forth, homeless, your occupation gone, your promise lapsed into success: close your eyes, and you may glimpse the poem there, in the head, stirring, just outside reach, perfect and intolerable as that heaven that loured above us in our infancy.[16]

Presences attend such lines—those of Coleridge, of Donne, of Eliot, of Shakespeare, of Traherne—and they all belong: they do not represent sites quarried but selves's echoes: they, too, are traces. And when in turn one remembers them, the memory is not principally of flourish or flair, but of wrestle, retrieval, generation, blood put to words. Psychologists are familiar with the phenomenon of the "Presenting problem"—the issue offered by the client either as hurdle in front of, or a metaphor for, the real issue. Whenever I read Buckley's poetry I have a sense that most even finely-tuned and gravely-intended poetry that I know of is, as it were, dealing with a presenting problem. By contrast, what he was up to, whether or not he invoked the company of earlier poets—Catullus, Nashe, Yeats, Keats—was a personal redefinition of the self and of all that englobes it. The more original this is, the harder it is to trace. There were things to be learned from Hopkins whom, in an earlier version of "Lament for the Makers," he describes as tracing the world which he left: and whose vivid sense of the contours of both landscape and psyche could not but appeal to Buckley. There were things to be learned too from contemporaneous poets like Heaney or Kinsella, whose apprehension of microcosm or of macrocosm was neither blurred nor gentled by time, and with whose ethos, pathos or eros he could take fruitful imaginative issue. But in the end you are on your own, if you are to be truly one of the makers. I once used as a summarizing image of the ancient Irish bards the figure of their composing, as they did, in the stone huts or kennels of their musing—cold, dark, and fruitful. Thinking about it now, it seems as good an image of this man about his vocational task as I can get.

It is to be hoped that a collection of estimations of his work will appear. Such a book, above all but not exclusively about his poetry, would have to find ways of talking tellingly about the rhythms of his mind and mouth. He did this sort of thing himself over many years when trying to work out what was going on in the poetry of others, when alluding to motions of the kind and the body in literature at large, and when asked to speak of his own art. Vincent O'Sullivan, in a valuable paper given not long after Buckley's death, has written about his "singing mastery": anyone who knows the poetry well will recognize how little this is to be identified with an easy musicality.[17] When he was buried, by his wish the *uillean* pipes were played: not the easiest of music. His writing and his memory go on making their way amongst people who had, in some cases, supposed that they had done with all that. He would be doubly glad that this should be so—because like all who have not despaired of themselves he hoped to be remembered, and because remembering was both his *métier* and his blessing. It seems good, then, to end with one of the fine poems from *Last Poems* which will, surely, go on making its own way:

A man, a woman

A man, a woman, straighten up from where
they have been dragged by a kerosene tin
they cooked and did their washing in. Their shoulders
are bent and lifted by it. Now, on the fire,
it makes a yellowish steam spitting around
its rim and sides; the cauldron of the poor. . . .

They raked twigs and stalks to catch the fire.
They sat round telling Depression jokes
of pannikin bosses, flash clobber, and winning Tatts.
Memory is unreliable and self-serving,
as the critic said. But I recall the flame-core,
the cores of all the flames, as vivid yellow
turning to vivid orange, like cordial in the water,
like the new gush of petrol in the old puddle
like meaning in a quarrel. I won't forget that.[18]

NOTES

1. Most of Buckley's writing is the evidence for what I have to say here. A couple of articles which bear interestingly on the matter are his "The Strange Personality of Christ," *Quadrant*, Sept.-Oct. 1970, Vol. XIV, No. 5, pp. 11-25; and (with Robert Wilson), "Persona: The Empty Mask," *Quadrant*, Nov. 1975, Vol. XIX, No. 8, pp. 81-96.
2. *The Discovery of God*, trans. Alexander Dru from *Sur les chemins de Dieu* (Aubier) (Darton, Longman and Todd, 1960).
3. Irene Harvey, "The Welisprings of Deconstruction," in *Tracing Literary Theory*, ed Joseph Natili (University of Illinois Press, 1987), p. 133
4. *Cutting Green Hay* (Penguin, 1983), pp. 134-35.
5. *Ibid.*, p. 149.
6. See especially Emmanuel Mounier, *The Spoil of the Violent*, trans. Katherine Watson (Harvill Press, 1955) and *The Character of Man*, trans. Cynthia Rowland (Rockcliff, 1956).
7. "Stroke" in *Arcady and Other Places: Poems* (Melbourne University Press, 1966), p. 9.
8. *Conversations: Interviews with Australian Writers*, ed. Paul Kavanagh and Peter Kuch (Angus and Robertson, 1991), pp. 17-18.
9. *Memory Ireland: Insights into the Contemporary Irish Condition* (Penguin, 1985), pp. 78-79.
10. *Ibid.*, pp. 86-87.
11. G.K. Chesterton, *Autobiography* (Hutchinson, 1937), p. 158.
12. *Essays in Poetry Mainly Australian* (Melbourne University

Press, 1957) p. 1.
13. *Poetry and the Sacred* (Chatto and Windus, 1968), pp. 137-38.
14. *Ibid.*, p. 227.
15. *Cutting Green Hay*, p. xii.
16. "Pen-sickness," in *The Pattern* (Oxford University Press, 1979), p. 48.
17. Vincent O'Sullivan, "Singing Mastery: The Poetrics of Vincent Buckley," *Westerly*, June 1989, Vol. 34, No. 2, pp. 50-57.
18. *Last Poems* (McPhee Gribble, 1991), p. 129.

The Poetry of Robert Adamson

MICHAEL WILDING

Robert Adamson's first book, *Canticles on the Skin*, appeared in 1970. Its impact was immediate. The first poem, "The Imitator," opened:

> Dirty hypodermics rattle in the glovebox: morphine flows
> over the top of your brain. An artery collapses
> and migraine floats out of your eyes—Alright, there'll
> always be glib explanations: cashing-in on experience again?

The shock opening, the starting off at full throttle, has its revered literary tradition—Donne's "Spit in my face you Jewes,"—but is nonetheless effective for that. And the danger of the device, that its very traditionality should now run the risk of being the somewhat hammy, the overblown, the too blatantly posturing, is something that Adamson has taken account of and exploited. Writing a poem involves not only producing the powerful line, but countering the variable reactions to the line from the variable audiences. The proclaimed bad boy stance, with the insignia of hypodermic syringes and hard drugs, moves in the moment of its telling from a low life realism to a surrealism with all the inexactitude of the expressively exaggerated account—

> An artery collapses
> and migraine floats out of your eyes

in which the self-dramatizing is seen by the poet as absurd and nonetheless destructive for that. When we move from this poem to part one of the poem, "The Imitator," the dramatic rhetoric, the romance of powerful cars and drugs, is suddenly resituated. Now we are on a train, under the control of the child welfare department. The juxtaposition says so much.

"The Imitator" is an extraordinarily powerful poem. The themes and imagery announced here—cars, drugs, sexual ambiguity, crime and punishment—recur through the later volumes, though far less frequently than the received impression of Adamson's work might suggest. Adamson was uneasy about writing about these materials. He had no wish to perpetuate the image of a life of crime and prison. "Cashing-in on experience again?" as he asks himself sardonically. It was something he preferred to leave behind. When he does write about it, it is with an awareness of the self-delusions involved, the young boy imitating the bad boys; and then the necessary imitations, the acts that are learned to survive in gaol.

Running throughout "The Imitator" sequence is a powerful tension between the materials employed as lived experience, autobiographical, confessional; and the material employed generically—the given scenarios of prison novels, crime movies, television police procedure shows. There had been so many movies, novels, newspaper accounts of petty crime and juvenile delinquency by the time Adamson came to write "The Imitator" that the experiences were in no way fresh or unique. They were comparatively unknown to Australian poetry but not to literary and cultural production in general. The paradox provided a problem for the poet; of the materials being both too raw and new, and at the same time too old and cliched. They required all the available skills of the tightrope line of literary balancing. "Make it new" was Ezra Pound's poetic prescription. The task for Adamson was to make new for poetry materials debased and cliched and distorted by the media archetypes. His solution was to treat the materials allusively. There is the shadow of a narrative sequence, but the details are not spelled out, the crimes and courts and cells are not replicated with a documentary realism. Instead they are evoked from the reader's shared memories of prison movies and newspaper reports; evoked with poetic economy and the most accurate selection of appropriate image, gesture, implication.

In gaol Adamson had begun to write. He began, like all poets, imitating the available models, Shelley in particular. We recall how Henry Kendall had called his early works "imitations," the necessary exercises on the way to discovering his own voice. As Adamson moved to more contemporary models he discovered Robert Lowell, another writer of imitations. Lowell wasn't exactly the model Adamson wanted. But Lowell had made acceptable in established literary circles the introduction of new experiences, new expressions, new language.

Every new generation of writers has to create its new language, has to take from the living, spoken word the components that can bear a literary resonance. Lowell had moved in his own verse to a much more colloquial mode than had been acceptable, creating a new poetic out of living language rather than working within an inertly inherited range of idiom, vocabulary, and acceptable material. For there are conventions of material as well as of expression which the poet has to confront. The pressures against including hypodermics, V8s and prison cells in poetry in Australia in 1968 were huge. The range of allowable material had become so narrow. In England Philip Larkin had evolved an idiom for bicycle clips and Sunday morning church, an image of the joyfully accepted narrowness of human possibility eagerly endorsed by the connoisseurs of contemporary poetry. To write about drugs, getaway cars and gaol was to risk being seen as rather crass; disrupting the poetic moment with the unnecessarily self-dramatizing. This was the end of the age of what A. Alvarez had called "the gentility principle" that had atrophied mainstream English poetry; it was no less dominant in Australia.

And so Adamson used that tight stanzaic form in "The Imitator," a form that gives the illusion of rhyme; and the envoi was composed in tight half-rhymes, to show that he was capable of the traditional crafts. The binding of the explosive into the tight framework of emphatic rhythmic return creates its literary tension. The strict formal structure, with its rather prissily archaic poem and envoi were the necessary price to pay for the introduction of the raw content. Now a free man, Adamson found he had to put his muse behind bars in order to write about being behind bars.

Artistic freedom, freedom of expression, these slogans of the free world had a particular poignancy for Adamson, embarked on his poetic course. In one sense the freedom of the artist as we see it in our contemporary world seems ideal. No patron requiring a topic, no state or party requiring a line. The world lies all before you. But it is the freedom of the freed slave, who finds there is no role, no function there; a free market economy that offers no support. This was the problem that confronted Henry Kendall. What does a poet do in this society? How do you be a poet? Kendall tried by celebrating the deaths of public figures and the topography of local landscapes to attach poetry to the world of public affairs, to places that might develop a significance in the worlds of geographers, bush walkers, tourists, developers. He tried to materialize his belief in the social function of the poet. He cannot be said to have succeeded in most of the public poems of memorial and occasion. But the invocations of the bush, the rivers, the plants and birds, the natural topography, survive as romantic correlatives for private feelings, feelings for all their privacy there to be shared. Kendall is read and remembered for those plangent, weird, watery invocations of nature and for the story of his own sadness.

Confronted by this same lack of a public role for poetry some hundred years later, Adamson like Kendall was uneasy about making himself the centre of his poems. There was a temptation to exploit the prison years; the sensation value of them was a way of gaining attention, and a poet has to gain attention. But it was not the attention he wanted; he wanted attention turned away from those experiences onto the poetry. But in the absence of a public role for poetry, to reject those ready-made materials would seem wanton. There was a waiting place for poems of imprisonment in the literary world. But was there any place for poems of freedom?

Prison poet, latter day Villon or Genet, was not an image Adamson cared to exploit. "The Imitator" achieved wide currency. It was a poetry accessible, forceful; a strong metrical energy, a living language. But it was the formal issues that primarily concerned Adamson; this was the dominant concern, the critical consensus of that time. And so there was careful emphasis on craft, on verbal effects, on idiom ringing true, on cadence, all this done with as new a language as possible, a living vocabulary of contemporary speech. When he turned to the prison materials in his second book of poems, *The Rumour* (1970), it was even more wryly, even more sardonically:

> As the crack up came on
> There was nobody to blame and I confessed for hours
> Until the police were in tears.

For the concern of *The Rumour* was poetry itself; poetry, and the writing of poetry, were now foregrounded as the subject. "Seven Odes to Themselves" begins

> So the first ode kicks off
> into its own life.

The title of the first ode, "Should avoid coming to grips with love," indicates an awareness of central evasion in this self-referentialism, the avoidance of the subject, of the human. In one sense it was in happy avoidance of the subject—the institutional years he would rather forget—that Adamson entered his formalist period. He welcomed the socially accepted evasion.

But it was also because he wanted to become a poet. Becoming a poet was the new subject. And with "The Rumour," the twenty-five page title poem of his second volume, he writes about this. The abstract mode, and his questioning of it, record the process of his engaging with open-field poetry, moving away from Lowell to the post-modernism of the Black Mountain poets like Charles Olsen and Robert Creeley, and to the work in particular of Robert Duncan. The poem was a dialogue with the work of Duncan especially, an attempt to make connexions over there, just as Brennan had written to Mallarme with the same hopes. But instead of writing a letter enclosing poems, as Brennan had, Adamson made the poem his personal communication, packing it with the results of a minutely close study of Duncan's poems. Following the aesthetic of the priority of the poetry to the life, of the created artefact and imagination to lived experience, to the confines of realism, Adamson proposes to enter Robert Duncan's existence by ordering the lines of his verse; if poetry is so powerful and all important as they say, then he will take them literally and attempt to manipulate social reality by poetry.

Adamson's attempt to manipulate social reality was successful. Robert Duncan came to Australia to visit him in 1977. And in *Ground Work: Before the War* (1984) Duncan's "Go, My Songs, Even as You Came to Me" is glossed as "(after Robert Adamson's opening song in his *Swamp Riddles*)." But at the same time this verbal play must also work as poetry— "this is the point/where whoever's reading this/ is forced into deciding/whether these lines are/turning to poetry." Adamson declares his complete commitment to the mode, though not without recognizing the cost, the exclusions—writing "as an american," and "those intricate/evasions"—and not without admitting his sense of how problematic an experiment he was engaged upon. It is this wider, warier sense that gives "The Rumour" its tension.

Historically we can now see this poetic moment of self-referential poetry, of poetry about its own processes, as the verbal equivalent of abstract expressionism in painting. They can both be seen as the aesthetic of the cold war, with social and political content firmly excluded, and modernist abstractions and commitment to spontaneity privileged. The asserted freedoms were freedoms of the will, displays of anarchic individualism. The mode's usability by the governmental apparatus suggests its innate politics. In the end it doesn't say very much, other than express a dehumanization, disintegration and decadence.

Yet at the same time the self-refrentialism of the poetry also contained a potentially progressive aspect. It reveals something of the nature of poetry. It has its analogies with Bertolt Brecht's alienation effects. By revealing, by foregrounding the literariness of the poem, the poetic can be demystified. We are reminded that this is fabrication. Adamson was later to write "The Glorious Lie." Is imitation the basis of art? Is there a difference between creation and imitation, between inspiration and fabrication? And can anyone tell the difference? The strength of Adamson's poem lies not just in the successful imitation of the open-field poem, but in the questioning of it; turning the self-referentialism of the poetry a further turn, so that "The Rumour" is a poem about whether poems about poems are the way to go about writing poems. The open-field poem, the words filling the area of the page, shrinks to this doubtful, unconfident column trickling down the page:

> so what to make
> of that.

With "The Rumour" Adamson successfully established himself as a postmodernist poet. He distanced himself from the quasi-autobiographical figure of "The Imitator" by becoming a new imitator. And yet having had, and put aside, those experiences, he wondered about the implied discounting of experience and privileging of poetry and pure language. This wondering about the open-field poem, the true dialogue with it, gives "The Rumour" its life, where the merely inert imitations of the mode, the replications of its visual appearance, without that questioning, now as ever have little to say to us:

> the new mode.
> To ride the Open Song.
> So the ideas slanted against war
> struggle free; the lyric

> obstructed by sexual fury breaks forth, leaps
> insatiable

At this poetic climax, sparks of meaning are struck into life: social and psychological, political and emotional reference is reasserted even at the moment of the final abstraction. The war in Vietnam, the sexual revolution of the late 1960s, could not be repressed. Issues of life and death, destruction and creation, refuse to be displaced by the preoccupation with the aesthetic of surfaces. Or is it a case of the proper preoccupation with aesthetic surfaces leading to the release and expression of reference, of content, of issues of life and death?

Having discovered the poetry, there was still the search for the subject. Self-referential post-modernism might gain the respect of other poets of that aesthetic, but was comparatively obscure for a wider audience. Of course, obscurity was still, at this point, highly valued as a mark of art. Satire had traditionally been obscure, partly since pejorative references to individuals and politics were necessarily allusive, oblique. Persius's Latin was hard to understand and translate, so the Elizabethan and Jacobean satirists cultivated obscurity to seem like Persius. But by the time of the modern movement there was little satire, little political reference left in poetry. Obscurity was appropriated as the mark of high poetic art, the insignia of the elite, while the problematic content that once had necessitated the obscurity was silently left behind.

In the mid-1970s, prison writer had become something of a vogue. Here was Adamson with his hot, fashionable material which he preferred to forget, did not enjoy recollecting, and the cult of which he deeply suspected. Already Bruce Hanford had locked Adamson up and co-written with him a prose account of his prison experiences. Locked up again to write about being locked up was all very traumatic. The ensuing work, *Zimmer's Essay*, veered between the poles of expose journalism, American sociological study (Hanford was an American) and railway newsstand fiction used for committed ends. Serialized in *The Digger*, it had considerable impact. Again, the success was ambivalent to Adamson. He wanted to be loved for his art not his sufferings; for the imagination, not for receiving society's blows. Sardonically he produced "Sonnets to be Written from Prison" which he included in part 2 of *Zimmer's Essay* when it was published in book form—a complex qualification and enhancement of the prose work. They are in Part II; "Some More Experiences,"

Adamson laconically entitled it. Experiences came to have the resonance in Adamson's vocabulary that "adventure" did for Tom Sawyer: "it was a grand adventure, and mysterious, and so it hit him where he lived." The enigmatic quality of the experiences is underlined by the title of the book of poems in which Adamson collected them, *Swamp Riddles* (1974). "Sonnets to be Written from Prison" are hypothetical future poems to exploit the journalistic vogue for prison writings, poems that in their hypotheticalness were poems about poems, poems that privileged the imagination.

These are powerful, caustic poems, poems in which the poet argues with himself and with those around him, with the media focus on prison writers, with the liberal assumptions of prison reform groups.

Again a strict form is used, as with "The Imitator." Now a sonnet serves as the imprisoning grid. But that formality, that strange harking back to a traditional renaissance form like the sonnet is qualified and confronted by the sardonic diction, with the almost contemptuous, derisory observation of the troublesome bondage of rhyming:

> Here's the world—maybe what's left of it—
> held together by an almost experimental sonnet.
> Surely there must be some way out of poetry other than
> Mallarme's: still-life with bars and shitcan.

In that collocation, "Mallarme's: still-life with bars and shitcan," so much is said; it is a hieroglyph of compression. The contemptuous diction and the perfunctory rhyme of it/sonnet have their honoured tradition, too, of course—via Byron back to Samuel Butler's *Hudibras*.

And for all his resistance to dealing with the prison material, Adamson nonetheless does confront it: "I won't be clever—/ all the clever crims are not inside the prisons."

That is the social message to take away. While the repressed issue, the avoided issue, is the suffering. In these imaginary sonnets, or these sonnets of an imaginary prison, "I'm not in pain." The point being that in the real situation there is a lot of pain. And what are motives of those who want to write or read about pain?

The tone of these sonnets is unique. They are an amazing blend of irony, self-mockery, Baudelairean contempt for the hypocrite reader, and wonderment at this world of poetry, at this occupation where making fake confessions was so publicly rewarded.

The social issues are inextricably intertwined with the issues of poetry and abstraction. At the moment when he is discovering literary abstraction, pursuing the successors of Mallarme, there has arisen a cult of realist prison writing. Or supposedly realist. Suddenly Adamson has perceived the possibility of making it all up in a way both satisfying that symbolist privileging of the imagination, and the true realism of prison—making up stories, statements, confessions, lies. "There I love confessions." "My *story* so glib it made/no sense." Here is a practical use of the imagination: survival. The socially acceptable lie, the publicly acclaimed evasion. Art for art's sake, the poem concerned with poetry, has its social relevance and uses after all.

As much as "experiences," "the imagination" was one of Adamson's recurrent touchstones. And *Cross the Border* (1977), his next collection, is nothing if not a work of the imagination.

Cross the Border was very much an experimental volume, continuing the post-modernist open-field of *The Rumour*. Included, too, were wider explorations, tentative verbal and technical experiments, cut-ups, partial erasure, spontaneity, pastiche. These are experiments that show an openness to trying something new, to revitalizing the old, an eclectic Poundian openness to the huge variety of literary tradition and effect.

In *Cross the Border* part of the effect and purpose was the enigmatic. The enigmatic, the mysterious, the intimations of a withheld secret knowledge, permeate. There are implications of magic, conjurations of myth. Here was the grand old man of the sea of Sydney's new poetry, broken armed, forked tongued, medicine man of curses and hunter of the Holy Grail, driving an Alfa Romeo and living in Elizabeth Bay.

Kendall is the poet of rills, running water, fast flowing rivulets, mountains. Adamson is the poet of the mangrove swamps, that ambiguous region half underwater, half exposed, half river estuary, half salt water, the primal soup, visions of mud wrestling, the liquid larva of some Pompeian setting, outcast, woebegone, ramshackle. And this primal landscape, seascape, mudscape, riverscape became the setting for poems of sexual discovery, outlaw adventure. The themes are announced in *Swamp Riddles* and developed in *Cross the Border*. Kendall's images of running water, refreshing streams in secret places, represent both alcohol and sexuality—the warring poles of joint distraction from his central pursuit of being a poet; and the private themes, inexpressible in any other way, are displaced into implicit imagery. Adamson, writing in a less inhibited age can write explicitly about sexuality, alcohol and drugs. But his mangrove swamps and mudflats bear no less than Kendall's rills and torrents the same burden of resonance, the same associations of sexuality and of muddy oblivion.

In *Where I Come From* (1979) Adamson broke through into a brilliant, firm clarity. The experiments with poetic possibility had been absorbed. The haunting images of the Hawkesbury are now focussed onto childhood events—real or imagined, revealed or fantasized; the archetypes of what might have been. Here speaks the spirit of the mangroves and the mudflats. The setting is the correlative for a mood: the events express a certain attitude.

This was childhood regained and mediated through LSD-25—not the unrecoverable experience, but a fabrication by chemical means. The image in the electron microscope is no less a fiction and our science is built on it. It is not easy to write about childhood trauma, about parents, about families. The necessary ambiguity of fictionalization, fantasization is there for protection: the retractable truth of the surreal. And what in our dramatizations of childhood hurts and fears, trauma or melodrama, is the creation of rhetoric and self-justification, and what the truth ever was, who knows? These are stories about a story-teller, poems about a poet, telling stories is part of the subject matter.

The images bear their symbolic overlay—not just the Freudian interpretations which for all their familiarity we cannot for that reason simply reject, but also less conceptualizable fears, anxieties, threats.

It is a remarkable spareness, a simple, clarity of language, an absolute dispensing with unnecessary words, yet without moving into that cryptic minimalism that becomes obscure in itself. There is no hiding behind flashy image, verbal ambiguity, literary allusion. This is very hard to do, psychically as much as technically. Such verbal clarity can come only from many, many pages of writing, from a continual immersion in the medium to be able to use its essence so clearly, confidently, accurately. The return to childhood is not an easy nostalgia. The ambience is far more menacing than that would allow. Fear, violence, aggression permeate the episodes. There is a sure, firm, spare clarity—something won through to, something perfectly achieved.

The mangrove celebrations, the Hawkesbury world, are the establishment of a distinctive, Australian image that will stand equally with the contemporary international—something Kendall was similarly trying to do with the same district. Adamson's "The Mullet Run" in *Cross the Border* is set in that same Mooney Creek celebrated by Kendall; there is a shared blackness, but a century of difference in language. It is a hillbilly, backwoods world Adamson evokes. And hillbilly culture in its various manifestations was a major part of Adamson's musical interest—the electric Vilon balladiers like Jimmy Buffet, Doug Kershaw, J.J. Cale and various strands of country music, part of the folk heritage Bob Dylan led into, Johnny Cash perhaps the best known of them. Hillbillying troubadors, the bohemians of a new world, not cafe society but more like the poor white origins of an Elvis Presley. River people, marginal people: Adamson evokes a distinctive and recognizable aspect of the world of poor.

A haunting concept Adamson has worked with in his poetry is that of the imitator, the forger, the con man. Perhaps one of the reasons for the uneasiness about Adamson's work amongst the reviewers and academics and arts adminstrators is the fear that he may be putting them on: Robert Creeley—whose presence is much felt in *Cross the Border*—tells of a poet being asked at a reading, "Is that a real poem or did you just make it up yourself?" Of course it is a mark of contemporary, literary insecurity, the uncertainty about values and meanings, the lack of any shared sense of what poetry is, what cultural production is, or could be, that this eroding anxiety should have created such an abysm of unease. And Adamson plays on this anxiety. But the playing is not merely a provoking of the defensive reader, a challenge to hypocrisies: it is a questioning of what constitutes art, or what poetry is. The theme is confronted in "Beyond the Pale," the opening poem of *The Law at Heart's Desire* (1982).

This privileging of technique, this technological vision of art for art's sake that would ultimately judge the world's cultural production by the standard of a Disneyland, is the aesthetic of our society materialism. It follows the model of engineering and architectural functionalism, without the admission of any prior function. Well made, but for what?

A central theme of *The Law at Heart's Desire* is marital relationship; the issues of form and formalism are urgently there for the poet, but they are issues of discovering the appropriate form to write honestly, as well as powerfully, of human relationships, human dishonesties. That is not easy. There have been many centuries of poetry about love and marriage, but how much of it has been honest? How much was idealizing, rationalizing, self-justifying, self-dramatizing? The simplicities of language and form that Adamson attains to in these poems are simplicities and clarities reached through to after the consideration of other possibilities, other models. As with the poems of childhood in *Where I Come From*, there is a sure, transpicuous poise.

This concern with the function of art, the role for poetry, continues in *The Law at Heart's Desire*. It is not an issue on which Adamson ever sits back with comfortable certainty. It is always problematical for him, as surely it is for any serious artist. In "Friend" he looks at what forces, what images, an artist draws into being. In "A Final Spring" he looks at the illusions. The invocations and addresses and allusion to poets like Robert Creeley and Robert Duncan running through the poetry of his formalist preoccupations are now absent. Their influences have been absorbed, now Adamson writes with the confidence and sureness of an accepted practitioner, without any colonial, dependent status. "Visiting Francis Webb" pays tribute to the poet he admired most of all his Australian predecessors—yet another tragic figure in that long line from Kendall onwards.

The Clean Dark (1989) marks a distinct and substantial development from his previous volumes. The personal themes of *The Law at Heart's Desire* are still powerfully addressed; and the topography of the Hawkesbury region that Adamson has so successfully celebrated in the past is the site of a return to a new depth and seriousness. The natural environment is succinctly and indelibly recorded, and the works and acts of humanity in that environment are recorded in a clear-eyed, unforgettable way. "The river is like a blank page"; and Adamson is able to continue his modernist project with this creation of poetry out of absence, this recourse to the "imagination." The epigraph from Mallarme is not out of place.

Poetry itself, of course, is always a conscious theme in Adamson's work; and the moving "Quartet of Sonnets: for Robert Duncan 1919-1988" is a major testament to poetic commitment and the agonizing doubts and despairs consequent upon such a choice.

Other poems return to the scenes of childhood, families and relationships that had been opened up in *Where I Come From*, and evoke a social reality not routinely encountered in contemporary poetry.

Adamson moves out from the private world into public events, offering a powerful, inward meditation on social violence; and the theme is addressed with a deep sensitivity to suffering and experience, with an extraordinarily powerful resonance of sympathy, in "Canticle for the Bicentennial Dead," a landmark of poetic understanding.

What are the characteristics of Adamson's tone? It is knowing, self-knowing, self-aware. There is a mockery of delusion, a self-mockery. There is a commitment to the overriding demands of art and a quizzical wondering that art can be seen to be prior to the demands of life. There is a delicate evocation of sensuality, and sense of the way this pursuit of the sensual life is an illusion screening us from things we find convenient to be screened from. Wars and revolutions are only ever marginal; but that marginality is not unaware, not unconscious. It is not that war or revolution is perceived as the real issue, more important than love or art. Though it might be. Certainly repressing consideration of it by a focus on love or art is no way ever to find out. The social is always there as a context, even in as seemingly formalist a volume as *Cross the Border*.

Robert Adamson has been a powerful force and focus of poetic activity for twenty years, and this new collection amply confirms this stature. His work remains an inspiration to others, readers and writers alike.

NOTE

Quotations from Robert Adamson, *Selected Poems* 1970-1989 (St. Lucia: University of Queensland Press, 1990).

"The Glint and the Shadow": The Poetry of Dimitris Tsaloumas

ENRIQUE MARTINEZ

I

With the recent publication of the first full-length study of Dimitris Tsaloumas's poetry,[1] the scant and somewhat repetitive treatment by critics of this Australian poet writing in both Greek and English has received a more exacting due. Much of the critical work published in English on Tsaloumas to date belongs, in fact, to the synoptic review type and, with the exceptions of the more innovative and lengthy approaches by R.F. Brissenden[2] and John Barnes,[3] we can say that the critical appreciation bestowed upon his work has been slight.

As Brissenden has said in a short review of Tsaloumas's *Falcon Drinking*[4] for the "Weekend Australian," his is the "authentic poetry." Authenticity will no doubt be the passport to acceptance and perhaps even to wider recognition; the latter being a condition which, although sought by many who enter the fields of literature, does not necessarily presuppose entry by poetical means; nor—where indeed the poetry is to the fore—does this assume the strength of the thing thus elevated. The endeavour of critics like Castan, Brissenden and others who have sougnt to push into the reticent circle of literary debate the poetry of a man deserving of our esteem, then, has nothing to do with literary politics (since Tsaloumas is the most self-effacing of men, and in retirement from teaching). But it is worth recording the plaint that the debate over Tsaloumas's poetry is still confined to a narrow circle of admirers and friends, thus lacking an ecumenical, as well as a generic poetological, response. Some might argue that Australia is still on the whole devoid of an aesthetics of reception. The only vigorous of such responses come from Sweden and England. Arthur Lundkvist (a former member of the Nobel Committee of the Swedish Academy) and Oxford professors Peter Levi and David Constantine are, by far, the sole beacons that give direction to the poetry and the man. Lundkvist strikes the right key in his review of Tsaloumas's *The Observatory*[5] when, disowning traits which have defaced the poet's image into a grimace between the exile's and the migrant's (and which have equivocally come to form the kernel of all criticism of his poetry), he says:

> In his poetry Tsaloumas appears as a rugged and proud man reluctant to compromise or to underrate his own talents. He remains a true son of Greece, drawing on his origins in the island of Leros, so rich in tradition.[6]

Lundkvist's tone is pithy enough to render a truth without attracting polemic. Everyone who knows Tsaloumas, knows that he will not, poetically speaking, bow down in the house of Rimmon. But here perhaps the road bifurcates: without an aesthetics of reception, there is much groping in the dark. Although circumstances of the poet's life might aid an appreciation of his poems, they sometimes impose a hindrance, in the same sense in which knowledge that some of his works are translations confuse the scholar, for the cultural and linguistic assumptions are difficult to undo from the webbing. It is not so much the spectre of authorial fallacy dropping from the closet, but that the result of our disquisitions are wont to fall outside the rigorous sphere of the poem. Yet the author, of course, cannot be completely removed from his text, though biographical overinsistence runs risk of promoting an attribution of false values to words not intended to bear such meanings, and derives the poetry of its highest reach, that of ushering to contemplation:

> Beating a buzzard's wings
> I now land at the ebb of light,
> neck drawn in contemplation,
> scanning the silent harbour.
> Gorged to the gullet's extent
> I suffer delusions, choose not to observe
> shapes that drift past guardian rifts
> and rips to burrow into darkness.
> Nights are restful. There are no dreams
> in catastrophe's plenty.[7]

Need we dwell on the fact that such "catastrophic" *mise-en-scène* may have something obliquely to do with the effects of migration, which tenuous sociological studies still wish to prorogue and postulate as informing the text in some vital relation? Sure enough, we have within the same poem a slender stalk, to prompt to such a reading:

> This is an innocent land
> Cruelty stalks in the wilderness
> in a splendour of flesh.[8]

Yet surely the poem has loosened the grip on a single cause; it achieves an expansive movement through the multiple meanings of "gorged" and "gullet" revealing landscapes which perilously shadow the speaker's physiognomy; or "drift," "rifts" and "rips": the cuff of waves against the shores of some dark mental activity. Simultaneously, their intense consonances—akin to the sharper contrasts among consonants reminiscent of the Greek tongue—tighten the poem to the point in which the *tenuis* preceding the concluding lines shortens our breath, leading us back to the collectedness of contemplation. One could easily believe the poet to be vulcanizing his stoic self in the "relentless and rending rhythm which ravages the writing," were not the line "Nights are restful" and the dreamless sleep a see-sawing assurance of emotional stablity which instils the poem: the hub of rest and fixity at the centre of a chaotic periphery.

We need not look too far into Tsaloumas's work to understand that control over the most pusillanimous feelings or experiences within his writing has purged the poems of all semblance of frivolity.

In "Pre-dinner meditation in an Aegean courtyard"[9] Tsaloumas juxtaposes metaphors of youth and old age to construct a Byzantine dream: a splendorous scene, with light bathing the sensuous play of opulence. Yet the last stanza is no genuine part of the dream; it belongs with a terrestrial element. The poet chooses the most tactile and tangible of materials, which he chances upon: flesh, and communicates through it—through its stench and an array of displaced metaphors—an impartial end to the dream-game:

> Too weary now for sterile vigils. This breeze
> is wholesome. Lighted time makes a sphere
> too smooth for roughened hands,
> too slippery. Only this morning, friends
> walking together to the beach and all

> the way beside us the bloom of dead flesh.
> Only a dog, admittedly.
> Carcass maturing in the heat.
> But in the jasmine, my friends, the jasmine,
> the hibiscus lane stammering ahead
> cicada-mad?

The presence of death is, of itself, strong enough; yet, Tsaloumas speaks of a carcass and dead flesh in the midst of metaphors of light and scents of flowers. It is in the use of "bloom" and "maturing," in the repetition of "friends" with the innuendo on "man's best friend" that the poet's mastery, his control over the poetic line, wryly asserts itself. Up to this stanza the poem had been an apologia of life in the flesh, and the metaphors of the last stanza match the general movement of the piece while treading the route of bittersweet scents to the bier of meditation. Although there is no apparent difference in the rhythm, here the connotations flood the mind to an acquiescence of death as a life-long companion: "maturing in the heat"; "all the way beside us." The paradox of the parallel play of life vis-a-vis the sweetened decay of death is resolved in the focussing on the somewhat preternatural (and appropriately onomatopoeic) "cicada-mad."

Such subtlety is the result of a process of distillation and of an exacting choice. Thomas Mann's remark in *Death in Venice* apropos the nature of solitude marks the brilliance of Tsaloumas's poetic disposition: "that it gives birth to the original in us, to beauty unfamiliar and perilous—to poetry." But also, "to the opposite: to the perverse, the illicit, the absurd."[10] In the corpus of Tsaloumas poetry there is indeed always a natural ordering at work, an affinity or variance—as the case may be—with the seasons and earthly cycles.

II

The contemplative in poetry is a shared bedrock throughout the ages and in every tradition. The Tang poet Meng Hao-Ran could be living in the Australia of the late twentieth century. What follows is a translation from his five-character "cut-short" poem "Spring Dawn," which finds inclusion in all the representative poetry anthologies of the Tang Dynasty, and conveys a contemplative mood often encountered in Tsaloumas:

Spring sleep spares not the dawn
All around I hear bird songs
Night came rowdy, wind and rain
Who's to know the flowers strewn.[11]

Compare it, if you will, to "Winter Song," included in *Falcon Drinking*, here are the last five lines:

This is the muffling season, the ultimate

earplug. Taps drip in the house.
I can tell by the stalactite above

the sink. Its growth in the morning
informs me of the night's duration.

Even though the poets speak of different seasons and with altogether different voices, attention can be drawn in both to the source and the arrangement of the material. In Tsaloumas's poem, the final lines—as is the case with much of his poetry—recapitulate the governing metaphor of the piece, in verse honed to great poignancy and pith. Here the colophon brings to our attention both reason and consequence. Not only is the sentiment (which might be considered quite commonplace) itself presented, but (much to our delight) the disposition of the mind, its attentiveness is portrayed in the conscious reckoning of time. Ian McGilchrist, commenting on the role of the imagination, so aptly said that— "Its effect is momentarily to integrate the conscious and the unconscious, as it integrates our whole being, body, emotions, intellect and soul."[12] The poems are the sovereign poetic experience that both poems retail are set against an unremitting radiance. It is the radiance of unmoved contemplation. When Meng Hao-Ran attempts the tallying of scattered flowers after a night of rain, he is gathering a universe of Spring and compressing it into a (singular) vision of abundance. Yet his choice of words is simple; there is no obtrusive philosophic speculation, as in much contemporary clever verse. The clue to such sweeping strength is the order of the poem, a temporal conception which mimics nature: awakened by bird-songs past the hour of dawn, the poet recalls the sound of wind and rain and imagines the fallen flowers. "Metaphor," as Ernest Fenollosa has said, "the revealer of nature, is the very substance of poetry. . . . The beauty and freedom of the observed world furnish a model, and life is pregnant with art."[13] Metaphor here is not bound to a single line but encompasses the entire piece, an *ensemble* playing. Similarly, total experience is tentacular; in "Winter Song," the season's "presence" places an embargo on all other detail. The "model" observed in the world is tinged with irony: the fruit of long seasons of endurance. It is not difficult to suppose the reason for the poet's choice of metaphor. We have bare-bone poetry: activity has been pared down to the marrow, but it is not minimalist, for the sensuality has been allowed its sempiternal glow. Snow, when it falls, falls silently on the bed of previous precipitations. No animals are heard, and not even the water, frozen in the taps, disturbs the stiff tranquillity. As with Meng Hao-Ran's Spring, the Winter here remains the sole reality, a harsh presence, insufferable and overwhelming, but yet weathered in the magnificent flight of abstraction to an antediluvian cave, whose stalactite measures time. That *stalaktikos* means in Greek "dripping" tacitly underscores the oblique pertinence of the referent, but in this there is yet no diminution of a bonding that is quintessentially phantastical, a feat of poetry.

As Costan has pointed out apropos the "To the Reader" poems which I will shortly introduce, Tsaloumas "creates a dramatic situation in which the speaker and the person spoken to are pronominal, unnamed and unplaced in particular time and place."[14] Such is the working of generalization, a beacon which Chinese poetry has looked to for centuries. The comparatist Wai Lim Yip explains:

> Much perhaps of the art of Chinese poetry lies in the way in which the poet captures the visual events as they emerge and act themselves out before us, releasing them from the restrictive concept of time and space, letting them leap out directly from the undifferentiated mode of existence instead of standing between the reader and the events explaining them, analysing them.[15]

In applying this kind of statement to Tsaloumas's poetry we need to reconcile ourselves to the face that although the pronoun "I" often appears in the poems, it is only a referential superfluity predicated by rules of English grammar, without bringing greater subjectivity to bear (something not mandatory in Chinese). Furthermore, expressions adverting to time are but a telegraphing of an "undifferentiated mode of existence'' of the poem's intense locus, and they simultaneously shuffle time-frames to bestow a remoteness on the creative intelligence— ''Its growth in the morning/informs me of the night's duration.''

When such technique is used to retrieve the deeper concerns of the poet and not just to visualize existence, as it were in the conceptual realm, we are rewarded with the exalted beauty of the ''To the Reader'' poems. The directness of their address to the reader compels a challenge with authorial license. As we have seen, such liberty has been wrested through detached observation, where the object (ap)perceived is not meddled with but singled out and examined. Yet, whenever Tsaloumas addresses his reader, there rise terms of admonition from the verse which allow a prophetic element to possess the poems:

> If when you walk through the mist you notice birds
> ablaze like pomegranates
> in the window and on the bearded roof of winter,
> if sometimes the dark tunnels
> let you out on to the balconies of the Amazon
> to see without fear flesh-eating leaves
> swallowing alive the straying beams of the sun,
> and if your rights are trampled
> or for your country's sake you're led away
> to gaol and see how blood sets fire
> to the despairing blankness in the poeple's eyes,
> then know that you're indebted to me, that it you doff
> the music I clothed you in, the shudder will crack you,
> the mists will flood you, and you'll perish.[16]

As has been noted in Australian literary circles, such despotism on the part of the poet would need to dodge more than one blow in order to resist the post-structuralist and deconstructive terms of the contemporary literary debate.[17] For Tsaloumas avers that language cannot be but the poet's own; it should be traced back:

> not to the universe of grammar
> and the republic of dictionaries,
> nor to the wilds of textual anarchy
> where my substance is another's sign,

but where the word is born
and things become and are
because I call them mine.[18]

III

Tsaloumas, resistive in song to the heresy of the play of signifiers, breaks through the shell of declamation to a dramatic soliloquy. The beauty of wealth and suffering cannot be shared, but they can be turned in such a manner that the reader takes refuge in his own experience and probes until his eye is recalibrated with the intensity described. Poetry has returned its due to adventure and fiction, yet these are only metaphors of the potentiality which remains the nucleus of poetic creation, breathing in the chosen word, the *mot juste* of true creators. Scrupulous attention to the birth of the right word is at the hub of Tsaloumas's craft, a poetic raft that is durable to weather any storm of theory, and has the seaworthiness to call the world its home:

In monasteries I studied
Ancient maps and corsairs' chronicles
epics of nations and martyrs' miracles
and one morning among the wrecks of ships
and the conch-horns of victory
with the inextinguishable lamp of my desire
I descended, and from the lap of the abyss
I pillaged its most precious pearl
to enrich the brow of your youth
for all eternity.[19]

Here indeed the classical inheritance is at work. The imperative "desire" of the poet is being reconciled to the world in the offerings made to the ideal, as suggested by the intensity of words like "pillaging," "abyss," "eternity," encompassing a fertile tension implicit in the quest and themselves part of the offering. The poetic persona, while delivering itself into the hands of what seems an illimitable quest, only does so by playing the gambit of fulfilling the ritualistic demands of classical form. The parable of the well-earned reward figures in the triple themes of study, adventure and the attainment of fame. This would appear to buttress Castan's contention. For Castan speaks in terms of "topos," and situates the poet's production within the sphere of influence of so rich a concept:

> as well as meaning "native place" it bears sense of continuity, of a single life lived continuously within it, and of the continuity of that life with the lives that were lived there before it and will be lived there in the future. In short, the concept "topos" is very strongly tied up with pre-capitalist notions of tradition, which are not alive today among English speakers and which are not capable of expression in the language.[20]

To live in the "modernist" world means perforce to have abandoned contact with a traditional past. Such concepts as Castan introduces belong to the realm of history, and the study of etymology. The relevance of the concept of native place to a person born in the West after the Second World War is not at all evident in world literature. Ideas pertaining to familiarity with soil, or one's own "mother-land," have to conted with two major shibboleths of present-day interest. Firstly, the reality of a mondial awareness for issues, aided by information technology seguing with the consequences of foreign influence. Second, and more importantly, the schism between Church and State, betwixt religious and cultural spheres, which have been dabbed ineffective in the face of the contemporary social and political problems and the spuriousness of current sociological paradigms. Tsaloumas still belongs to the old world, which has become (since the present never ages, and there is no past) the world of present concerns. Hence a genuine abandonment of tradition is also (perhaps paradoxically) a tolerance with an older time, an abiding with Bergson's pure time. But it is of course via the truth of genuine mythos and poetry that the pastness of the past eats its way through to the timeless concerns of the present.

The surge of modernism and the immediate success of works like *The Waste Land* (duly tempered down by Eliot himself in later years) have encouraged a trend for a poetry of transition. Such poetry pretends to know no other permanence than that of change, yet fails in most cases to remain serene in the midst of incessant revolution, thus joining the tumult, ever unaware of its own traditional function as a bridge towards what permanences there be. Much of Tsaloumas's translated poetry remains fixed to the stake of tradition, holding out with exasperation against what seems a demonic disposition in literature, bending, at moments, to undeclared self-pity; perhaps an evolution from a sense of impotence to grasp the Protean *Zeitgeist*. The poem "Carelessness" is a case in point:

> In winter, mother, I set out: I was turned back by floods,
> by angry hail, a ruinous dawn, my soul's own mulish spite.
>
> But if the winter put you off, my son, how did you come
> in summertime, when death is harsh and parting hard to bear?
>
> I went for solace to the sea, rode pick-a-back the wave;
> the swell it rocked me fast asleep, the whirlpool sucked me down.[21]

For all its despair, this is not reactive verse, but firmly controlled; the rhythmical resonances of "pick-a-back" crown the drowning scene which in spite of its tragical quality retains the robustness of the Grecian mythical dolphin swimming allusively by. Tsaloumas's poetic self knows well the impossibility of alleviation and only his passion, pure and unquenchable, leads to the resurrection of youth. He creates a world of poetic wealth to invigorate the suffering soul; avalanches of beauty rise up, knitting image and sound together in a flux of expression, yet unlocking another (more resistant) form of negation where sadness lies unmoved as on a bier. The twelfth poem:

> What overflowing of anthers
> what balsam the melancholy jasmine
> afternoons
>
> what whispering of poets
> and blessings of immortal loves
> in the domed walks of heaven
>
> what exquisite shimmers of water
> what marbles and ascension of wings
> on the facade of light—
>
> from the far shore will come to my door
> no man in pride of youth to call
> God bless all here

from the peaks of the Marathons
where you kept watch
the Pleiades of dawn salute you

and from the garden's ageless cool
in the City you pillaged
the nightingale sends greetings.[22]

Somewhat Yeatsian in tone, Tsaloumas doesn't flinch before the contradictions baiting his mind; instead, he devotes himself to the word, knowing it to be companionable beyond the frailty of beauty as the sole lodestar of desiring. It is in this unfulfilled bridging action where the shoots of Tsaloumas's irony lie hidden. Many of the contradictions of his verse are only resolved at the level of the poetic line, and more often than not there remain the dregs of an unresolved dilemma, a fencing with abstraction or doubt, of which the poem "Elegy" is a good instance. Here the poet discovers for the reader a psychological truss built on the splendour of music and with the solidity of metal. Reason and passion are playing side-by-side in an unlikely metaphor of harmony:

Full nine time like the silent river
  round the nether world,
and thrice, like night, this ancient sorrow girds
  the threshing-floor of your days.
Over the castles, the waters and pastures
  of my prosperity, day breaks
where constellations set. But what irony
  will conquer the steel of truth
in your remoteness, where melodies walk
  like rivers over the *pizzicatos* of strings
and the horns tumble dying into the depths
  of valleys? I don the eagle's wings
but lack the courage, the claws of the wind
  but shrink in fear. At night
whispers stir abroad to bridge the moat, scale
  the fences of sleep. Yet my knowledge
seeing them won't let them in, and at dawn's door
  they spend the night in vain.[23]

Irony underlies much of Tsaloumas's poetry, but I would postulate here that such integral irony is only given full reign in the more recent English originals, and not in Grundy's translations from the Greek. The volume *Falcon Drinking* offers us numerous examples of an ironic undertone sanctioned by the poet himself and quite different from the more sharp occasional thrusts of the derisive vein which infiltrate the poems of *The Observatory* and *The Book of Epigrams*. In *Falcon Drinking* the poet has accepted his fate, a hard-earned skepticism has settled in this seemingly never-ending transition through landscapes of the mind. From this volume onward Tsaloumas takes with him wherever he goes the Thespian's trunk for what have become by now performances of a seasoned dramatist. The poems produce monologues and occasional dialogues or engage the poet's resourcefulness in all kinds of disquisitions (with an increase in the use of parentheses or asides) which only touch on the philosophical to resume lyrical expositions. There are signs of completion of the double process of modernization and anglicization which have made possible his success in Australian literary circles. Con Castan explains these changes through a redefinition of the concept of Modernism within which he accords Tsaloumas a place of excellence:

> Tsaloumas' rejection of the role of a political activist and his preference for the role of the "chronicler"—complex and contradictory as that role actually is as he conceives it—places him perhaps most profoundly of all as a Modernist. For as our century has proceeded it has become more widely and more deeply felt that what we call politics does not provide the answers to our problems and is nothing but vanity and vexation of spirit.[24]

"The Inhibition":

> Because a crow's been roosting in my head
> which, though a metaphor, troubles sleep
> and makes waking miserable, I thought
> I'd go for solace to the bush. And there,
> sitting under a gum at noon
> I began to observe the swinging cow
> and study at last the bright bird's mockery

at the unanimous sheep, when swoosh!
subliminal through the corner-sight
this whir of black,
turning to day-concrete crow that flaps
to a stop on the tall gate
across the path, then settles,
and scanning me with cockeyed sadness
jerks up its tail and shifts at once.[25]

Tsaloumas explains his terms of comparison because, as a poet using a "new" medium (*Falcon Drinking* was Tsaloumas's first English book) he is confronting a new audience; and because, since he might have expected a poor reception,[26] he does well, in all humility, to presume that the reader will not understand his return to the roots of the mythical Crow. The poetry in *Falcon Drinking*, assured though it is, still requires preambles in the form of explanation addressed to the reader. A return to the original Greek element exemplified by Aesop's fables is required, and the poet's explanations provide an excellent poetic bridge to cover the time-lapse, making plain the range of imlications. This is not Ted Hughes's demonic hero; at least, it has not yet been garbed in human disguise. It remains the instrument of doubt and the unripe fruit of unfocused perception: "subliminal through the corner-sight." It is powerful because, contrary to Hughes's Crow, it does not submit well to scrutiny but holds instead the heightened position of the examiner "scanning me with cockeyed sadness." The projection of the above scene on the reader's senses, moreover, gains intensity by making the pastoral landscape previously set as an already derisive scenario recapture the more realistic traits of nature through a further turn of irony extremely well-calculated to startle first with sound: "swoosh" and "crow that flaps;" and later with a sudden cuff to the reader's sensibility: "and shits at once." All this is necessary to inscribe the actuality of superstition, and of its origins in our mind. There follows an imaginary monologue with the crow in which the poet points to the sentiments latent in the crow's cry: "the sagging *aaah* of your cadence" which probes "the fear in living things,/the darkness in the soul," and a return to the lyric mode via a reference to others who also "held discourse" with the bird of ill omen. In this return to lyricism, Tsaloumas gathers the wool of his unanswered questioning and seeks to make an even stronger imprint by fusing dream-like elements of darkness and intellectual pain in an image of dawn which not only resists explanation but reinforces the myth magnifying the life of the crow to more than literary dimensions:

> For he'd be back
> to roost, to grumble in fitful sleep,
> start up and peck about and spy
> and hone his beak against the flint
> of fossil thought, then grow to black
> mad moon through winter orchards
> and rise rooster-big and crowd the brain
> till feathers spill out the narrow skull
> and crested dawn comes scraping on the pane.[27]

Although the prompt for Tsaloumas's poem has its root in superstitious notions of the mythical "crow," the concern of the poet does not remain nailed to the literalist. There is an eavesdropping on the wider implications of his own remarks; he basks in the dismemberment of the myth and in its reconstruction—the verbile stevedorage of all poets—lingering there, dazed at the achievement of a form which though not unlike the general outline of the myth, has been woven entirely anew into a yarn to suit his own poetic mind.

Paul Ricoeur in *The Symbolism of Evil* has established an astonishingly similar pattern for the recovery of myths.[28] Adverting to the characteristics of the modern mind, he says:

> because mythical time can no longer be co-ordinated with the time of events that are "historical" in the sense required by historical method and historical criticism; because mythical space can no longer be co-ordinated with the places of our geography, we are tempted to give ourselves up to a radical demythization of all our thinking. But another possibility offers itself to us: precisely because we are living and thinking after the separation of myth and history, the demythization of our history can become the other side of an understanding of myth as myth.[29]

But even Ricoeur's more particular working thesis, though bent on an exegetical analysis of mythical texts, seems to coincide with the core of Tsaloumas's thinking:

> It is in gnosis that the simulacrum of reason attains realization. Gnosis is what seizes upon and develops the etiological elements in myths. The gnosis of evil in particular takes its stand on the ground of reason; as the word itself makes clear, gnosis tries to "know." Between gnosis and reason a choice must be made. But perhaps there is a way of recovering the myth as myth, before it slipped into gnosis, in the nakedness and poverty of a symbol that is not an explanation but an opening up and a disclosure. Our whole effort will be directed toward dissociating myth and gnosis.
>
> We are encouraged in this attempt by the great example of Plato. Plato inserts myths into his philosophy; he adopts them as myths, in their natural state, so to speak, without trying to disguise them as explanation; they are there in his discourse, full of enigmas; they are there as myths, without any possibility of confusing them with knowledge.[30]

It is in the poetry that we recognize the man, his standing among other poetic figures and his congeniality with our own deepest responses. There is much of T.S. Eliot's idiom in the more concise verse by Tsaloumas. In *Falcon Drinking*, the author's admired poet of youth has made his way elegantly at various points into the poems. "The Survey" speaks the language of "Prufrock": "across the sterile sky/ the monocled beard observes"; while "Exercise for three voices"[31] owes its technical twist to *The Waste Land*. However, these are little more than acknowledgements. The poem "Falcon Drinking" has already taken secure footing in a style that will affirm itself throughout Tsaloumas's first English book of poetry, and the poetry he has been writing since:

> Awakened to this other bleakness
> I sit to read my daily portion
>
> of the wall. Sometimes it's voices:
> women disputing a place at the head
>
> of public fountains in years of drought,
> Orpheus pleading in the basement,
>
> the anguished bidding at the Change

Sometimes it's touch:

shuddering flesh and silken skin,
the clammy passage of darkness

in night corridors, forgotten scars
and varnishes on old violins.

Today is seeing time. Knife-sharp,
a cruel blade of light cuts through

the brain's greyness, sweeps over mists
and hints at ridges, distantly.

Close in, at the stone-trough
hard by the spring of language where

the cypress stands, a falcon drinks.
The cypress ripples in shattered water

nights of many moons and nightingales.
The bird stoops shivering to sip

then tilts its head back skywards,
stammers its beak and trills

the narrow tongue. Spilt drops
hang bright in midair, hard as tears.

In a form which recurs in his poetry, and mostly in the pieces reflecting a more modernist slant, the poet speaks his mind openly as he would to the friend or to an interested interviewer. Perhaps the greatest quality of the poetry here is that youthfulness—the crisp succession of images providing the reader with an inexhaustible source for contemplation. Yet these images are never independent; each is integral to the tale; if we decided to unearth them from their context for inspection, many of them would pass us by, misunderstood. A mixed metaphor like "the clammy passage of darkness" can only be linked to the tactile sense, to touch in its broader meaning; that is, the one that recalls the sensory faculties to their mental origins. Similarly, "the spring of language" refers to the classical metaphor only indirectly, since the landscape has been recreated as an experience where foreground and background propose themselves as the mind's fulcrum of truth, portending freshness of vision as their sole origin.

As has been said, Tsaloumas introduces his theme and gives a chance to share in the intensity of the poetic turn. The first part of the poem, where the general humour is exposed, serves as an introduction; but it is only in the second section of the poem that the novelty of the piece emerges. With "close in, at the stone-trough" Tsaloumas achieves his objective, returning to the Mediterranean reality, to the world where he belongs and from which arise most of his expectations. Tsaloumas's poetry feeds from Leros (as Lundkvist had said), the Mediterranean basin, and its character is thus open, independent and adventurous, only attached to Nature, where it basks; its pathos is the truth of the world, which the imagination cannot quite redeem to smelt into joy: but there it sits, proud and disdainful, on the edge of the abyss, celebrating the ceaseless nuptials of time beside the bier of casual living.

In more recent poems Tsaloumas's Hellenic background, magnified by images of travel, beside some superb satirical flights,[32] gathers the glitter—at times Byzantine—of gilded wood, sombre because of the remoteness of its roots, but unquestionably precious both in design and finish. It is no wonder that before any of the English originals had seen the light, Thomas Shapcott had already spoken of "the glint and the shadow" in Tsaloumas's poetry, something vivid in the unpublished lines of "Interlude":

> Those alien tracts breathe peopled
> with voices I thought I'd reared myself
> to test the pitch of my ears; furnished
> with things responsible to my touch
> exclusively, from private worlds.
> This, to the resentful mind, is loss.
>
> But I consider the lily of the valleys.
> In my native barrenness of autumn hills
> I see them fringe the brow of ditches,
> the thirst-cracked barley strips.
> The fiction's truth is in the absence
> surely, valid in the return of spring.

NOTES

1. Con Castan, *Dimitris Tsaloumas*: *Poet* (Melbourne: Elikia Books, 1990).
2. Australian Broadcasting Corporation Radio Drama and Features, *The Poet's Tongue* (n.d).
3. Meridian special issue, 1990.
4. Tsaloumas, *Falcon Drinking* (University of Queensland Press, 1988).
5. Tsaloumas, *The Observatory* (University of Queensland Press, 1983).
6. Arthur Lundkvist, "A Migrant Greek Poet," *Svenska Dagbladet*, 7 June 1985.
7. *Falcon Drinking*, "Three Night Pieces for Thomas Shapcott I" (University of Queensland Press, 1988), p. 7.
8. *Ibid*., p. 6.
9. *Ibid*., p. 18.
10. Quoted from memory.
11. My own translation. The 5-character "cut-short" style was one of the six types of prosody practised during the Tang Dynasty. The "cut-short" was a reduced version of the traditional 8-line poems and could be compared to an epigram since it was meant to convey its full meaning with only those few words. I have tried to retain the rhyme in lines 1, 2 and 4 while altering as little as possible the sequence of the original Chinese characters.
12. I. McGilchrist, *Against Criticism* (London: Faber and Faber, 1982), p. 39.
13. E. Fenollosa, *The Chinese Character as a Medium for Poetry* (London: Stanley Nott, 1936), p. 27.
14. Castan, p. 66.
15. Wai-lim Yip, *Chinese Poetry: Major Modes and Genres* (Berkeley: University of California Press, 1976), p. 11.
16. Tsaloumas, *The Book of Epigrams*, "To the Reader II," trans. Philip Grundy (University of Queensland Press, 1985), p. 115.
17. To glimpse the convoluted workings of current deconstructive practice, Spivak's introduction to her translation of Derrida's *Of Grammatology* (1976) gives a telling account: "To locate the promising marginal text, to disclose the undecidable moment, to

pry it loose with the positive lever of the signifier; to reverse the resident hierarchy, only to displace it; to dismantle in order to reconstitute what is always already inscribed. Deconstruction in a nutshell. (p. xxviii)

One need only place against Spivak's assertion Yip's idea of the leap from the undifferentiated consciousness to note deconstruction's fundamental unserviceableness to Tsaloumas's dispositions.

18. *Falcon Drinking*, "Six Variations VI," p. 67.
19. *The Observatory*, "Eleventh Poem," p. 105.
20. Castan, p. 2.
21. *The Book of Epigrams*, p. 133.
22. *The Observatory*, p. 107.
23. *The Book of Epigrams*, p. 175.
24. Castan, p. 144.
25. *Falcon Drinking*, p. 23.
26. Such reasoning is not unfounded since we now know that in the year Elizabeth Jolly won "The Age" Book of the Year Award, ALL the judges, Thea Astley among them, had voted in favour of Tsaloumas's book, and it was only after the then editor, Stuart Sayer, overrode the judges's verdict that Jolly was awarded the prize.
27. *Falcon Drinking*, p. 25.
28. Paul Ricoeur, *The Symbolism of Evil*, trans. from the French by Emerson Buchanan (Boston: Beacon Press, 1967).
29. *Ibid.*, p. 162.
30. *Ibid.*, pp. 164-65.
31. This poem was the one chosen by the author to represent himself in an anthology of Australian poetry he selected and translated into Greek. See *Contemporary Australian Poetry* (University of Queensland Press, 1986), p. 44.
32. See *Portrait of a Dog* (forthcoming with University of Queensland Press, summer 1991).

Healing the Wounded Sea: A Study of Satendra Nandan's *Voices in the River* and *The Wounded Sea*

TIM DUNLOP

> The other night . . . my wife turned on the radio and heard the announcer offering cash prizes for the best television plays of five minutes' duration, written by children . . . at such moments it is difficult to find one's way around the kitchen.
>
> Philip Roth

The poetry of *Voices in the River*[1] and the novel *The Wounded Sea*[2] are concerned with the infinities of life and death reflected in the minutiae of daily life. In writings that are largely autobiographical, the concern is always beyond the personal. There is a startling consistency of theme, and this seems to stem from Satendra Nandan's view of the "artist as healer." This essay will therefore deal with those themes and then attempt to assess the poetry and prose in light of Nandan's conception of the artist in society.

The writings occur in a continuum, bracketed at one end by the Indian-Fijian experience of exile as a result of indenture, and at the other by the further displacement after the Coup d'etat of Lieutenant-Colonel Sitiveni Rabuka. That these are major events is not denied, but their influence on the writer's society is shown to us in the form of personal details from individual lives. Nandan expresses alienation, racism, prejudice, even death, in "a landscape of little ruins." The poem, *Inward Death*, tells us:

> the death of a king
> a cataclysmic event
> the holocaust

of Auschwitz-Shatila-Sabra
all made by men like you and me
a shipwreck on Nasilai reef
a tempest in a Shakespearean sea

these are not necessary
for a tragedy
happens anywhere, anytime.

Dr Subramani, of the University of the South Pacific, has written: "Nandan's poetry is an affirmation of his double inheritance."[3] This double inheritance leads not only to tension between the races in Fiji, but also seems to cause a dilemma for the children and grandchildren of the original indentured labourers: particularly when the contrast between the generations is highlighted by education and the influence of western traditions. In *The Old Man and the Scholar*, the poet tells us that:

authentic history cannot be written
with words from living mouths.

This paradoxical statement, indeed, the whole poem, seems to be affirming *experience* over understanding achieved through second-hand means such as written accounts. That such an affirmation necessarily brings into question the role of the artist is one of the problems that Satendra Nandan addresses quite directly in the autobiographical/fictional form of much of his work, especially in *The Wounded Sea*.

It is perhaps not surprising that an artist so deeply concerned with the problems of his society, should be in some way prescient. Ezra Pound's notion that artists are "the antennae of the race" is given some credence in the poem *The Village is Burning*:

the village is burning

will the sun fall
to char us all?
will the ocean rise
in a blue bloody tidal wave?

The poem provides an almost perfect spiritual segue into the concerns of the novel *The Wounded Sea* (*TWS*). And the lines:

> only the fish will live
> unless we learn to forgive

illustrate Nandan's concern with forgiveness and healing. And concerns that were being explored in the poetry are considered in a new light—or under a darker shadow—in the novel *The Wounded Sea.* As with Nadine Gordimer, writing is the "essential gesture," a phrase that is a wondrous juxtaposition of the fundamental and the ephemeral.

One strength of *TWS* is that it makes a coherent whole from a narrative form that is essentially fragmented and piecemeal. This approach often presents the reader—or at least the western reader—with difficulties, as it flits from one time frame to another, in and out of reminiscences, anecdotes, facts and storylines. The narrative owes more to an oral tradition than it does to the conventional European form of the novel, which of course is one of the refreshing and appealing aspects of post-colonial literature in general. Salman Rushdie describes the pattern of the oral narrative:

> It isn't linear. An oral narrative does not go from the beginning to the middle to the end of the story. It goes in great swoops, in spirals or in loops, it every so often reiterates something that happened earlier . . . then takes you off again . . . summarizes itself . . . digresses . . . then comes back to the main thrust of the narrative.[4]

This approach, this fragmented narrative, is integral to the *particular* story being told. As Marion Halligan noted in her review in *The Canberra Times, TWS* is "an account which is also an attempt to puzzle out meanings." The puzzling out is being done by the author as he writes and tries to put into words the experience he has lived, and it is also being done by us, the readers, as we try to puzzle out the connections between, for example, the installation of a flush toilet in a village home and the election to parliament of a Labour politician: or that between a new pair of shoes and a masked gunman.

What the book is telling us is that ultimately all these things are connected, the little things as well as the big things, and that we ignore the connections only through ignorance—sometimes wilfully, sometimes innocently.

What is probably of more significance in the way the book is written is in the area of the cross-over between it being a novel and an autobiography. Though it is hard to read it as anything other than autobiography, it is obviously something more than that.

TWS blurs the line between fact and fiction, novel and autobiography, and it isn't simplifying too much to say that *TWS* is autobiography written by a novelist—or more correctly, history written by a poet.

The distinction between novel and autobiography has relevance in the overall critical history of literature. Harry Levin says: "The increasing demands for social and psychological relevance made upon the novelist can only be satisfied out of his experience."[5] Satendra Nandan, and other post-colonial writers, particularly those in exile (voluntary or otherwise) come from the opposite angle to this: it's not so much a demand for social or psychological relevance, but the demands of the writer's own experience that requires him to seek means of expression that are psychologically and socially relevant. In this sense, the autobiographical novel is an ideal form because it allows the writer to deal with the sometimes very hurtful, or even dangerous, facts of his own life, in an artistic way that allows the "mere reality" to be transcended. As Scoles and Kellog have said: "It is in the knowing and the telling, and not in the facts, that the art is to be found."[6] And we find some justification for this point of view in *TWS* itself: "Words can give tremendous distance and objectivity to events too close to the heart." (150)

In a sense, everything that is thought and felt, everything that is going to happen in *TWS,* is given to us in the first two pages of the book—the coup, the exile, the fears, the doubts, and the hope—they are all there. And this is more in keeping with the techinque of a novel than it is with that of autobiography. By foreshadowing all that is to come. It is necessarily implying a structure, a plot, a storyline, a sense of impetus that goes beyond the general recording of a life that is usual in autobiography.

The sections that deal directly with the coup are the most obviously autobiographical parts of the book, yet the childhood memories clearly belong to the same narrator. So where is the line drawn between fact and fiction?

Some devices are obvious, such as the use of fictionalized names, but consider the sections that deal with the recollections of childhood. In terms of the overall structure of the book they are not simply childhood memories. It is not simply a book in parts, one of which is an account of a happy childhood. The childhood is actually bracketed by the disasters of, in the past, indenture, and in the future, the coup: a point that was made earlier in regard to the continuum between the poetry and the novel. Such references within what could otherwise be described as straight autobiography give an overall textual cohesion: they are rhetorical devices that justify applying the term *novel* to the book. This sentence on p. 6 is an example:

> Feasting after a funeral is—or was—a Fijian way of life.

The insertion of—*or was*—reminds us that what we are reading has a structure beyond that of simple reminiscence.

The structure of the book parallels the real world. The plot hatches throughout the early stages of the book in the same way the *plot*, the coup, was hatched in the early days of Fiji, right back to when the *Leonidas* arrived with its first cargo of indentured labourers. The author shows us that in these simple, apparently carefree days, the ground was being readied for what turned out to be the bitter harvest of the coup. And all of this is present, too, in the themes and subject of the poetry. Consider these lines from *Ruins*:

> It takes generations, they say,
> To create even ruins.

The Wounded Sea most clearly draws the line between autobiography and novel in those sections, and there are many of them, where the narrator, ostensibly relating facts from his own life, suddenly becomes privy, and allows us to become privy, to events that he probably had no access to. In other words, there are times when the narrative becomes the work of a conventional all-seeing—though not necessarily all-knowing—omnipotent narrator.

For example, the narration of Jaddu's seduction/rape of Chanchal on pp. 56-57 is told as if the narrator was not only there but was perfectly aware of what each character was thinking. The same sort of thing happens on pp. 74-75 where we are let into the secret of Jagat Mahajan's mysterious powers. It is apparent too, in one of the most effective sequences in the book, which begins on p. 109 and tells ostensibly of Gautam Gounder moving into the Chief Executive's office. (This section is also a very good example of oral narrative influencing literary design.) Through the words of the omnipotent narrator (it is virtually a third-person narrative) we hear of GG's rise to power, his affair with Pauline, his meeting with Indira Gandhi and a range of other personal details and thoughts, presumably none of which would be available to other than the imagination of the writer. The section climaxes on p. 121 where GG wonders why today of all days his mind is full of recollections of reading about Mahatma Gandhi's assassination. The question is answered for all of us on p. 122 when GG receives a phone call informing him that "the deed is done."

A further advantage of merging autobiography and omnipotent detached narrator is that it gives a sense of the village nature of the lives being described and of Fiji in general. Even in the places where the narrator becomes completely omnipotent, tells us things he couldn't possibly know, there is still a sense that, 1) it is real and it all happened, and that, 2) the narrator could easily have been hiding in the bushes watching the comings and goings of Jagat, or could have been a fly on the wall in the offices of GG. It gives a sense of a community that is small enough, and significantly, close enough, for the most private thoughts and actions of people to be known by everyone. And it is this sense of "community," that makes the planning and the execution of the coup all the more sinister and divisive. How was a treason of this magnitude so thoroughly hidden from its victims? Ultimately it leaves a sense that although the ties that bind in such a community must be strong, the wounds that divide are very deep indeed.

And the "wounds" are an abiding theme running through Satendra Nandan's work. Obviously, the novel deals with a deeply wounded society, but as a metaphor for use in the novel, the wound has extra significance. At the risk of imposing a Western Christian framework on the book, a quote from the Bible may illustrate the point being made. The section is John 20:25. It is after the resurrection when Jesus has appeared to the apostles but when St. Thomas was absent. Thomas, doubting Thomas, says: "Except I shall see in his hands the print of the nails, and put my finger into the print of the nails and thrust my hand into his side. I will not believe."

In this way, "wounds" are necessary to dispel doubt, and it is the sense of doubt that is important in the context of the novel. "Doubt" is a word with many connotations: it can imply cynicism and mistrust, as it does in the example of St. Thomas, but it can also imply innocence, and it is in this sense that it has significance in *TWS*.

The wounds of the society are summarized on p. 137:

> Our world . . . has been full of cannibalism and colonialism, savagery and slavery, convictism and coolism, genocide and racism, religious bigotry and intellectual dishonesty, moral hypocrisy and political treachery—these ills have been integral to our seascape.

They are there from the beginning of the book and they are there from the beginning of the indentured labour system. At no time are they ignored, but their significance is only really appreciated in the aftermath of the coup:

> We were such ignorant, innocent people: we had so little understanding of *realpolitik*.

So the wounds provide a way of describing the ills that may beset a society and they provide a touchstone for the reality of those ills. They also provide the starting point for Nandan's view of the role of the artist.

The essay, *The Artist as Healer*, concerns itself with the works of three major post-colonial writers, namely V.S. Naipaul, Wole Soyinka and Patrick White and at one stage it says:

> These three writers are profoundly conscious of the nature and origins of their societies and, in their art, are attempting to heal the wounds which have touched the very springs of our communally exacerbated consciousness and individual being.

It is doubtful that when these words were written, Satendra Nandan would have thought that one day he would be participating in the process of "artist as healer" under the exact circumstances in which *TWS* was written—the prescience of the artist is ultimately limited. So it would be unfair to take his essay as theory and see how it stacks up against the practice as represented by *TWS*; but it is interesting to consider the notion of the artist as healer in regard to the novel.

It says earlier in the essay: "Where mortality is the one fatal fact of existence, the artist attempts to transcend it through creative effort:

life is essentially concerned with the overwhelming reality of death." And death is one of the wounds that runs through the book. It is present—as it is in life—in all forms, from the most personal through to the most distant; from the individual through to the collective. The deaths most exquisitely recalled are those closest to the writer, his father, his grandfather, his brother; whether it be in the novel or in the poetry.

Death can be a matter of great personal concern, or it can be a matter of individual neglect. The opening two pages of the book mention at least four deaths and they run gamut of these variations. What comes through is the ambiguity of feelings towards death—it is at once a loss and at once a celebration, as the juxtaposition of the sentences on p. 4 illustrates:

> I felt as if I had clambered from a life raft onto a cruise liner.
> I was leaving my country, at Christmas, with death on my mind.
> I asked the Fijian air hostess for a bottle of champagne.

As death is the one overwhelming reality of life, then it is the one wound nothing—including art—can heal. But "the pain of death is for the living" and it is to the living that the artist addresses himself.

So what of the other wounds—racism, colonialism, savagery, slavery and the others—what can the artist offer to salve these? One answer might be that suggested on p. 153: "History was unimportant to us. It hadn't even become a witness to our manacled destiny." Through writing, the healing process can begin simply by the artist bearing witness "to our manacled history." Even the doubting St. Thomas acknowledged the resurrection once he had seen the wounds. And maybe Jesus's admonition to Thomas that "blessed are those who have not seen and yet believe" is a little unfair, because in the secular world this involves a faith that can easily be betrayed.

So is the artist taking on too big a job in attempting to be a healer? In some ways he is, but this is no reason to abandon it as a notion. Even if the best the artist can actually achieve is to treat symptoms—wounds, if you like—then it is worthwhile. Because sometimes in the process of seeking causes or reasons, victims can be forgotten. What books like *The Wounded Sea* and *Voices in the River* do, is to remind us that there are always victims.

It says at one point in *TWS* that "without crucifixion there can be no resurrection." And in a sense, *The Wounded Sea* represents the resurrection, or at least the start of a resurrection, after the crucifixion of the coup. What the book offers, then, is the wounds in the hands and feet and the side of society, and it gives us a chance to place our fingers in those wounds and to doubt no longer that such things are possible—crucifixions and resurrections.

NOTES

1. Satendra Nandan, *Voices in the River* (Fiji, Suva: Vision International, 1985).
2. Satendra Nandan. *The Wounded Sea* (Australia: Simon and Schuster, 1991).
3. Subramani, in *South Pacific Images*, ed. Chris Tiffin (Queensland: St Lucia, SPACLALS, 1978), p. 43
4. B. Ashcroft, et al, *The Empire Writes Back: Theory and Practice in Post-Colonial Literature* (London: Routledge, 1989, p. 183).
5. D. Lodge, in *The Novel Today*, ed. Malcolm Bradbury (London: Fontana Paperbacks, 1969), p. 90.
6. *Ibid.*, p. 100.

Knock, Knock

MICHAEL WILDING

There they were in bed when the hammering started. Not just a knocking. From the beginning it was a hammering. And then there was the gooseflesh, and the tightening in the stomach, the fear in the bowels. Very Biblical.

They lay there still, not talking, holding their breath, not wanting to give away that they were in there.

It came again, hammer, hammer, hammer, too loud for a visit, the hammering of a proclamation.

Police never hammer that long. They would have been in there by now, the door frame splintered, and he would have been up against the wall, his mouth bloody from pistol whipping, while she was being raped on the bed. He rejected the image of her whimpering into a sheet in the corner of the room as presenting an unacceptably stereotyped sex role, the wailing woman. And being raped by police was more acceptable?

Or she could have opened it, the door, to a messenger with flowers from an absent lover, the room suddenly burst into deep rich red life with the explosion of roses, bunch after bunch, a florist's van heaped with them outside and they kept carrying them in till they covered the floor as deep as the bed and she could lie on them.

I fall upon the thorns of life, I bleed.

Now it changed to a slow, steady, knock knock knock knock.

He could see the arm flailing there, just dropping on the door with its own weight, the huge paw, the old grease stained greyed jaket, the straw sticking out of the shirt, the ears, and behind the lolling scarecrow, the wily lunatic, the smiler with the knife, the man behind the mawkin.

She sat up in her tower plaiting her hair and her lover climbed up a rope and spirited her away astride his powerful black mare, the clouds were inky blue across the moon's face, and behind at the inn or chateau or castle they were hammering on the door trying to waken her guardians to say she'd been taken away.

Now the woodpecker tapping on the windows, a coin cracking against the glass with the resonance of threat, waiting for the vibration that will shatter every pane, the ultrasonic devastation.

Once this is the first time this happens, once maybe you decide right this is the last time this is going to happen, she draws up the white sheet to çover her breasts, and then draws it up higher to chew on the edge, and the fact that the man in bed looks despite all his efforts absolutely terrified, and knows it, hunched in a foetal position there, exposed as she draws the sheet up to her teeth, dragging it off him, the fact of his naked terror before the unknown lunatic at the door, with his woodchopper's axe, or escaped from his daily dose of largactil, or flown in from out of state or outer space, still without his daily dose of largactil, or hourly, or maybe very drunk, very drunk from drinking all the way up on the flight, this fact of his naked terror in bed there doesn't especially diminish him in her eyes at all, the man at the door is no longer of any great interest to her, but that he can imagine her to be connected to a man who fills him with the terror of the unpredictable, this gives her an edge, this is like one she'll keep up her sleeve when she puts one on, that's what he figures anyway, hunched into a foetal position and wincing every time the door is hammered or the window pane tap, tap, tapped.

'Maybe if you're into amyl nitrate it's great. Personally I don't like these adrenalin rushes, I'd rather he just stopped hammering and went away.'

Maybe she doesn't need amyl nitrate, maybe her life is a succession of hammered on doors, waking to the sudden howl of the highspeed saw in the timber yard, or with a friend at the door to show her how she'd shaved off her pubic hair and what did she think, maybe now she'd turned up in drag, top hat and tails and was whacking away with the silver headed cane.

The beating is like the piston strokes of an old steam engine, billowing out thick black clouds of smoke against the green hills, a splendid red and black apparition with its single carriage, likewise with fine red detail on the gloss black background, as she rushed off to escape retribution or to meet her heart's delight.

Then the knocking and the tapping and the hammering stopped and there was the great unearthly peace, the waiting for the next onslaught, the suspicion, the knowledge of a trap, the transparent sense of false security lulled past the window like a blanket flapping smoke messages from the signal fire, and she curled up in front of it, Catherine Tekakwitha, Pocahontas, Minnehaha, bound at wrists and ankles, otherwise naked, maybe a feather in her headband.

The rocks started raining down on the roof. They bounced down the tiles. Crack, crack, crack.

It would have been worse in the trenches. Or as an urban guerilla under siege. Mortars lobbing napalm over, spew, pow, flam-blam. Squads of special anti-riot police climbing in at the windows, tossing in smoke bombs, firing first, laconic types.

Or they were sailing through mysterious waters and this was the larva from an unknown volcano, raining down in the soft tropic night, and the flap of the taut canvas, waiting for the cry of some weird nightbird.

So there were two men so there were two men, they could sort it out between them, she'd end up with one of them at least, unless they fought to the death and each delivered fatal blows, or rejected her in new found male camaraderie, so which ever one got left behind, that would be fine, why would she need to worry, the piquancy of uncertain expectation in itself was enough.

'Though I don't like it when you talk about being tied up and watching me being raped in front of your eyes, I don't like the way you keep coming back to that scenario, I think you like the idea too much, I wouldn't put it past you to try and set it up.' 'I don't play those sort of games.' 'Well, we could open the door and see. Perhaps I do.' She got out of bed and walked to the door, touched the catch, turning it back. 'Clothes?' 'What, you want to watch them being ripped off me?'

The Old Magic

VICTOR KELLEHER

"D'you see that?" Gramps said, gazing up. "It's the old magic that's in him."

High above us, on a narrow ledge projecting from the back of the terrace roof, my Great Uncle Frank was standing with outstretched arms, a tin rattle in one hand, a scoop of dried peas in the other. With a flashing and fluttering of wings, the pigeons descended upon him, settling on his arms, his head, his shoulders. He gave them no time to feed, pushing them off impatiently, urging them towards the line of traps and into the loft built beneath the roof. Only half a dozen birds remained in the sky, drawn down in a tighter and tighter circle by his waiting figure, yet somehow resisting the temptation to land.

"There'll be hell to pay now," Gramps growled.

Sure enough! Uncle Frank began to jump up and down, his reedy voice raised in a barely human cry of anger. Straight away the wheeling birds broke ranks and spiralled towards him, though not this time to be ushered into the loft. As the first of them settled, he took it deliberately in both hands and wrung its neck, stuffing its lifeless body into the side pocket of his jacket.

"Isn't that the magic for you?" Gramps said admiringly. "Look at them, queuing up for the hangman."

And so they were: roosting contentedly on his head and shoulders as he reached for them one by one. The last of them he tugged at so fiercely that the head and body sprang apart. I saw something break from the severed neck, like a thick speck of dust, and arc towards me, landing with a plop on the polished toe of my Sunday boots. I stared down at the livid bloodstain, then up to where Uncle Frank, only a moment before, had stood black against the sky. But the traps were already closed and he too was coming down, as only he knew how—his back to the ladder, the outside of his boots sliding on the polished rails, his heels clicking against the rungs to slow him down.

He hit the ground with a thump, landing in a half crouch that absorbed most of the shock. Not a big man like Gramps, but small and wiry: his wrists covered with black hair; more of it pushing out from the neck of his collarless shirt; the thick stubble on his face reaching to just beneath the eyes. Only his head was free of hair, smooth and shiny except for two stiff black tufts that jutted above his ears like horns.

"These youngsters," he said, giving us one of his sly and winning smiles, "they're not worth the feeding." And he patted his distended pockets. "I'll tell you what, Mick," he added, laughing freely now, "the others'll fly the faster for it."

"You're right there, Frank," Gramps agreed as he shuffled towards the lane at the bottom of the garden, which we all knew was the quickest route to the pub.

I was about to follow when Uncle Frank clapped a hand to his bald head. "Me cap!" he broke out. "Will you fetch it for me, Micky love? I'm still too much the Catholic to enter the Devil's house uncovered."

He smoothed my cheek fondly, which made it impossible to refuse. Not that I wanted to. It was just the thought of venturing into the house alone that I dreaded, The raw animal smell of it so enticing when someone was there beside me; so forbidding at any other time.

Nervously, I entered through the dingy scullery and peered along the darkened passage. I could make out the shape of a cage protruding from the space beneath the stairs. On tiptoes I tried to sidle past, my body hugging the wall. Yet still the hand shot out, thick fingers grabbing at my hair and clinging on, a heavy chimpanzee face pressed against the bars.

I did my best not to scream . . . and failed. My obvious distress bringing the others running.

"Charlie, you godforsaken creature!" Uncle Frank shouted.

Picking up a stick kept in the passage for that purpose, he thrust it between the bars and began beating the animal about the head and shoulders. I'm not sure what made me ask him to stop. Perhaps it was the low moan which burst from Charlie's lips. Or it could have been his eyes, the liquid glint of them in the half-darkness; eyes not so very different from Uncle Frank's, or even my own.

"There y'are, Charlie," Uncle Frank said, withdrawing the

stick. "There's mercy in this babe's heart even for the likes of you. So show him what you're made of. Thank him kindly."

Although he was instructing Charlie, it was me he took by the shoulders and pushed towards the cage.

Charlie's wrinkled old face, hairless except for a straggly fringe about the ears, loomed before me. His breath like the smell of Uncle Frank's jacket. His rubbery lips puckering grotesquely as they reached through the bars, for my flaming cheek, their touch unexpectedly warm and soft. Then, as if that were not contrition enough, he was hunkering down, groping for my ankles, his tongue surreptitiously gathering up the blood spattered on my shoe.

"Will you look at that Mick," Uncle Frank said wonderingly. "Kissing the boy's feet! Now isn't that something."

"If y'ask me," Gramps said, "he's earned his pint today."

"And a pint he'll have."

There was a rattle of keys and Charlie was dragged from the cage, his massive hand pressed into mine. As always, I had mixed feelings about minding him: his savage presence peculiarly exhilarating; his cracked yellow teeth, his great arms, stronger even than Gramps', making me quail inside. Hand in hand, we followed the adults down the garden—leaving behind the bleating nanny goat in its pen; the ducks and geese, their long necks yearning after us; the tethered, dejected figure of the dog, Raggles, whom I then loved best of all Uncle Frank's pets—the four of us heading for The Spotted Cow at the end of the lane.

Because it was summer, most of the men were in the cobblestoned yard behind the pub, standing around the walls in their dark coats and caps, or crouching on their hams, their smooth-glassed pints beside them. Some had brought along singing birds in tiny covered cages, and the main contest of the day was in progress. At the centre of the yard there was a small heap of coins; and in an effort to win this wager the contestants were uncovering their cages one by one, the birds bursting into song as the light flooded in upon them.

Our arrival was greeted with cries of welcome.

"What do you say to standing in for me, Frank?" a stout middle-aged man called out. "There's a brace of pints in it for you."

"I say you're on," Uncle Frank replied, licking slyly at his thin lips.

Accepting the proffered cage, he did not whisk off the cover, which was the normal practice. Rather, he slid his hand beneath it, eased open the door, and drew the bird out—its yellow plumage brilliant within his dark hand. For a full minute he held it to his lips; mumbling softly. His finger and thumb, I noticed, were held pincer-like on either side of the creature's throat, cradling and threatening the neck in a single gesture. Slowly, with everyone in the yard watching, he lowered the bird to his open palm, fractionally relaxing his pincer-grip, his touch as delicate as the throat itself. Instantly, as if by magic, the tiny beak opened in a chattering, whistling call so loud and sure, so eager in its responsiveness, that I knew from past experience that the contest was over.

Amidst applause and laughter, there began for me a typical Sunday afternoon: a seemingly endless round of pints; the raucous singing of old Irish songs; an unlimited supply of lemonade and crisps thrust upon me by red faced drunken men. And as if that were not enough, still there was Charlie, who had learned to manipulate his fellow creatures with a skill almost equal to Uncle Frank's.

His method was infallible. Shuffling around the sunlit yard on his leathery backside, he would take up any unguarded pint, run his tongue around the rim of the glass, and then pass it to its owner. I never saw anyone accept it. Amused, they would wave it away, a look of feigned horror on their faces; and Charlie, a look of faint surprise on his, would down the pint in a single gulp.

By the end of the afternoon it was hard to say who was more drunk, Uncle Frank or Charlie. Even Gramps, despite his reputation, was no match for them. with me half-crushed under the reeling, reeking weight of Charlie, and Gramps supporting his brother we took the front way home, staggering past the old bald-faced terraces. Every few paces, Charlie, his eyes startlingly human in his drunken state, turned towards me and mouthed my cheek. "Get off!" I yelled, "Get off!"—foolishly believing that it was little more than a learned gesture; that there was no place in his animal mind for true affection.

Relieved, I deposited him on the front step, only to be accosted by Uncle Frank, his reddened eyes flat and blank. Drawing me near, he kissed me lovingly.

"Here, Micky lamb," he slurred. "A present for your Nan. And a lovely woman she is. Tell her . . . tell her. . . ." As words failed him, he fumbled in his still distended pockets and pulled out two limp bodies. "Just the doings for a pie," he mumbled, pushing them into my hands.

I didn't thank him. One of them was headless; and at close quarters I could see it wasn't a racing pigeon at all. It was what he called his "flirter": a white, fan-tailed dove which he kept as a pet, to lure reluctant pigeons into the loft; which I'd fondled and petted on many an occasion.

I suppose it was stupid of me to be disappointed. Already half-way through primary school, I wasn't a baby any more and should have known better. Also, as I'd had opportunities enough to observe, encounters with Uncle Frank, for all their magic, frequently contained that same dreadful element of surprise.

LIke the day I spent romping in his narrow garden with the dog, Raggles: the broad bull terrier head, magnificent in its ugliness, pursuing me through the miniature wilderness of unpruned apple trees and overgrown animal pens. Towards the end of our frantic play I fell into the duck pond and had to be fished out by Gramps—with Raggles barking excitedly in the background, and Gramps and I drunk with laughter as he picked the snails and bits of weed and slime from my hair and clothes.

At the time; it struck me as the culmination of a glorious afternoon. Not for some days did I learn otherwise. How Raggles, still feverish with excitement after our departure, had attacked and killed two of the prize geese; and how Uncle Frank, having enticed him with a piece of meat, had split his head with the garden axe.

I learned of that incident from Gramps, who recounted it to Nan in the kitchen. Lingering just outside the door, both drawn and repelled by the story, I heard my Nan sigh. "He's a hard man, Mick," she said, "and no mistake."

A hard man. Yet not quite hard enough, it seemed. Not for his own strange lifestyle anyway. For soon afterwards he too joined the list of casualties. It happened, Gramps informed the assembled family, during a pigeon race. Going up to the loft to check the traps, Uncle Frank found to his astonishment that his prize bird was home in record time. The official clock, evidently, was still in the house; and in his eagerness to record the bird's time, he descended the ladder a little too fast—his feet slipping off the rails, the bottom of his spine catching the lowest rung just before he hit the ground.

"But do you know?" Gramps added with pride. "He never dropped the ring. Blind with pain he was, and still he clocked it in and won. That's the kind of man he is. Pain means nothing to him."

I was probably misled by Gramps' tone, lulled into false security. Because when I next saw Uncle Frank his changed appearance came as a real shock. His face pinched and closed, his eyes as dull and blank as when he was drunk; his body so twisted and bent that he was hardly taller than Charlie.

"It's a doctor you need, Frank!" Nan told him

We were sitting in the front room, the curtains drawn wide, the dusted furniture gleaming in the afternoon light.

He shook his head so that his hornlike tufts of hair quivered with indignation. "I'll not be going to any doctor, Polly. Before you could drop your hanky, he'd have me under the knife. Then where would I be?"

It was during that same afternoon that I tried catching sparrows in our back garden—the idea of it inspired by Uncle Frank's presence. With the help of Boy Tizzard, who lived next door, I'd set up a simple trap: scattering of breadcrumbs, as bait; and directly above them the garden sieve, one side propped on a piece of stick to which a length of string was attached. It seemed too cunning to fail, but time and again the birds escaped. We were on the verge of giving up when Uncle Frank suddenly came staggering down the side path, each faltering step forcing from him a grunt of pain,

"Let me show you the trick of it," he said, taking the string from me.

Within minutes, as I might have guessed, he was successful, a quivering sparrow held in his dark hand. He raised it to his lips in his usual way, to calm it, his finger and thumb poised on either side of its throat. But while he was still crooning softly, a spasm of pain took him, his whole body clenching shut. When at last he looked up, the bird was lying crushed and dead in his open palm.

He tossed it onto the garden bed and ruffled my hair consolingly. "Never mind, pet," he said, "there're plenty of sparrows left in the bush."

That must have been the last time I saw him at our house, and because of his worsening condition I never spent another Sunday in his garden. It wasn't fun there any more and I took to making excuses in order to stay away. At the last, though, excuses weren't enough.

"He's your great uncle," Gramps said in admonition, "and he likes you by him."

So late one afternoon in autumn, I again accompanied him to the dingy little terrace three streets from ours. As we neared the side gate, the local priest came walking towards us, his cassock blowing in the damp wind. Releasing my hand, Gramps stood in the opening to bar the way.

"We've no call for the likes of you, paddy-muck," he said fiercely.

The priest hesitated and stopped. "Be reasonable, Michael," he remonstrated. "It's a man's soul we're talking of here. A man! Not the beast you'd have him be."

Gramps stamped on the hard pavement. "You're forgetting this is English soil," he said. "He'll rest easy enough without your say-so. You can save your belessings for the sheep and goats you're forever ranting about."

He roared the last words so loud, his fists half raised, that the priest ducked his head and backed off. And all at once I was alone on the pavement—the cassock swinging away out of sight, Gramps having already disappeared down the side alley.

I hurried after him—too late! Forced now to enter the house alone. The scullery as dim as ever; the passage a line of shadow in which only the edge of the cage was discernible, outlined against the frosted glass panes in the front door. I edged past it, expecting at every instant to feel Charlie's fingers groping for my hair. But there was no movement from within the cage and as I grew accustomed to the gloom, I spied Charlie sitting hunched and still in the far corner, his eyes, alive and watchful, catching what little light there was. He had the air of someone who was listening intently and, following his example, I became aware of murmur of sound filtering down through the house.

Cautiously I mounted the stairs, the murmur becoming a low moan; the moan swelling suddenly into a demented shriek.

"Take me out of it, Mick!" The voice barely recognizable.

"For the love of Jesus, I'm begging you! Take me out of it!"

"Hold on, man!" Gramps shouted. "It'll pass!"

"What's a little bit of life worth, Mick?" The voice shrill and pleading now. "Nothing! Not a spark in hell! You could finish it if you had a mind."

Gramps made no reply. His footsteps hurrying across the landing and down through the darkness to where I waited. "Here," he said, pressing money into my hand. "It's whiskey he needs right now. Fetch yourself to the pub. And quick!"

Another of the shrieks drove me from the house. Shaken and confused, I ran down the lane to The Spotted Cow where I was given the whiskey, but my offer of money refused.

"For auld lang syne," the publican said sadly, sliding the bottle across the polished counter.

Fortunately, I was saved a return journey on that particular evening, for only a few steps from the pub I ran into my Great Aunt Kate. The bottle, plus the expression on my face, must have told her all she needed to know.

"Give it here, darling," she said, an uncharacteristic tenderness in her voice, "and get yourself off home."

Again I needed no urging. Our kitchen, with its smell of boiling haddock and freshly cut bread, like a sanctuary in the falling dusk. And best of all, Nan's special brand of fierce warmth to ward off the nameless evils of the coming dark.

"You can sleep with me tonight, lamb," she said, snuggling me down beside her in the feathery hollow where my Gramps normally lay; sleep quickly rescuing me from the shrieks and moans of a world gone disturbingly awry.

When Nan woke me soon after dawn, Gramps was still absent from the bed. "He's not been back the night long," she said. "Be a good lad and take him a bottle of tea. He'll need it after what he's been through."

So armed with a very different kind of bottle, I made that journey for the last time.

Aunt Kate was just leaving when I reached the house. With a shake of the head, the slit of her mouth straight and hard, she let me in at the front door and closed it after her. Immediately the rank scent of the place enveloped me, cutting me off from the outside world. As on the previous evening, I was aware of a low moaning sound, louder than before and more persistent. Mistakenly, I believed it was coming from the upper landing; and I was halfway up the stairs before I realized that what I was listening to was Charlie—his wordless offering of grief.

More fearful than curious, I crept across the landing and pushed open the bedroom door. Early morning sunlight was flooding into the room, its occupants trapped within its dustry bars—Gramps slumped in a chair, his head buried in his hands, and lying close beside him, unclothed upon the bed, the figure of Uncle Frank. I had never seen him naked before: his whole body, from feet to neck, covered with a sheen of finest black hair, soft and downy in the sunlight, like the sleek fur of a young animal. The face alone revealed his true age and the passage of his pain. A grimacing mask, wrinkled and stubbly, it leered monkeylike through the swirling motes, gazing with an awful fixity of purpose at the stained ceiling.

I stayed only long enough to deposit the bottle on the threshold. My legs carrying me back down the stairs, past Charlie's cage (the glint of his eyes following me longingly), and out into the untainted air.

The magical stillness of a Sunday morning was upon the garden: the tethered goat facing the house, its bearded head raised urgently; the heads of the ducks and geese strained in the same direction. Like them, I tipped my face to the sky and began to climb, moving steadily rung by rung up to the loft high above. The traps were closed, but I could hear the birds cooing and milling about within. Turning the lock, I flung the hatch wide; and the pigeons, cooped up for days, burst eagerly through the opening, their wings buffeting my face, exploding about my ears, making me reel to the very edge of the platform. I don't know what scared me more: the thought of death, waiting just beyond my groping fingertips, or the idea of the fall itself, of being drawn down, like Uncle Frank, to the dark earth and beyond. With a desperate lunge, I grasped the edge of the hatch and hung on. A faint moan escaping from my lips. My finger suddenly as hard and unyielding as Charlie's when he gripped onto my hair. While above my head, the pigeons, freed at last, rose dovelike into the sky.

The Bell-Ringers

They converge by bus or car,
strap-hanging parodies of the ritual
or waiting their right to go in the gamut.
Almost no-one lives close now.

They meet, for centuries it seems,
one with the jokes his father told,
the tall kid with his nose in a motorcycle manual
and Cath from classes.

They take their place in the workings,
firm-twisted, cast, a good fit.
The counting games start,
the regulated smooth pulls

on heaven that lives sluggish in a low tower
earthed by counting of stones,
heaven closer than in-flight meals.
And heaven lets down its milk,

the suns of sound rolling
on into the half-life of harmonics
and a word in the half-hour tour of plaques:
Here they ring bells.

As poets half-attend—
Shelley, timing his moment by Shakespeare,
Sor Juana, Neruda, Whitman,
Euripides by Ibsen:

facing, chosen by the sequence, they count
and take the strain, ringed round
a bell in the forging, blows
of the original O.

Hairdo

Someone told her she needs height.
Or else it was getting in her eyes.
She's reined it up tight in a band—
aimed it up, out of this world—
teased it out, raining all round.
It's curled to beat a fernery.
Her friend's looks like a bin
stuffed with scraps of rope.
These art works move into lifts.
They're finished with fringes below
and huge dangles. They bloom in classrooms.
They're the Institute's hanging gardens.

JUDITH RODRIGUEZ

The Bird

I

There is great softness in pain
And few people can grasp
The complexity
Of madness
Simply because they place themselves
Beyond its clear
Distortion

Fear
Concentrated and fatal
Has no other role
Than to be a harbinger
Of pain
It is tragic and morose
And yet mysteriously necessary.

II

When I was three
I saw a man sail through
A pane of glass
And shatter to the street below
I had no idea
That an exploding furnace
Had propelled him skyward
Only that the result was
Nothing
Less than peaceful

I watched reds and reflected golds
Mix in a glorious
Collison of light.

My mother
Shielded my eyes
Held my body
Clutched tightly to her breasts
As would a thief her newly stolen
Treasures
I was engulfed
In horrifying and unnecessary silence
Her screams pulsing through my body
Into my bones
And I wanted to tell her that her fear
Was more frightening to me
Than the great bird a-sail
Through morning diamonds.

III

I discovered
Seven months later
That the bird I had watched
Was my father
Borne

To new and ironic heights
At four I failed to grasp
The significance
Of my father's
Graceful flight.

IV

From his absence
I unknowingly drew strength
Pulled myself up
I was turned to music
And
Like a needle
Felt it push artificial courage
Through my blood.

V

My feet scraped
Tripped
I stumbled
Blowing my desperation through
A soundless reed
Into a hollow clarinet
Even as I fell
I knew
I had blown all I could expel
From the instrumental tunnel
Unable to hear impending silence.

VI

I fought my step-father
As he carried me
Tucked beneath an arm
Like a wind instrument
Along dead grey roads

I could feel the blood that traced my lip
The swell where reed
Had cut and splintered

VII

That night I crawled to an open window
And smashed my left hand
By bringing the window
Down so hard
That glass flew
And pierced
My wrist.

VIII

With that pain I knew the softness
Of a peace I would never re-discover
And if I cried
My tears were not because I would never play
Again
Nor because I knew
That I would lose
The use of my left hand

Rather
I cried because
For the briefest instant
When the moonlight
Caught the exploding glass
I found my father again
As I best remembered him
A giant
Graceful bird
A phoenix
Piercing infinity.

GERRY TURCOTTE

Savoy Truffle
(Greenwich, 21 July 1969)

By one o'clock they've kissed, and run
around in circles, and begun
to grow more passionate, but slowly—
a couple of times he tests her coyly:
all seems well. And though the faintest
voice advises some restraint, he's
never been one to heed advice
and infiltrates her in a trice.
Once again the night is turning
on its axis, and the burning
at the geologic core
takes the pinfall to the four
before they know the thing is finished;
by the five the fire's diminished
to an afterglow, that licks
against his throat by count of six,
and by the seventh stroke they find
the moment dwindled, a divine
regret beginning to create
a kind of panic; on the eight
she squirms uncomfortably below
as if to disengage—or so
it seems to him, while "Revolution
9" recalibrates their cushion,
record-player now reminding
them the disc (the tenth) is winding
toward the centre of its spin.
He rolls away, and she from him.

Letter to a Child of the Future

You asked me once about insanity,
stretching to understand

with the imperfect puzzled earnestness
of one thirteen years old
the night-time of the soul, the sad profanity
cornered already in your eye.

Too much awake to suffer lullabies
you waited. Vanity,
your captive presence, plus a certainty
the *Rubaiyat's* demands
were not beyond your intellect had made me bold,
and I'd amassed an eagerness

to touch the magic text again, no less
for you than for what I
remembered once, watching the book unfold
its rich tonality.
But now your awkward question had to force my hand—
I scrambled for reality.

What could I tell you? Partiality
to fobbing off the best
evasive maxim a moment could land
was not at all my style,
nor academic posturing—formality
can quench a thirst for knowledge cold.

And yet something, somehow had to be told. . . .
I said: Humanity
means constant war on the brutality
waiting within, or else—
Eat, drink and be merry, for tomorrow we die!
The vast majority will band
somewhere between these two: they can command
the label "Sane" to hold
together as their sacred alibi.
But such normality
is what the mad fall short of, or have in excess;
that, son, is their calamity. . . .

I understand, you said. Yet, a profanity,
like something old and tired of earnestness,
licked at my eye. A lizard on the noon of sanity.

ALEX SKOVRON

Loose Talk

A can of *Victorian Bitter* beside a thick
tumbler. She flicked a black look
straight through the rag of her fringe,
one eye blue from being punched.

She rocked back, muttered from a chair—
"We're all creeps when the chips get cashed,
sick to get rich, even grabbing
with our mouths. Oh sure, talk can be

a kind of money. Floating in the air.
Hey mate, you're looking real crook,
no wonder, drinking that shit." A bubble
breaks and pocks the creamy froth, a spark

of light flecks the red line of her lip.
On the fake-wood wall, the *scene of Italy*—
and by its torn paper lake, a detail—
Alpha's emblem in the alpine atmosphere.

A page ripped from the menu, a lip-stick
script, it's her best classified.
Who's game to say what they imagine
she might dare? It can only get worse

the waiter thinks. Tell her something now
She doesn't know. O shit, yes—a word
that's unbecoming to us feminists—
muses of paper, words and printer's ink.

She takes a knife out from her purse,
the handle's pearl, see if it twists.
All this rhetoric's fit for Rimbaud's hands.
Give back his beer, rancid old misogynist.

Petrol Sniffing

A red shell on a yellow can: a joke
before experience—and all the money boxes

left in a corner, jagged open.
The children bumping soft foreheads

in morning steam; a prickly scent trickles
from a cap, hands too young to shake

tremble: the heavy metal fumes sink home.
We have tomorrows to eliminate,

though who knows how long the brain
can take the fingers of vapour

that soothe the pain—Any bad dream
dissolves to the touch of a rubber snake

that dribbles its menthol from cracked lips.
Give it names and call us sick

but your real drugs cost a sister's lunch,
and the whiskey's in your sin-bin;

Southern Comfort's for that lucky bunch
who can afford their own extinction

in style, oh sure it's a luxurious joke—
though you can't joke when you're flat broke;

it's a plastic bag when you're on the nod—
Don't think we can't see you getting off on misery.

Social Realist

There's no one in charge, so I'll do the talking
there are some things you could put
into words, just in case
not that you'd ever use them. This is no
flash race-course where even the punks
have resumes—I might get out of it
but just give me the nod and I'll speak
with a shocking accuracy
just to pester your cynical awareness with
raw fact. These impressible words exist in a desert
called "life-style," it's difficult for me
not to resort to mockery, waste more paper, write
and they call you Headspace: up the road
a movie flickers inside a post-modern cinema
directed by some fashionable bent-german,
it shows how gullible imaginations fall
to a designer's "look"—this destructive nymph
splashes black right across the screen
yet somehow she's been pasteurized
to get them in, she's what passes for a muse
and is loved for her elegant implausibility. Though
today she's head down in astro-turf,
blown out by posing for some B grade pornography—
who knows what city she is in, her head shaved,
beyond time, squinting through the new conjunctivitis.

ROBERT ADAMSON

Sydney Brick

The city's rich with one Lancastrian thing—
And that's red-brick. The good-bad-poem sort:
Some looks like raw rump steak, some's lobsterish,
Some's rosé pale; some shines like ruby port;

Some's apoplectic mauve and cheek by jowl
With glazed red-brick with Kranski sausage hues;

A red mosaic sprawl across the hills
From Ryde to Marrickville to La Perouse;

Maroon or fiery or plain ruddy-brown,
Each one's red-brick beams out its different glow
In Bronte, Abbotsford and Woolstonecraft
From school, shop, duplex, block and bungalow;

With constant startle, eyesight almost aches,
As Sydney brick in Sydney sunshine bakes.

Sydney Opera House: There She Goes

The long-span joists, the concrete struts corrode,
With flashings worn and sealants gone to pot;
How long is it the frame can bear the load,
The halls, the glass, the marvellous roof, the lot?

The broadwalk's shaky, skirting panels grim,
The precast beams show stains from outside leaks;
Salt air and blazing sun and weathering
Are testing out our skilled space-age techniques

(Our high hopes, too; the pride of New South Wales),
As cancer gnaws now at the structure's heart;
The scrum of nuns—the pachyderm—the sails—
The temple on the harbour built for Art.

See sunset light her, flowering. There she goes.
I pray she will not go like Blake's Sick Rose.

Mooney Mooney

Bloody Marys, Sheaf Stout and Black Velvet
in your garden by Mooney Creek,
where we talked about Kendall, whose country this was,
and Furphy and Webb (and the meaning of *Voss*)
and bush ballad and free verse technique;

your verandah, tame magpie and trellis
with its purple and red morning glory,
and drink priming talk so our penny-plain words
shine coloured in hindsight like so may shards—
now for it—of millefiori;
swamp harriers on high I remember,
Over Mooney's olive-grey banks;
its oyster-lease calm relecting huge skies,
and all day long mullet, rising to flies—
Bob, Lyndy and Michael, thanks.

SIMON CURTIS

Silkworm

The memory of flight
a severed thread

as you spin
cradle, house, tomb.

All will be unwoven,
rewoven, dipped into

plum, aquamarine,
blue of early summer,

emerge with moon—
glean still intact.

Centuries of immobility,
attending with subtle

patience to the fabric
of things (that is so

perishable): the Self
serves and weaves,

with instinctive vision
shapes its rebirth.

Praying Mantis

Prophet at prayer
worshipping stillness,
forwards, backwards,
swaying like a leaf.

A camouflaged god
with all-seeing vision;
uplifted forelegs
await holy communion.

For the Bushman people,
spirit of the moon,
a trickster weaving
in and through the visible.

Carnivore, cannibal:
violating laws that
in war and love
we violate, over and over.

With reptilian chill
its triangular head
swivels to observe
from green or pink eggs:-

sleek alien, dwelling
in a different time,
belonging in the air
of some other planet.

Fireflies

Happy the tree
illumined by candles, warm stars.
The lights
go on and off
in concert—
seeking attention, inviting
interest. From here and there,
a green brightness flashing back—
she knows, she's watching.
Gradually,
lights disappear
from the tree—the brilliant
collective lost
in the humble ceremony.
Now the makers of light
revel in its absence—
instinct equally at home
with either.

The cosmic tree
silhouettes itself against
many darknesses,
waits for the dawn
as it waited for night.

DIANE FAHEY

Mackay Man Walks Towards Mud

Each meticulous step is planned
as carefully as a moon landing.
Leaning on metal sticks, labouring
towards the beach—half crab, half man—
he takes an hour to get there.
Arriving, he will watch the sea
then limp back to his fibro shack

with his friend who carries the chair.
No lunar glamour, no healing touch
of TV lights awaits. Just mudflats
at low tide, mangroves, the pewter chop
of distant, dirty sea—not much
when each step sweats. Perhaps it's mud
he's after, a strong syllable
to match the stroke which slowed him,
anchoring moondust in his blood—
mud's wet muscle, unkillable.

On John Donne's Conversion to Oatbran

Batter my heart, quick-fingered God,
wrap it in that ageing Sun, flog
it with the fish and chips to sods
with low cholesterol. What blood
hast thou given me, Lord, what fats
so lipid-loaded? Must mystics
of the Chiko roll's intemperate vats
now relish oats, revere statistics?
So what if my count is seven?
Bran-mad I hammer at your door
beseeching Hamburger Heaven—
one small dimmie, Lord, just once more?
Cease, starved heart; I hear the bell toll
your death by damned cholesterol.

The Way

The way happiness appears out of nowhere
like a high white cloud travelling east;
the way you bounced and jiggle-danced
in the hall this morning with windmill arms,
crying, "Like this? Like this" nonsensically;
the way that young woman working in the bank
collapses forward on her hands, laughing

and laughing, her dancing holiday eyes;
the way memory plucks a file from the shelf
unasked, spreads it on the counter, says "See?
Once you were driving across America,
here is the friend's farm in West Virginia
where you stayed that night, here is clover
glowing in fields where you walked at dusk."
Outside, the street has faces like blossoms.
Through the mid-morning bustle I drift
from bank to chemist to supermarket
the way light sifts through an orchard.

TONY LINTERMANS

Mouth Feathers

Once shy, twice bitten, ten times bitten.
The old sayings twist in the mouth
like a dry feather shoved in
making you spit.
"Only joking!" they said in the playground,
"Can't you take a joke?" That's what they said.

I take this odd feather. It has floated in from outside.
Nothing could be more ordinary:
like a playground of kids, teasing.
Nothing could be more strange.

I hold it up in finger and thumb. It is a science
of intricate connections, a nib
inviting the words, though we have forgotten nibs
and there are no more knuckles blotched with ink. It is
one strong channel thrusting its point down
till we think of darts, arrows, the skin pierced
and a sort of necessary ritual that has
something to do with taste.
Or it is the last dream, feathers as wings
and flight into the ventilation points of the stars
or at least an eagle's glide. Why did we lose

on the genetic graph towards flight?

He who hesitates is pinned to the ground forever.
Even in orbiting satellites we hold a little cup
of our weighted atmosphere like the kid
gripping six marbles in his pants' pocket, knowing
they are his only security against the Big Boys
and the feather torture.
He who hesitates is not lost to a lot of fantasies
and one tiny boon of fate: he who hesitates
can have the power to look, look again, to review
and consider strategies for next time.
Daedelus hesitates before affixing wax to the wings,
Christ hesitates before the final commitment.
Ten times bitten and always shy
the doves of this world have outpopulated
those endangered eagles. An eagle's feather
is the quill, and the doves' soft down
fills the pillow on which I lie.

THOMAS SHAPCOTT

INDEX